THE
EVERYTHING
WEDDING
BOOK
5TH EDITION

Dear Reader,

You're engaged! There is no other feeling quite like it. Now the planning begins and all the fanfare that goes with it. While wedding planning may seem like a daunting task, if you have the right tools, it can actually be a lot of fun. Remember—it's a day dedicated to the two of you and your families!

Don't worry, this book is here to guide you every step of the way. The earlier you start your wedding planning process, the easier your engagement will be (and the more time you will get to actually enjoy it). Think of this book as your wedding secretary to help you manage all the to-do lists for your wedding day.

After planning thousands of different events throughout my career, I can assure you that there is a wedding design and plan for every type of bride and every type of groom! Whether you have a month or two years to plan your wedding, this book will guide you from the big-picture basics to the smallest of details.

Congratulations and happy planning!

Katie Martin

Welcome to the EVERYTHING® Series!

These handy, accessible books give you all you need to tackle a difficult project, gain a new hobby, comprehend a fascinating topic, prepare for an exam, or even brush up on something you learned back in school but have since forgotten.

You can choose to read an Everything® book from cover to cover or just pick out the information you want from our four useful boxes: e-questions, e-facts, e-alerts, and e-ssentials.

We give you everything you need to know on the subject, but throw in a lot of fun stuff along the way, too.

We now have more than 400 Everything® books in print, spanning such wide-ranging categories as weddings, pregnancy, cooking, music instruction, foreign language, crafts, pets, New Age, and so much more. When you're done reading them all, you can finally say you know Everything®!

QUESTION

Answers to common questions

FACT

Important snippets of information

ALERT

Urgent warnings

ESSENTIAL

Quick handy tips

PUBLISHER Karen Cooper

MANAGING EDITOR, EVERYTHING® SERIES Lisa Laing

COPY CHIEF Casey Ebert

ASSISTANT PRODUCTION EDITOR Alex Guarco

ACQUISITIONS EDITOR Brett Palana-Shanahan

SENIOR DEVELOPMENT EDITOR Brett Palana-Shanahan

EVERYTHING® SERIES COVER DESIGNER Erin Alexander

Visit the entire Everything® series at *www.everything.com*

THE
EVERYTHING®
WEDDING
BOOK
5TH EDITION

Your all-in-one guide to planning
the wedding of your dreams

Katie Martin

Avon, Massachusetts

This book is dedicated to Elena, Derek, and Thomas.
May I be blessed enough to be part of planning all of
your weddings one day!

An Everything® Series Book.
Everything® and everything.com® are registered trademarks of F+W Media, Inc.

Published by Adams Media, a division of F+W Media, Inc.
57 Littlefield Street, Avon, MA 02322 U.S.A.
www.adamsmedia.com

ISBN 10: 1-4405-6958-4
ISBN 13: 978-1-4405-6958-6
eISBN 10: 1-4405-6959-2
eISBN 13: 978-1-4405-6959-3

Printed in the United States of America.

10 9 8 7 6 5 4 3 2 1

Library of Congress Cataloging-in-Publication Data
Martin, Katie
The everything wedding book / Katie Martin. -- [5th edition].
pages cm
Includes bibliographical references and index.
ISBN 978-1-4405-6958-6 (alk. paper) -- ISBN 1-4405-6958-4 (alk. paper) -- ISBN 978-1-4405-6959-3
(ebook) --
ISBN 1-4405-6959-2 (ebook)
1. Wedding etiquette. 2. Weddings--Planning. I. Title.
BJ2051.M38 2014
395.2'2--dc23
2013031061

This book is available at quantity discounts for bulk purchases.
For information, please call 1-800-289-0963.

Contents

PART II
DETAILS FOR THE BIG DAY

21 **The Married Life / 357**

Acknowledgments

A huge thanks to Grace Freedson and Stefanie Manns for helping make this fifth edition a reality for me. I could not have done it without you Stefanie! Of course, as with everything I do in life, I am eternally grateful to Miguel for creating space and time for me to write and God for providing opportunities for me!

The Top 10 Mistakes That Engaged Couples Make (But Are Easy to Avoid)

1. Skimping on photography: This is the start of your family history!

2. Ignoring advice from married friends and family: Consider all the advice you are offered and choose what is good for you!

3. Not having a backup plan for an outdoor ceremony: Just do it!

4. Thinking you will be able to set up your reception venue the day of your wedding: Why would you even want to?

5. Trying to do your own flowers: Again, why would you want to?

6. Not having a realistic budget from the beginning: Unless you want to just elope right now.

7. Skipping a honeymoon: You will need one, even if it is just for a couple of days!

8. Using an MP3 player for your musical entertainment: Electronics have a way of malfunctioning at the wrong time—at least get a DJ!

9. Not asking for help: Ask a friend, relative, or hire a planner!

10. Forgetting about the environment: Even one small green choice can make a huge difference!

Introduction

YOU HAVE EITHER SHOUTED it from the rooftops or just made a few calls, either way—you are officially engaged! Being engaged comes with a slew of questions, advice, celebrating, and a whole lot of planning. For you, this may be the first big event you have ever planned.

With an ever-growing base of wedding professionals in the world with all sorts of ideas and options comes the knowledge that you can truly have a unique wedding day. A wedding should be all about bringing your two families together to showcase your love for one another. Take all the unique event vendors, your style, and your heritage, mix them all together in one room, and you will have the makings of a dream wedding. While envisioning this dream wedding is often easy, it's finding your way through all of the details that is typically the problem. How can you make your dream day a reality when you have never done this before? Sure, there are a ton of wedding professionals out there, but how do you choose?

It's perfectly normal to feel a little overwhelmed. Couples get married every day all over the world. Does that mean that they were not nervous and that they had a plan from the beginning? Nope! It just means they started the wedding planning process, just like you, and went out with their to-do lists and got the job done. For some people, wedding planning is a breeze, for others it is an absolute challenge. No matter which camp you are in, you just need a little bit of time, patience, and excitement.

Wedding planning is really just information gathering. Your budget and style are what dictate your criteria for the best possible wedding vendors. Just like school or work, you have a project and you have to manage it. With your wedding, it is the same. The biggest difference is that this day is part of your history and typically one of the most important days of your life! So it is completely understandable to be nervous and excited all at the same time.

The Everything® Wedding Book, 5th Edition provides you with the best possible tools and a wealth of information about all of the major aspects of planning a wedding. From how to announce your engagement to planning your honeymoon—each chapter is a guide. Take one chapter at a time and then go back and review as needed. This book is filled with worksheets and information that will help keep you on track and stay organized along the way.

This book will help keep you sane and I hope let you actually enjoy your engagement instead of sitting through countless unnecessary meetings. Being engaged is one of the most thrilling times in a person's life—savor every moment of it. Don't let wedding planning overshadow the end goal: getting married and living happily ever after!

PART I

Planning Your Wedding

CHAPTER 1

Wedding Planning 101

Congratulations! This is an exciting time in your life! Don't let the (sometimes daunting) task of planning your wedding day take away from the excitement of being engaged. This chapter will help you lay out a plan as you begin the process of designing your big day. Take your time as you consider your options and be sure to enlist the help of your fiancé along with your family and friends. Let the planning begin!

Two Families Coming Together

Once you are engaged, the most natural desire is to shout it from the roof-tops! Take special care and make sure to tell the most important people in your lives first. The last thing you want to do when announcing this momentous occasion is offend anyone. There are right ways to announce your engagement and there are wrong ways as well.

Telling Your Parents

If possible, it is always recommended to announce your engagement to your parents in person. If both sets of parents are far away from you (and each other), try to set up a weekend for them to get to know each other. If arranging a meeting is too difficult to do before the week of your wedding, make plans for a personal get-together before your rehearsal.

QUESTION

What should I do if my parents are divorced or remarried?
Try your best to inform all parents on the same day. Traditional etiquette calls for telling the parents of the bride first followed by the groom's parents. Be sure to speak to your parents directly and not through a stepparent.

Telling Your Child or Former Spouse

If applicable, the first person you should tell about your upcoming nuptials is your child (or children). Whether this is your first, second, or third wedding, your child has the right to know before anyone else does. The hope is that you have prepared your child for this possibility. The most important thing to communicate to your child is that you are not trying to replace a parent. The second thing you need to communicate is how your lives will change during the planning process and after the wedding.

In the case where you have a former spouse, it is always best for you to be the first person to inform them. Do not send the word through someone else, especially through your mutual child. If there is no child involved and communication is difficult, an e-mail or handwritten note is sufficient. Be prepared for renewed discussions of alimony and child support. Consult your attorney before discussing these issues with your ex.

ALERT

The issue of a former spouse can be a source of great difficulty for a couple planning their wedding. The best course to take is to be open and honest with your fiancé and both of your families. After discussing the possibilities, you should be able to decide what is best for all involved.

Formal Announcements

After proper etiquette has been followed in announcing your big news to family, the fun begins! This is the time to celebrate with your family, friends, and coworkers. Enjoy this time of engagement!

Start Spreading the News!

The easiest and most formal way of letting the world know about your upcoming nuptials is, of course, through the newspapers. The parents of the bride (for traditional weddings) usually submit newspaper announcements. Typically an announcement gives general information about the couple, including their schooling, careers, how the couple met, and where the wedding will take place. Many couples include an official engagement photo along with the announcement.

The announcement information is usually sent to the newspaper's lifestyle or society editor. Every newspaper has different guidelines for submission so be sure to check out the website or call the administrative office before you send the information. Some newspapers announce for free and some charge to print the announcement. Check with your local publication for specifications and details. Following is an example of a standard published announcement:

Engagement Announcement

Mr. and Mrs. (bride's parents) of (their city, state) announce the engagement of their daughter, (bride's first and middle name), to (groom's full name), son of Mr. and Mrs. (groom's parent's names) of (their city, state). A (month/season) wedding is planned. (Or: No date has been set for the wedding.)

If your fiancé's family lives in another city or state, be sure to send them a copy of the engagement announcement (wording and photo) so they can have the opportunity to announce the good news in their local newspaper as well.

ALERT

Typically newspaper announcements tend to be short and sweet. However, some announcements can be long and pretentious. Announcing your upcoming nuptials should give your guests (and onlookers) just a taste of who the two of you are and what is to come to whet their appetite for the wedding day!

Timing It Right

If you are planning a very long engagement (one year or more), you may want to wait before publishing a newspaper announcement. Most announcements are usually printed no earlier than a year prior to the actual wedding day. Every newspaper has specific (and different) timing guidelines. In larger cities, it is best to research this information sooner rather than later as they will have a larger number of submissions and can only allow a certain number in each printing.

A general rule of thumb is to make your announcement anywhere between three to six months prior to the wedding day. Even the best-laid plans can change due to special circumstances, so the closer to your wedding date your announcement is, the better! It is also perfectly fine to make the announcement after the wedding using a photo from your wedding photographer.

Setting the Date for the Big Day

Some couples prefer not to announce their engagement to the masses until they have a date in place for the wedding. When people learn of your engagement, the first thing you are likely to hear is "Congratulations!" followed by "When's the date?" You cannot make arrangements for any of your family, wedding party, and professionals without a date. If ever timing was of the essence, it is when you are planning your wedding!

Availability and Seasonality

The most obvious place to start is your own calendar! Between you and your fiancé, you are likely to have a few dates that can be completely scratched off. Then it is off to the parents and your closest friends in your wedding party for their weekend preferences. It may sound overwhelming, but your family and friends are the ones who will be surrounding you that day, so you'll want to consider their availability.

ALERT

Keep your family and wedding party part of the process to help your wedding planning go smoothly. Letting them help in simple areas will allow you to have more control over the bigger decisions later. Avoid giving them too much control by asking their opinions about two or three options that you have narrowed down for them ahead of time.

Now that you have the calendar dates that are available for you, your family, and wedding party, it is time to zero in on the date! Here are a few questions to help you narrow your search:

- Which seasons do you prefer?
- Do seasons matter at all to you?
- Do you like snow?
- When did you fall in love?
- What kind of food would you like to have served?
- What are your favorite colors?
- Is there a particular time of year that your families find meaningful?

- Do you want an outdoor ceremony?
- How much time do you have to plan your wedding?
- Do you like the heat or cold?
- Do you want a strapless dress?
- Are there military commitments to consider?

Believe it or not, all of these questions play a role as to the seasonality of your wedding.

Once you have settled on a season and you have weeded out dates that don't mesh with all of the familial calendars, you will be off to the races. It is important to be as flexible as possible with your date as you start the search for your ceremony and reception sites. Your date and venues are really what set the tone for your event, so be careful in your selection and the rest of the planning process will be much easier.

FACT

Wedding season is typically April through October. Keeping this time-frame in mind will help you pick a date and prepare yourself for the possibility of some of your favorite wedding professionals being booked more quickly. In comparison, off-peak weddings are often easier to plan.

In general, the most popular wedding months are June, August, September, and October. Keep in mind that this is only statistically speaking and can change from city to city. Depending on where you live, December may be popular because of the holiday season or February because of Valentine's Day. Every city and couple is different! The key is to be as flexible as possible at this point in the planning process and to be open to what your families' needs are. Remember, the two of you are getting married and entering each other's families. Start off on the right foot and you will be thankful after the wedding.

Happy Holidays?

Should you have your wedding day on a long holiday weekend, such as Memorial Day, Labor Day, or Columbus Day? Does the sound of a festive holiday-season wedding sound incredible to you? What about a New Year's Eve celebration or a romantic Valentine's Day theme? There are pros and cons to each of these ideas.

In regard to the long holiday weekend wedding, there are three major pros. The first pro is that your guests will appreciate a wedding on a long weekend. The long weekend will give your guests an extra day of rest after the wedding before they have to travel back home (if they are coming from out of city, state, or country). The other pro is that you get to celebrate a major holiday with all of your family and friends, and it will give you extra time to do other activities that are not associated with the wedding. Another fantastic pro to consider is your honeymoon! Having your wedding on a holiday weekend means an extra day for your honeymoon or saving at least one of your precious vacation days from work for another future getaway.

ESSENTIAL

If you live in a major city that celebrates a holiday with festivals and other free activities, be sure to do your research ahead of time. If you end up having your wedding on a holiday weekend, be sure to include these activities in your Save the Dates, phone conversations, wedding website, and e-mails!

Unfortunately, with every pro comes a con. Realistically, you will not be the only one who has thought of all these pros for having a wedding on a long holiday weekend. Along with you, will be a long list of other couples wanting the same venues, photographers, florists, etc., for the same date. You will have to make quick decisions if your date falls on a holiday weekend. With this in mind, the next con will be obvious. You will have less negotiating power with your wedding professionals. It is as plain as supply and demand. Some wedding professionals may even charge more for these weekends as they end up having to pay their own staff more on holidays. So be prepared for a higher price tag. The last con is that you will be in competition with longstanding vacation plans that your guests may already have. Both Memorial and Labor Day weekends are popular for beach getaways. Columbus Day weekend is a little easier on families; however, some college students may find it hard to pull away from studying for impending exams and some cities do not celebrate Columbus Day, therefore it may not be a long weekend for all of your potential guests.

In regard to other holidays for your wedding (the winter holiday season through Valentine's Day), be sure you know the pros and cons of these as well. Weddings during the winter holiday season can work best for large families that tend to get together for the holidays anyway. However, this would mean that both sets of families would have to be on the same page for celebrating together (not such an easy task!). If you are looking for a small, intimate wedding, the holiday season could be your best bet. The holidays are generally filled with traditions, spirituality, and normally a great deal of stress. The stress of a wedding on top of family holiday politics may make you consider eloping. Another con is that gifts are traditionally given during the holiday season to family in general. It might make it harder financially for your guests and wedding party to pay for travel and formalwear in addition to all of the gift giving they might have to do (never mind a gift for your actual wedding). You really have to keep your guests in mind more when it comes to getting married during the holiday season.

ALERT

At certain times of the year, major religious holidays can really affect whether or not some of your guests can attend your wedding. If people in your wedding party have strict religious beliefs, be ready to not only check their calendars, but their diet, and other possible observances as well.

One other big popular wedding holiday is New Year's Eve/Day. Many weddings are held on New Year's Eve as it is a great reason to have a big party! Your guests will delight in being able to dress to the nines for your wedding day and you will have a great excuse to get together for the same holiday in the future. The guests love the possibility of being together in the same hotel and not having to drive anywhere after midnight! Some of the same cons will apply to this holiday. Many wedding professionals charge more and traveling on or around this date can be very hectic and costly. Also, many couples see New Year's Eve as a truly romantic night and want to keep it private. You know your guest list better than anyone. If you tend to have a party-all-night crowd, New Year's Eve could really be a fantastic date for you.

ESSENTIAL

When having a wedding on New Year's Eve (where the average alcohol intake is normally doubled or even tripled), the best place to have your wedding is at a hotel or resort. If a hotel is just not your style, make arrangements for transporting all of your guests back to their hotels for safety and liability purposes.

When thinking of the most romantic day of the year, the first day that comes to mind for many people is Valentine's Day. The biggest pro for having a wedding on Valentine's Day is that it is not typically a very popular time of the year to get married and therefore you will have more options for your wedding. The second pro is that couples love to dance, eat, and drink on Valentine's Day. What better way to celebrate than a wedding? In contrast, because Valentine's Day is centered on couples, once again you may find couples that simply want to keep Valentine's Day private. Valentine's Day is not always on a weekend either!

Keeping all of these different things in mind will help you in your selection process for the best possible date for your wedding.

Wedding Consultants versus "On Your Own"

Undoubtedly by the time you have read to this point in the book, you may have thought, "I am going to need some help!" Should you hire a wedding consultant (also known as a wedding planner) or invite a friend or family member to help you plan your wedding? Professional wedding consultants in your area know everything about the wedding industry and specifics about what will work for your wedding in your particular city. A friend or family member knows you best and will help offset the amount of time that you will need to research and interview prospective wedding professionals.

Making the Decision

The most important days of a person's life are buying their first home, getting married, and having a child (not necessarily in that order, of course!). For every single one of these events, there is normally someone helping you. Whether you hire a wedding consultant or have a friend or family member (with some wedding experience under their belt), it is wise to enlist help sooner rather than later.

Not everyone needs or wants a consultant. You should not feel pressured to hire one simply because you are getting married or because someone else you know hired one. Every couple's experience is different and some really enjoy the planning process and have plenty of time to do it on their own. If you fall into this category, you are most likely a very organized and resourceful person. You get excited as much about the process as the actual wedding day. Other couples who may just need a little help, and love having family and friends around to help them make important decisions, may not need the help of a wedding planner. If you fall into this category, you are probably thinking "Why should I pay for advice when I am surrounded by people who have been recently married and have tons of experience in the wedding department?"

There are couples that do not have any time or anyone who can help them plan or design the wedding that they want. With today's busy schedules and dual-income couples the norm, hiring a wedding planner has become more affordable and sensible. Some couples may not live near their families and the mere thought of finding the right caterer or florist induces stress. Hiring a wedding planner is a welcome relief to many couples and can help bring back the excitement of being engaged!

Whether you love the process, and need a little or a lot of help, make sure you are enjoying both the planning process and being engaged too!

Hiring a Wedding Consultant

Should you decide to hire a wedding consultant, there are several things you should keep in mind. The first thing you should know is that an independent wedding consultant is your representative in the wedding industry. Do not confuse an independent wedding consultant with a wedding consultant that is part of a store, reception site, or caterer. These consultants normally cannot advise you on wedding professionals outside their area of expertise, products, or particular services. For example, there may be a specific wedding staff person at a hotel who specializes in weddings for that particular location. That does not make this person a wedding consultant. Remember, the money you are paying the hotel is strictly tied to the contract you sign with them. These contracts typically only include the banquet event order (BEO), which details what the hotel will be providing—not what outside vendors will provide. Essentially, an independent wedding consultant is the only professional whom you will hire that makes sure that all of your vendors have the tools they need to make your wedding the day of your dreams and that they are fulfilling their contractual obligations to you as a couple.

Questions, Questions, Questions!

Once you have narrowed your search for a wedding planner, you want to make sure to ask as many questions as possible before deciding. Your chosen wedding planner needs to understand what you are looking for on your wedding day and your personalities should be compatible. Your wedding planner will be walking alongside you in every aspect of the planning process and you want to make sure you feel at ease in communicating your desires.

ALERT

If you are in the process of hiring a wedding planner, the most important thing to note (before hiring them) is their list of what they cannot provide for you. Every wedding professional will tell you what they can do, but finding out what they will not do for you after you hire them is too late!

Here is a list of a few key questions that you should ask before hiring your wedding planner:

- How long have you been in business?
- Are you a part-time or full-time consultant?
- How many staff members do you have?
- How many weddings do you handle per weekend?

- What are your fees? (Hourly? Flat fee? Percentage?)
- What is included in your package?
- Will you be the person coordinating the day of? If not, when can I meet my planner?
- Do you have photos of any recent weddings you have planned?

Levels of Service

There are normally different levels of service that each consultant can and will provide. The most popular packages are full consulting, partial consulting, and wedding coordination "day-of." Make sure you review what each package includes and communicate to your planner what you need the most help with. Full consulting normally helps in planning the entire event down to the tiniest detail, while day-of consulting can mean just helping the week of the event.

FACT

Etiquette will play a major role in every aspect of the wedding planning process. Some socially acceptable rules of etiquette, manners, and protocol are written and others are not. Wedding planners will help you navigate these rules.

A *full wedding consulting package* typically includes the following:

- Unlimited consultations in person, on the phone, or online
- Wedding planning timeline
- Expert guidance on etiquette
- A customized budget
- Wedding professional recommendations
- Scheduling of wedding professional appointments around your availability
- Review and negotiation of vendor contracts on your behalf
- Logistical management
- Cuisine selection and help at any tastings

- Ongoing communication with your wedding professionals
- Event design of overall décor scheme
- Design of all guest amenities, including welcome bags, favors, programs, etc.
- Scheduling of salon and spa services
- Creation of a detailed itinerary for your wedding weekend
- Timeline distribution to all wedding professionals prior to the wedding
- A walk-through at your ceremony and reception locations
- Final wedding professional confirmations the week of your wedding
- Oversight and management of wedding day installation
- Rehearsal coordination and direction
- Coordination, management, and troubleshooting on your wedding day
- Follow-up with all wedding professionals and your wedding party as needed after your wedding day

Typically a full consulting package will include a head consultant with an assistant for the day of the wedding.

A ***partial consulting package*** typically includes the following:

- Initial planning timeline
- Initial budget design
- Vendor referrals
- Review of all vendor contracts before signing
- Vendor negotiation hints and tips
- Coordination of all décor, linen, and/or tent and supply rentals
- Detailed itinerary creation
- Walk-throughs at ceremony and reception sites
- Vendor confirmations
- Point of contact for all vendors and key individuals
- Rehearsal management and week-of-wedding coordination
- Organization and coordination of all events related to your wedding weekend
- Day-of coordination

As with full packages, most partial planning packages include a head consultant and an assistant for the day of the wedding.

Finally, a typical list of what is included in a ***day-of coordination package***:

- An itinerary and timeline assistance meeting
- Scheduled walk-throughs at your ceremony and reception sites
- Rehearsal management
- Vendor confirmations
- Complete day-of coordination with a head consultant and at least one assistant

Is This My Wedding?

Make sure that no matter whom you ask to help with your wedding day, whether a planner or a friend, you are in charge of the decision-making process. In the end, you are the one (or your parents are) who is paying for all of the services that day and it is *your* wedding day! Although it is not typical for wedding planners to make contracts with wedding professionals on your behalf, there are planners who do. If your planner has the power of the checkbook (or credit card), be sure there is a written agreement that you have final say as to who is being booked for your wedding day.

It is important to note that a wedding planner should really be behind the scenes the day of the wedding. You should be the one who shines and the planner should just be there to help facilitate the day.

ALERT

Be careful and avoid any consultant who seems likely to disregard your wishes and gives off the feeling that she is in charge of "the show." Your wedding day is not a show and should reflect the two of you as a couple, not the style of the planner!

If you are having difficulty selecting your wedding planner, references are normally the best bet! The best references for a wedding planner are, of course, past couples. Some other great resources are venue managers, as they normally work the most with wedding planners (if at a popular venue). Some venues even print brochures with their list of recommended planners among other event professionals. In the end, if your planner is one of the best in the area, venue managers will know. Parents of past couples are also a great barometer of how a planner will treat your family during the planning process and the day of the wedding. The best wedding planners have a wide range of styles and budgets in their repertoires.

How Much?

The price range of wedding planners today is amazing. With the advent of wedding reality shows on TV came the influx of wedding and event planners. Some planners are weekend warriors and have full-time jobs during the week. They tend to be less expensive and usually less experienced. The weekend warrior is normally your best bet if you are on a tight budget and really just looking for some help the day of the wedding but want a professional. Other planners are full time and have extensive experience and numerous weddings under their belts. With experience normally comes a higher price tag. A general rule of thumb is that you should never spend more than 10 percent of your overall budget on a wedding planner. Do not give up the thought of hiring a wedding planner based on budget. Prices really do vary, so don't be afraid to ask around. With so many places for references (books, magazines, and the Internet) it is easier for couples today to find wedding planners that fit within their budgets. In the end, your planner should be creative, communicative, easy to deal with, and within your budget.

FACT

For full wedding planning packages, some wedding planners charge a flat fee while others charge a percentage of your overall budget. Some planners even charge by the hour. In the end, a flat-rate package is typically the most cost-effective.

Remember, starting with your wedding planner, you should always come prepared. Take a look at the Wedding Consultant Worksheet at the end of this chapter to help guide you through the process of hiring a wedding planner.

Planning Checklist

Six to twelve months before the wedding:

- [ ] Announce engagement
- [ ] Decide on type of wedding
- [ ] Decide on time of day
- [ ] Choose the location
- [ ] Set a date
- [ ] Set a budget
- [ ] Select bridal party
- [ ] Plan color scheme
- [ ] Select and order bridal gown and/or groom's suit
- [ ] Select and order headpiece
- [ ] Select and order shoes
- [ ] Select and order attendants' gowns
- [ ] Start honeymoon planning
- [ ] Create bridal gift registry
- [ ] Start compiling the guest list
- [ ] Select caterer
- [ ] Select musicians
- [ ] Select florist
- [ ] Select photographer
- [ ] Start planning reception
- [ ] Reserve hall, hotel, etc., for reception
- [ ] Plan to attend premarital counseling at your church, if applicable
- [ ] Select and order wedding rings
- [ ] Plan rehearsal and rehearsal dinner

Planning Checklist (continued)

Three months before the wedding:

☐ Complete guest list

☐ Make doctor's appointments (if needed)

☐ Plan to have mothers select attire

☐ Select and order invitations

☐ Order personal stationery

☐ Start compiling trousseau

☐ Finalize reception arrangements (rent items now)

☐ Make reservations for honeymoon

☐ Confirm dress delivery

☐ Confirm time and date with florist

☐ Confirm time and date with caterer

☐ Confirm time and date with photographer

☐ Confirm time and date with musicians

☐ Confirm time and date with church

☐ Discuss transportation to ceremony and reception

☐ Order cake

☐ Select and order attire for groomsmen

☐ Schedule bridesmaids' dress and shoe fittings

Two months before the wedding:

☐ Mail all invitations to allow time for RSVPs

☐ Arrange for appointment to get marriage license

☐ Finalize honeymoon arrangements

Planning Checklist (continued)

One month before the wedding:

- [ ] Schedule bridal portrait (if wanted/needed)
- [ ] Reserve accommodations for guests
- [ ] Begin to record gifts received and send thank-you notes
- [ ] Purchase gifts for bridal party
- [ ] Purchase gift for fiancé if gifts are being exchanged
- [ ] Schedule final fittings, including accessories and shoes
- [ ] Schedule appointments at beauty salon for attendants
- [ ] Schedule bridesmaids' luncheon or party
- [ ] Arrange for placement of guest book
- [ ] Obtain wedding props, e.g., pillow for ringbearer, candles, etc.
- [ ] Get marriage license

Two weeks before the wedding:

- [ ] Mail bridal portrait with announcement to newspaper
- [ ] Finalize wedding day transportation
- [ ] Arrange to change name on license, Social Security card, etc.
- [ ] Confirm accommodations for guests
- [ ] Prepare wedding announcements to be mailed after the wedding

Planning Checklist (continued)

One week before the wedding:

- ☐ Start packing for honeymoon
- ☐ Finalize number of guests with caterer
- ☐ Double-check all details with those providing professional services (photographer, videographer, florist, etc.)
- ☐ Finalize seating arrangements
- ☐ Confirm desired pictures with photographer
- ☐ Style your hair with headpiece
- ☐ Practice applying cosmetics in proper light
- ☐ Arrange for one last fitting of all wedding attire
- ☐ Make sure rings are picked up and fit properly
- ☐ Confirm receipt of marriage license
- ☐ Have rehearsal/rehearsal dinner (one or two days before wedding)
- ☐ Arrange to have the photographer and attendants arrive two hours before ceremony if there are to be pre-wedding pictures
- ☐ Arrange for music to start one half hour prior to ceremony

On your wedding day:

- ☐ Try to relax and pamper yourself; take a long bath, have a manicure, etc.
- ☐ Eat at least one small meal prior to the ceremony; drink plenty of water
- ☐ Have your hair and makeup done a few hours before ceremony
- ☐ Start dressing one to two hours before ceremony

Wedding Consultant Worksheet

Name:

Address:

Phone:

Contact:

Hours:

Appointments:

Date: Time:

Date: Time:

Date: Time:

Date: Time:

Service:

Number of hours:

Overtime cost:

Provides the following services:

Cost:

Fee: ☐ Flat   ☐ Hourly percentage: _____   ☐ Per guest

Total amount due: Date:

Amount of deposit: Date:

Amount due: Date:

Gratuities included?   ☐ Yes   ☐ No

Sales tax included?   ☐ Yes   ☐ No

Date contract signed:

Terms of cancellation:

Notes:

CHAPTER 2

Creating the Budget

Once the excitement of getting engaged starts, it can easily be interrupted by thoughts of "How much will this cost?" Creating a budget that keeps all parties involved happy and carefree will be tricky. This chapter will help you with specific tools to keep all of your expenses in perspective. The key to successfully planning your wedding starts with a detailed budget. Leave your financial worries behind in order to enjoy your engagement by creating a rock solid budget!

Money Matters

Money is normally the first item on the agenda after announcing the engagement to family. Be prepared for a very long list of questions from the individuals who will be contributing financially to your wedding. If you are not having a traditional Western wedding (where the parents of the bride pay for just about everything), then you are either completely in control or will encounter more people to manage. Keep in mind that you have two families coming together. Money is no object for some families. For others, money can be a great source of stress and tension for all of the individuals who will be paying. Tread lightly!

When Money Is No Object. Really?

There are some very lucky (and rare) instances when couples find that their wedding budget does not have an upper limit. If you fall into the category of an unlimited-budget couple, you still need to set a budget. It may sound contradictory, but a budget is made for flexibility purposes. If you go over your budget in a certain category, you can make those adjustments as you go along. You need to make sure that your wedding professionals are not aware of this unlimited budget so they do not take advantage of you.

ALERT

If you find that you have a large amount of resources to put toward the wedding of your dreams, then you should hire a wedding planner. A wedding planner can help you make the right financial decisions based on your style rather than your budget.

If your parents are paying for your wedding (and money is no object), a budget will help them to see a clear picture of what your wedding might cost. The other issue to consider is that if your parents are in charge of the budget, they are also in charge of your wedding. Having an unlimited budget might give you limited choices. Be sure to communicate clearly with your parents from the beginning about your vision for your wedding day. If your vision does not coincide with their vision, difficult decisions and compromises will most likely have to be made.

Tighter Budget? No Problem!

The majority of brides do not have an unlimited budget. It is normal to have a finite budget. If money is especially tight, it's best to prioritize so that your wedding can have the things that are most important to you. First you must decide what type of wedding you want. Your job is to try to construct a budget based on your desires, using the resources you have available. Perhaps you and your fiancé don't want a big formal (or semi-formal) wedding. You may both shy away from over-the-top frills and opulent details, preferring to avoid much of the headache and expense by holding a small, simple affair. If this is the route you want to go, there are plenty of options: a backyard wedding at home, a simple dinner at your favorite restaurant, or a civil ceremony.

You may decide, though, that you want as much of the grand, traditional wedding that your budget will allow. In either case, planning expenses becomes particularly important. You'll want to make every dollar go as far as it possibly can.

Who Will Pay for What

Now that you know what your overall budget is and the type of wedding you want, you'll need to figure out exactly how you're going to afford it. Who will pay for what? This question is very important in the beginning stages of the planning process. You must have a face-to-face conversation (or phone conversation) with everyone who is paying for part of the wedding. Communication is essential.

Traditional Western Wedding Expenses

In traditional Western cultures, it is customary for the bride's family to bear the majority of the wedding expenses. If you fall into this category, the bride and her family traditionally pay for the following:

- Wedding gown and accessories
- The groom's wedding ring and gift
- Invitations, reception cards, and announcements (including calligraphy)

- Fee for ceremony location
- Floral designs for ceremony and reception (including flowers for attendants)
- Photography
- Videography
- Music for ceremony and reception
- All reception costs (including the location rental, food, décor, etc.)
- Transportation, accommodations, and gifts for bridesmaids
- Wedding planner expenses (if you plan to hire a wedding planner)

The groom and his family are traditionally held responsible for the following expenses:

- The bride's wedding and engagement rings
- Gift for the bride
- Marriage license
- Officiant's fee
- The bridal bouquet, mothers' and grandmothers' corsages, as well as the boutonnières for the groom's wedding party
- Rehearsal dinner
- Honeymoon
- Groomsmen's lodging (optional)

FACT

If you are holding a multicultural wedding, please note that you must consult with each set of parents to understand one another's culture. In some cultures, the groom's family pays for everything. In this scenario, the two sets of parents must come to an agreement as to who will pay for what.

Bucking Tradition

Even if you are having a traditional Western ceremony, you may feel uncomfortable asking your family to incur wedding expenses. There are several ways of handling this. It is not uncommon for a couple to bear the brunt of the wedding expenses themselves. If the idea of paying for your own wedding scares you (especially after you start finding out how much things can cost), just know that your own opinions carry more weight if you are the one writing the checks.

ALERT

Remember that if you are going outside customary cultural wedding traditions, you must keep all parties informed. Be aware that some other traditions will go out the window at the same time. For example, you may not have much say about the food if your future in-laws are paying for it.

If you are not paying for the entire wedding out of your own pocket, be sure you get set dollar amounts from each person that is graciously contributing to your wedding. This will help avoid confusion and will help you design an overall budget.

Setting Up and Sticking to a Budget

After you decide on the type of wedding you would like to have, you'll need to figure out exactly how you are going to afford it. The amount you allocate to your overall wedding budget will help you to determine everything from the number of guests you can invite to the type of cake you will have (and everything in between).

Running the Numbers

There are two ways to create a budget. The first is to determine the amount of money that is available right now. This will include any money that you and your fiancé may have squirreled away for the event, as well as any contributions that you are aware of. For example, you might know exactly how much your parents have saved up for your wedding day. The total of these resources is your total budget, assuming that you're planning on paying cash for the bulk of your wedding expenses.

If your parents have no wedding fund planned, then there is a second way of creating your budget. Maybe you are sure your parents will want to chip in and help defray the costs of the wedding. Try tallying up the cost of your ideal wedding before asking for financial assistance. You may find that you will get a better response if you have a ballpark figure to present (rather than asking for a vague contribution). The Wedding Budget Worksheet at the end of this chapter will be a valuable resource to you. It will give you a good idea of the amount of services and goods that many weddings include.

Doing Your Wedding Homework

If hiring a wedding planner to help you create a budget is not an option, you'll need to do your homework!

Although your budget numbers may differ from a friend's budget, asking newlyweds for their advice will give you an idea of what certain services might cost. For example you may want to spend more on photography than your friends did or decide to have a DJ instead of a band. Their choices will help to bring perspective to your budget.

After speaking with newlyweds, skimming magazines, and consulting parents, your next best bet is the Internet. There are several wedding websites that can help you determine what is the best budget for your city and number of guests. Most national wedding websites can help you navigate costs from wedding dresses to planning for gratuities. Several websites will let you set up your budget online so that your family can log on and see your budget and help you plan. Online tools are especially helpful for couples who have parents in other cities. A couple of the more popular websites are:

- *www.brides.com*
- *www.weddingwire.com*

Keep in mind that many bridal websites have budget calculators based on national averages. Your wedding and your city may be above or below the national average, which is why finding the right vendors and getting professional local advice is imperative.

ESSENTIAL

Sticking to a budget is always the hardest part. Be sure to include your fiancé and the parties involved with funding the wedding when making changes to the budget. You may find that you will have to make compromises to stick to your budget.

When looking online, be sure to take all advice with a grain of salt. Some websites have professional advice columns and some websites have advice from newlyweds. Wedding professionals are selling their goods or services and newlyweds are basing their advice on their budgets. Take all information into account, but be sure that the choices you make are right for your wedding. Also, don't let an online negative review about a wedding professional keep you from researching them. Nine times out of ten, if a wedding professional has more positive reviews than negative, they are a reputable company and deserve the research (especially if you have heard great things about them from other resources).

Tracking Your Expenses

After doing all the research, you can finally insert the cost ranges into your budget. The best bet is to set up a spreadsheet or table like the spreadsheet at the end of this chapter. Always start with the proposed budget amount and end with the most expensive scenario. This way there will be no surprises for you.

Proposals, Proposals, Proposals

The only way you will be able to figure out a real approximate cost of the services and goods you want for your wedding is to ask for proposals. Here are some hints on how to get reasonable proposals:

- Ask for proposals from two to three wedding professionals for each category of service or good you are looking for. This will give you more negotiating power and will help you to see the average costs of each type of wedding professional. If you see more than three professionals, things will really start to become a blur and you might actually be wasting your time.

- Try to get proposals from the same wedding professionals that your friends used. Wedding professionals love referrals and will be more apt to provide a discount or added value to the package of your choosing.

Decision Time

After receiving proposals and keeping all of your options in mind, the decision time has arrived. Many find that making a decision can be overwhelming due to the fear of buyer's remorse. Buyer's remorse, simply stated, is once a deposit is put down on a wedding professional, there is no going back, even if you want to! The best way to reduce buyer's remorse is always to weigh the pros and cons of each wedding professional. Here are a few ways for making the decision for each type of wedding professional:

- After speaking with vendors, evaluate how they each stack up against the others (within the same category of wedding professional). This way you can weed out which ones won't work for you, one step at a time.
- If you still have doubts, research their websites and other websites to see if you can find their pros and cons.
- Last but not least, always ask questions. Keep in mind your wedding professional wants your business. The only way they can confidently serve you is by knowing all of your needs and answering all of your questions. Communication is the key to a successful working relationship with your wedding professionals.

Traditional Gratuity Guidelines

From the minute you start planning your wedding to the time you go on your honeymoon, gratuities should be part of your overall budget planning. Keep in mind that this is the most important day of your life—you want to make sure that the wedding professionals you are using on this day are compensated for their extra effort.

What to Expect

Several wedding professional companies will include gratuities in their initial proposals. The most common are caterers and transportation companies. Another common area where you will see gratuities built in to proposals are at hotels. Don't be surprised to see gratuities built in to other proposals. In the case where a gratuity is not built into the proposal, you should consider cushioning your budget to make room for it.

The Gratuity List

- **Caterers/Facility Wait Staff**—Sometimes your contract will include a gratuity already. If your contract does not have a gratuity included, depending on the service provided, 10 percent of food and beverage only, before taxes, is traditional (no need to have a gratuity added for the rentals they provide for you). Remember your catering services are normally 50–60 percent of your entire budget and caterers do most of the setup of your event (tables, chairs, linens, etc.), breakdown, and cleanup. If you feel your catering sales manager did a particularly great job, an additional gratuity of your choice is always nice to help make your event a successful one.
- **Bartender(s)**—A caterer or hotel banquet manager might include their gratuities in your contract. If not, depending on the service and the type of bar, 5–10 percent of the beverage bill is customary. A bartender will likely be the first person to take care of guests once they arrive at the reception site or cocktail hour. Bartenders normally work the hardest the first two hours of the reception.
- **Florist**—Gratuity (not delivery charge) might be included in the contract. If there is no gratuity specified, a 5–15 percent gratuity is standard (before taxes, delivery, setup, and breakdown). Some florists will bring extra flowers to decorate in addition to what is in your contract, so take note and tip accordingly. Depending on the size of your wedding, most florists will bring additional staff to help create your

floral designs in a timely manner; this should be taken into consideration as well.

- **Religious Officiant**—Normally not tipped, however, if you have a personal relationship to the officiant or the church/temple where your ceremony is being held, consider a monetary charitable gift of their choice. Some officiants have a standard rate for services. If your officiant does not have a standard rate, consider an honorarium monetary gift, depending on your budget or affinity.
- **Civil Officiant**—Hardly ever tipped, as most civil servants are not allowed to receive tips due to local law. Consider giving a nice and appropriate gift for the occasion.
- **Musician(s) and DJ(s)**—Their gratuity might be specified in the contract. If not, consider a proportionate tip per musician or DJ (based on 10–20 percent of the contract), depending on each person's involvement.
- **Chauffeur(s)/Limo Driver(s)**—Almost always specified in event contracts. If not, depending on service, tip 10–15 percent of contracted price.
- **Parking Valets, Powder Room Attendants, and Coatroom Attendants**—Gratuity for the facility should include these tips. If you have hired outside vendors for these services, again gratuities should be included. If not, consider $2–5 per car.
- **Hairstylist/Makeup Artists**—If you are at a salon, tip as you normally would. If you have a contracted individual who comes to your home or hotel (and a gratuity is not already included in the price of their services), the gratuity should be between 10–20 percent.
- **Pedicurist/Manicurist/Beautician (facials, hair removal, etc.)**—10–20 percent each
- **Masseuse**—10–20 percent each
- **Photographer(s) and Videographer(s)**—10–20 percent depending on any extra effort. A photographer's or videographer's assistant (or second shooter) should be tipped as well. Some clients like to wait to tip on these two vendors until they receive their images and/or videos. However, tipping the day of the event will probably motivate them to pay special attention to the processing and have quicker delivery of images and DVDs for you.

ESSENTIAL

You can ask your coordinator to distribute gratuity envelopes for you. It is also appropriate to include your gratuity with a nice thank-you note so each of your vendors can show future clients for reference.

The Extras

Even after careful planning there are several expenses that can pop up a month before, a week before, or even the day of the wedding. The most important thing to note is that you have a choice in planning for these extra expenses or simply saying "no" to them.

The Unexpected Guests

After all the RSVPs have been counted and you made the calls, you have to make plans for last-minute, unexpected guests. Although it is not common for guests to show up at the last minute, it is also not unheard of! For instance, if all of your family is local (and the majority of them are coming) the tendency of family members is to think "There is always room for one more." There are all types of scenarios where unexpected guests arrive to a wedding uninvited. You simply have to be prepared to bear the costs of this and not expect guests to pay for it.

Gifts, Tips, and Repairs

In your budget you should always make room for giving gifts and saying thank you to those who are helping you during the wedding process. However, there is always a nice next-door neighbor and a generous coworker (who may not necessarily be on the guest list) who will surprise you with a nice card or wedding gift. You can have an extra invitation available for these people or simply have an extra thank-you note available. Either way, this is an extra expense that you need to prepare for.

Other tips and gratuities will pop up along the process of engagement and wedding planning. A couple of typical examples include the fantastic bartender at the bachelor or bachelorette party or the bellhop at the hotel who helps you unload your five suitcases full of wedding paraphernalia.

Finally, the one thing that engaged couples dread planning for: the worst-case scenario. The worst being: doing any kind of repair to your dress, suit, the bridesmaids' dresses, the groomsmen's suits or shoes, or any other wedding party clothing. Always having a backup option is the key to a flawless wedding day. Being prepared financially for this will help ease your stress and keep you prepared for the big day!

Using a Wedding Budget Worksheet

The following spreadsheet can be used to plan out your wedding budget from start to finish. Take the advice from this chapter and put it into practice here. You can either rip out these pages and place them in your wedding notebook, or create a spreadsheet online or on your computer for effortless changes along the way. This spreadsheet is meant to be a guideline and not law for your wedding. Again, budgets need to be flexible, and if you keep that in mind during your engagement you will have less stress and financial anxiety.

Wedding Budget Worksheet

Item	Projected Cost*	Deposit Paid	Balance Due	Who Pays?
Wedding Consultant				
Fee				
Pre-wedding Parties				
Engagement**				
Site rental				
Equipment rental				
Invitations				
Food				
Beverages				
Decorations				
Flowers				
Party favors				
Bridesmaids' party/luncheon				
Rehearsal dinner**				
Site rental				
Equipment rental				
Invitations				
Food				
Beverages				
Decorations				
Flowers				
Party favors				
Weekend wedding parties				

*(including tax, if applicable) **(if hosted by bride and groom)

Wedding Budget Worksheet (continued)

Item	Projected Cost*	Deposit Paid	Balance Due	Who Pays?
Ceremony				
Location fee				
Officiant's fee				
Donation to church (optional, amount varies)				
Organist Tip (amount varies)				
Other musicians Tip (amount varies)				
Program				
Aisle runner				
Business and Legal Matters				
Marriage license				
Blood test (if applicable)				
Wedding Jewelry				
Engagement ring				
Bride's wedding band				
Groom's wedding band				
Bride's Formalwear				
Wedding gown				
Alterations				
Undergarments (slip, bustier, hosiery, etc.)				
Headpiece				
Shoes				
Jewelry (excluding engagement and wedding rings)				

Wedding Budget Worksheet (continued)

Item	Projected Cost*	Deposit Paid	Balance Due	Who Pays?
Purse (optional)				
Cosmetics, or makeup stylist				
Hair stylist				
Going-away outfit				
Going-away accessories				
Honeymoon clothes				
Groom's Formalwear				
Tuxedo				
Shoes				
Going-away outfit				
Honeymoon clothes				
Gifts				
Bride's Attendants				
Groom's Attendants				
Bride (optional)				
Groom (optional)				
Reception				
Site rental				
Equipment rental (chairs, tent, etc.)				
Decorations				
Servers, bartenders				
Wine service for cocktail hour				
Hors d'oeuvres				
Entrees				
Meals for hired help				
Nonalcoholic beverages				

Wedding Budget Worksheet (continued)

Item	Projected Cost*	Deposit Paid	Balance Due	Who Pays?
Wine				
Champagne				
Liquor				
Dessert				
Toasting glasses				
Guest book and pen				
Place cards				
Printed napkins				
Party favors (matches, chocolates, etc.)				
Box or pouch for envelope gifts				
Tip for caterer or banquet manager (usually $300-$500)				
Tip for servers, bartenders (5–10% of food and beverage lines only)				
Photography and Videography				
Engagement portrait				
Wedding portrait				
Wedding proofs				
Photographer's fee				
Wedding prints				
Album				
Mothers' albums				
Extra prints				
Videographer's fee				
Video/DVD				

Wedding Budget Worksheet (continued)

Item	Projected Cost*	Deposit Paid	Balance Due	Who Pays?
Reception Music				
Musicians for cocktail hour				
Tip ($50–$100)				
Live band				
Tip (optional, usually $25 per band member)				
Disc jockey				
Tip (optional, usually 15–20%)				
Flowers and Decorations (5–10% before taxes, delivery, set-up, and breakdown lines)				
Flowers for wedding site				
Decorations for wedding site				
Bride's bouquet				
Bridesmaids' flowers				
Boutonnières				
Corsages				
Flowers for reception site				
Potted plants				
Table centerpieces				
Head table				
Cake table				
Decorations for reception				
Wedding Invitations and Stationery				
Invitations				
Announcements				
Thank-you notes				
Calligrapher				
Postage				

Wedding Budget Worksheet (continued)

Item	Projected Cost*	Deposit Paid	Balance Due	Who Pays?
Wedding Cake				
Tip for delivery person should be between $20–$50				
Groom's cake				
Cake top and decorations				
Flowers for cake				
Cake serving set				
Cake boxes				
Wedding Transportation				
Limousines or rented cars				
Parking				
Tip for drivers (usually 15–20%)				
Guest Accommodations				
Guest Transportation				
Honeymoon				
Transportation				
Accommodations				
Meals				
Spending money				
Additional Expenses (list below)				
Total of All Expenses				

CHAPTER 3

Your Wedding Party, Family, and Guests

Your wedding would not be the same without your family, wedding party, and, of course, your guests. It is so important to choose your wedding party wisely as they will help you prepare for the big day. You can't choose your family, so you need to find ways to keep them involved. And last, but not least, your wedding guest list is a science all its own.

Choosing Your Attendants

The first thing every couple has to think about when choosing attendants is how to narrow down the number. Most couples have too many people in their lives to choose for their wedding party. You can't possibly offend your five best friends, brothers, sisters, or your extended family by not including them in the wedding party . . . can you? You're going to have to make tough decisions. No one said it would be easy, but you really shouldn't have forty bridesmaids and groomsmen coming down the aisle!

Since your attendants will have certain duties to perform, this will help eliminate anyone you feel would not want these duties. There are also costs that have to be considered such as clothing, travel, and gifts. The last thing you want your wedding to be is a burden.

As soon as you figure out the people you want to include in your wedding party, find the time to personally ask them as soon as possible. Sometimes, due to financial obligations or work or family conflicts, one of your first choices may have to decline. You want to make sure you have enough time to find a replacement. Above all else, try to select attendants who are not too opinionated and who have known you and your fiancé for a while. This is no time for surprises! If you are upfront about what you expect all attendants to do, you shouldn't run into too many complications.

ALERT

You may feel pressure to include friends or family members who have asked you to be an attendant in their weddings. You are not obligated to ask them to be attendants. However, try to find another way to include them by asking them to do a reading or give out programs, for example.

Special Circumstances

Planning a wedding isn't a walk in the park, obviously. You need help, and that is one reason you are asking certain people to be your attendants. What if your best friend lives overseas? What if your sister (your matron of honor) is going to be very pregnant on your wedding day? How can you include these people, and what should you expect of them?

- **Distant best friend**—Should distance stop you from having your best friend beside you on your special day? A maid of honor and a best man have considerable responsibilities before the wedding. You should keep in mind that an out-of-town maid of honor or best man can't be expected to help you with as much of the pre-wedding planning as someone who lives locally. Just establish, as early as possible, what it is you would like him or her to help with that they can do from afar. Spell out your expectations so each knows how to be helpful even without being in the same time zone.
- **Pregnant bridesmaid**—Most designers now offer maternity-style bridesmaid dresses. Bear in mind that if any of your attendants (particularly the maid or matron of honor) will be eight and a half months pregnant at the time of your wedding, you may want to consider a standby maid or matron of honor.

ESSENTIAL

If you are having a hard time deciding between two friends for the role of your honor attendant, dual titles may make your life easier. If you have two sisters, for example, and one of them is married and one isn't, your problem is solved! You have a maid of honor and a matron of honor. Divide the duties equally between them. The other option is to just call all of your female attendants bridesmaids and all male attendants groomsmen (with no maid of honor or best man).

Wedding Party Duties

Help has arrived! Your attendants actually have duties! Don't just assume that all of your attendants will help automatically. You will have to spell out for your friends and family the duties you hope they will take on. This way, you don't get left resenting an attendant for something that they did not even realize you wanted them to do. Here is a list of who does what (typically).

Maid/Matron of Honor

Historically these were the women who helped the bride get away from her overprotective family and other suitors so that she could be captured by the groom she wanted. (Kind of like when your best friend would wait with her car while you snuck out your bedroom window to go clubbing and meet your boyfriend.) Even after such difficult methods of getting the bride and groom together faded in popularity, the honor roles survived.

Nowadays a maid or matron of honor typically helps a bride address envelopes, record wedding gifts, shop, and take care of other important pre-wedding duties. She is also charged with arranging a bridal shower, with the help of your bridesmaids (if you have them).

The maid of honor helps the bride get dressed before the ceremony. At the altar, she arranges the bride's dress and veil, holds the bridal bouquet during the vows, and holds the groom's ring until the appropriate moment during the ceremony. She will also sign a wedding certificate (if needed) with the best man as a witness to the ceremony.

After the ceremony, the maid of honor stands in the receiving line (if you plan to have one). She helps the bride change clothes after the reception and takes care of the bride's gown by either returning it to her mom, her home, or to the dry cleaners for preservation.

ALERT

Reading through these duties carefully, you will realize that this is not a job for the faint of heart or for the lazy. There is quite a bit involved with being maid of honor. Unless you want to end up taking care of all the details yourself, both big and small ones, choose this attendant wisely.

Best Man

Let's start with a little bit of history behind the term *best man* or *best men*. The groom used to take a group of his friends with him while in pursuit of the bride to help him capture her.

Young brides were kidnapped from a protective family—which typically included a few big brothers. Sometimes there would even be a battle between competing suitors. If a potential groom wanted to show that he meant business, he took along the best men for the job of helping him fight for his love. Aren't you glad you live in this century?

Nowadays the best man's position has evolved considerably! The best man organizes the bachelor party. After that, he pays for his own formalwear, drives the groom to the ceremony, and holds the bride's ring until it's needed during the ceremony.

The best man is also charged with handing over the checks to the officiant just before or after the ceremony. He may also be asked to take care of paying other service providers such as the chauffer for the limo. If this is to be part of his duties, the groom or the groom's family will give the best man cash or checks ahead of time, which he will then pass on to the appropriate parties. The best man is also given the duty of giving the toast at the wedding reception.

Bridesmaids and Groomsmen

You are asking a lot of girls to become your bridesmaids, so make sure they are up to the task. Bridesmaids pay for their own wedding clothing and accessories and typically help organize the bridal shower. One of the bridesmaids will keep a record of the gifts at the shower for you. The bridesmaids will assist in pre-wedding shopping tasks. They will also help you get ready for the wedding; after the ceremony they will stand in the receiving line.

Groomsmen are sometimes overlooked, but they are given a significant amount of responsibility. For starters, they will need to rent or purchase their own formalwear. Groomsmen are asked to arrive at the wedding location to assist with the setup and finishing touches, such as lighting candles or taking guests to their seats. Ushers and groomsmen tend to welcome and seat guests of honor such as grandparents. Just before the processional, one or two of the groomsmen will roll out the aisle runner. After the ceremony, the groomsmen stand in the receiving line. Groomsmen will oversee the transfer of the gifts at the reception to your home or to your parents. Last, but not least, they will most likely decorate your getaway car.

Keeping Your Family Happy and Involved

It is easy to think that your wedding will be a huge celebration with your best friends. However, you need to keep focused on your family and how to keep them happy and involved. Keep in mind that your parents and extended family do more than just simply sign checks and send you gifts. This is a special day in their lives as well. They get to dress the part and even offer their opinions once in a while.

Parents of the Traditional Bride

On the surface, your father's duty is to accompany you to the ceremony and give you away. In reality, most fathers have very specific duties:

- Paying for all wedding expenses
- Walking the bride down the aisle
- Hosting the reception (along with the mother of the bride)
- Giving a traditional welcome toast
- Dancing a special dance with the bride (typically after the bride and groom's first dance at the reception)

These are only traditional ideas for your father, and your family may have a few customs of their own.

You may not realize that the mother of the bride is considered part of the wedding party. After all, your father gets his moment to shine, shouldn't the woman who endured hours of labor to give you life be included as well? At the onset of the ceremony, the mother is the last person seated before the processional begins. Just like your attendants, she has plenty to do for the wedding both officially and unofficially.

Your mother does all of the following:

- Helps you choose your wedding gown and accessories (as well as the bridesmaid gowns)
- Works with you and your fiancé's family to assemble a guest list and a seating plan
- Helps your attendants plan the bridal shower
- Helps address and mail invitations
- Greets guests at the beginning of the receiving line
- May act as hostess during the reception

Your mother will, of course, occupy a place of honor at the ceremony and at the parents' table during the reception. Her biggest official duty is to assist you with any of the hundreds of details you need to handle before the ceremony. Her unofficial duties also include providing the emotional support you may not find anywhere else.

The Traditional Groom's Parents

The traditional groom's parents play a different role during the wedding planning process. There are some budgetary items to keep in mind as well. Typically, the groom's parents will be in charge of planning and paying for the rehearsal dinner and helping the groom choose his suit. In addition to paying for the rehearsal dinner, the groom's family should also pay for the officiant, marriage license, transportation services, expenses for the honeymoon, as well as certain floral designs, according to traditional etiquette. Additionally, the groom (and his family) are supposed to pay for:

- Bridal bouquet
- Mothers' and grandmothers' corsages
- Lapel flowers for the male attendants

These are just traditional roles. Depending on your family situation, the groom's family may take on more or less responsibility.

QUESTION

What should my siblings do if they are not bridesmaids or groomsmen?
If your siblings are not attendants, find special ways to have them involved in your wedding. For example, if your brother has a small child, perhaps he or she could be a flower girl or ring bearer. Other ways to keep special family members happy: helping with programs, playing an instrument, or helping you with your makeup or hair the day of the wedding.

Even though you may not be close to all of your family members, you want to keep them as involved as possible. You risk incredible resentment and future problems due to high expectations that surround your wedding. Just as you are excited about marrying your fiancé, your family will inevitably want to be a part of that day as well. In whatever small way, have special family members involved. Keeping everyone involved will help you and your fiancé have a better future when your two families come together after the wedding.

Creating Your Guest List

Setting out to create your guest list sounds easy enough, at least until you sit down and try to do it. When you start to combine your list with your fiancé's list, your mother's list, your father's list, and your fiancé's parents' list, you start to realize that you may be in trouble. Then you start to think about adding your coworkers and your neighbors. You will finally realize there is simply not enough room for everyone. You will have to come up with a plan.

Capping the Guest List

If money is not an issue, you should be able to invite as many people as you want to your wedding, provided that your reception space will hold them all. However, if you are tied to a specific budget, you will have to do some creative planning.

Start out with a list of everyone you would ideally like to invite. It may turn out that the total number is not beyond your reach. Some couples do a better job of being more selective than others. If you do end up having to cut people, don't throw everyone's name into a fishbowl and eliminate anyone whose name is picked out. Instead, set boundaries for your list and stick to them. In most cases the guest list is divided evenly between the two families, regardless of who is paying for what. Couples often split the list three ways: the bride's parents, the groom's parents, and the couple. Each invites one third of the guests.

Don't forget to include your attendants and your officiant with his or her spouse in the final guest count. All of them should receive formal invitations even though they are all well aware that they are already invited.

Children on the Guest List

If you have decided not to invite children, you usually make this clear to parents by not including their children's names on the invitation. In order to keep all of your guests aware, it is perfectly acceptable to insert a reception card in your invitation that states "Adult-Only Reception." Just to be safe, however, make sure your mother and anyone else who might be questioned is aware of this decision.

Whatever you decide in the end, everyone needs to stick to the same rule. You can't make an exception for your favorite cousin, who happens to be under your determined age limit. If you do, it is a sure bet that other parents will ask, "What is she doing here if my son couldn't come?" The only exception to this rule is if there are children who are very special to you. For example if you want your nephew to be the ring bearer at the ceremony, it is perfectly reasonable to have them at the reception. You may want to consider a babysitter or nanny option as one little child by herself at a wedding might be bored, difficult, or unhappy. Not to mention the child's parents will end up not having a good time at the reception either if they will have to look after their child the whole time.

QUESTION

What is the cutoff point between children and young adults?
A typical age cutoff point for children at weddings is twelve. Young adults eighteen years or older will need to receive their own invitations— even if they are still living with their parents. When it comes to the age cutoff for an adults-only reception, make sure both families understand that they must adhere to that age (no exceptions).

Coworkers and Distant Relatives

When you're deciding which coworkers you want to invite, honestly evaluate your business relationships. Many people feel burdened by an invitation to an acquaintance's wedding. You may end up straining the relationship rather than strengthening it. You also run the risk of creating a problem with the other coworkers whom you have not invited.

Likewise, you may want to exclude your more distant relatives from the guest list. Again, be consistent. As long as your third cousins don't have to hear that your second cousins twice removed have been invited, they should understand your need to cut costs. If your distant relatives ask, tell them you would love to have them, but you are having a small wedding and it is impossible to invite everyone. It may be a little awkward, but it beats dashing anyone's expectations later.

Miscellaneous Guests and Last-Minute Invites

You will probably want to allow any attached guest to bring their significant others. It is also nice, but not necessary, to give unattached guests the opportunity to bring someone. This is especially appropriate for people who may not know many others at the wedding, as it will help them feel more comfortable.

Married guests should always be invited with their spouses. Always give your attendants the option to bring a date, even if they are not involved with anyone at the time you send out invitations. Your attendants work hard and take on a hefty financial burden to be part of your wedding. Do them the courtesy of allowing them to share the day with someone special to them.

Because it is realistic to anticipate (on average) about 10–20 percent of invited guests will be unable to attend, you and your fiancé may decide to send a second mailing of invitations to people on a "B" list. If so, your first set of invitations should be sent ten to twelve weeks before the wedding date. The second should be sent no later than six weeks prior to the wedding. Typical wedding invitations go out six to eight weeks prior, so your guests won't be offended if they get an invitation earlier or one that is close to the six-week cutoff date.

Be aware that if potential invitees become aware of the fact that they were not included in the first mailing, you may have some hurt feelings. Some guests will be flattered that you have thought of them at all, while others will assume that you are trying to fill seats after you received regrets. If a late invitee corners you, all you can do is be honest. You may choose to explain about your financial limitations, which may be just the balm needed to soothe these potential guests' wounded feelings.

Divorced Family Members

If your parents are divorced but amicable, be thankful. You won't have to plan around family tension. If, however, the relationship between the ex-spouses is at best unpredictable, you will need to map out a plan in order to deal with it. The best way to prevent problems before the wedding is to speak with the divorced set of parents or relatives openly and honestly. All you can reasonably do is request their cooperation and ask them to be on their best behavior.

QUESTION

If I am still friendly with my ex-spouse, is it okay to invite him to the wedding?
Even if you are friends with your ex-spouse, his or her presence might be upsetting to your fiancé(e). Former spouses and family members are generally an unpleasant reminder of the past. Your wedding day is a day dedicated to your future and not to your past.

The majority of parents will try to put aside their grievances for this one special day, but it is always best to take precautions. Remind parents and relatives how important this day is to you. Unfortunately, emotions can lead to tension the day of the wedding. To be on the safe side, don't require divorced relatives to interact with each other. Seat them in different places at the ceremony and at the reception. Be sure their own family and friends surround them. If necessary, have their tables situated as far away from each other as you can. One hopes you have a family member that can be your safety net the day of the wedding and stop tension before it starts. Divorce does not mean you should not invite parents or special members of your family to the wedding.

Relatives or Friends?

When inviting out-of-town guests, be sure you are keeping in mind the expenses that are involved for both them and your family. If it is a relative coming in from out of town, some family may feel obligated to house them. If a grandparent or cousin will be staying with a local family member, it is imperative that you offer financial help if it is needed to offset their costs for hosting a particular family member. They may not always accept the offer, but they will appreciate it!

If your friends are coming in from all over the world, try to get in touch with local friends to see if they will be willing to open their doors to friends that may not have the finances to swing a three-night stay at a hotel. Your friends will appreciate this especially if you try to communicate it in advance of sending the invitations or Save the Date cards!

Places to Go, People to See!

Not only will accommodations be important, but also finding things for your out-of-town friends to do outside of your family obligations will be helpful. Having a list of the best local golf courses for your golf buddies or the best place to get manicures for your girlfriends will be much appreciated through advance notice either via e-mails or handwritten notes. You want to make sure that all of your family and friends who are coming from faraway places feel welcome and appreciated. This will start with initial conversations about your engagement and be followed by information that you insert in your invitations and hospitality gifts (which are described in more detail later in the book).

Wedding Party Checklist

Number of Maids of Honor

Number of Matrons of Honor

Number of Bridesmaids

Number of Mothers

Number of Stepmothers

Number of Godmothers

Number of Flower Girls

Number of Female Readers

Number of Guest Book Attendants

Number of Best Men

Number of Groomsmen

Number of Fathers

Number of Stepfathers

Number of Godfathers

Number of Ushers

Number of Ring Bearers

Number of Male Readers

Number of Soloists

Number of Officiants

Other

CHAPTER 4

Social Media and Your Wedding

The reality for today's engaged couple is that almost every wedding makes its way on to some sort of social media website or app (whether you like it or not)! Everyone has apps on their phones to take that quick Instagram photo and automatically update all of their different social media sites simultaneously—especially Facebook and Twitter. Social media is also the number one resource for wedding ideas for most couples. Pinterest, Flickr, and countless blogs abound with millions of ways for you to customize your wedding! Some couples love the thought of sharing their entire weddings and planning process on social media. Then there are some couples who can't stand the thought of anyone tweeting about their big day. Finding a way to manage the pros and cons of social media is simply part of the wedding experience.

The Factors of Social Media

How will social media factor into your wedding plans? Will you use it to communicate with guests? Find vendors? Or do you want to trend on Twitter or Instagram? Just ten years ago e-mail and wedding websites were about the extent of social media any couple utilized to plan their wedding. Since then, the reach of social media has grown tremendously and has become more powerful than websites. Social media has afforded couples many advantages, but it also has its pitfalls. There are numerous ways to make social media work for you and your wedding while protecting your privacy at the same time!

Social Media Strategy

Social media can facilitate your wedding planning. On your lunch hour you can scan Pinterest for great ideas, you can send off a few e-mails to vendors, and maybe even tweet a couple of companies with questions. The ease and reach of social media is vast and can certainly make life easy, as well as cut down on hours spent doing research. It is absolutely true that in certain respects, social media has streamlined life and made a wealth of knowledge accessible at a moment's notice.

So should you incorporate social media into your wedding? Disseminating information is one of the key components of social media. You may not want everyone in the world to see photos of your bridal shower or know where and when you are honeymooning, but being able to communicate almost instantly with a vendor when you have a question, or research how to make those cute favors is quite useful.

ESSENTIAL

Be sure to check the privacy settings on all of your accounts regularly. Even if they are set to private or "Friends Only" sometimes system upgrades on social media sites reset your personal settings.

Psst . . . Pass It on

There are many ways to use social media to ease your planning and pass information along to friends, family, wedding party members, and vendors, for example:

- **Facebook:** Facebook has been around since 2004 and its impact and reach increases daily. Today, Facebook has over a billion active users. What may have started as a simple tool for (young) adults to interact has become a daily staple for people of all ages. Your grandma may even have a page! You can not only "Friend" your best friend from the second grade, but you can "Like" company pages to keep updated on deals, promotions, and new ideas. In regard to wedding planning, you can post updates to your friends on Facebook about what you have planned so far or ask questions that your friends might be able to answer for you.
- **Twitter:** How much can you say in 140 characters or fewer? It may surprise you at the amount of information that flows through Twitter as well as the relationships that are forged with those 140 characters. Users send over 150 million tweets every day. Twitter happens in real time . . . it moves fast. You can follow wedding experts and style mavens, and you can create lists with particular tweeters based on what you are looking for. You can make simple statements and ask quick questions for wedding planning help. You can even post questions to wedding planners and designers on Twitter and sometimes they will answer you directly.
- **Blogs:** Blogs are websites that have "feeds" that can be updated as often as their creators want. Blogging is a great way to interact with others and document certain aspects of your planning and preparation. You may not want to post photos of yourself trying on your gown, but you may want to share a few photos of the venue or a crafty creation. You can update a blog daily (or more often). There are countless wedding blogs run by creative editors, designers, and photographers who update their blogs daily depending on how popular their sites are. They are the leaders in the wedding industry and idea houses for engaged couples.
- **Websites:** Brides and grooms have been using wedding websites for a while now. Many companies offer free wedding websites and some

charge a fee; it really depends on the sophistication of the website you want. If you are tech savvy, you can even create and host your own. Websites are different from blogs because while you can update them, they are more static, meaning particular information remains constant. Couples use websites to share detailed, pertinent information regarding accommodations, directions/maps, and registry links with guests. Many couples also accept and manage RSVPs through their websites.

- **Newsletters:** Using a company like MailChimp affords you the ability to send out newsletters to your guests with updates on accommodation information, directions to events, changes in scheduling, and other important notices. It is easy to create a simple newsletter and send it off to your guests informing them of changes or updates (if all of them have access to the Internet and e-mail).

How It Can Help

Before you decide for or against using social media to help you plan your wedding, you must take a look at what it can do for you. When utilized correctly, social media is a great tool, but when not used correctly—when used without a "social filter"—social media can be hurtful and overwhelming too. Here are some of the ways it can help you:

- You can connect with wedding suppliers and wedding vendors via social media. "Liking" a company's Facebook page or following a Twitter feed or a blog may give you access to additional discounts, daily deals, insights as to how the vendors work, almost instant access to them, as well as a glimpse into what others are saying about them online.
- You can pass along information quickly and easily. This not only applies to your vendors and suppliers but to your invited guests and wedding party as well. Just think about how many people you know that are alerted every time they receive a text, e-mail, or a message/posting on social media. It's instant access!
- You can create a group for invited guests (or the wedding party, etc.) on Facebook and create private boards on Pinterest. If you are going

to use groups to disseminate information through social media, you need to make sure the groups are private so that not everyone can access them. You cannot assume that everyone wants to hear about the wedding, especially if they are not invited. You can also set up a private blog to share information.

- You can help faraway family members feel like they are a part of the planning. Maybe your mom lives out of town, or maybe your sister has always imagined being by your side but she just can't be there. You can snap and share photos, upload videos, and share all the other details as you plan to help make distant relatives feel like they are included.

How do I decide which social media tools to use when planning my wedding?
Chances are you are already familiar with many social media channels. If so, use the ones you prefer and that most of your friends and family have access to for planning and sharing information. You may find you want to add one or two additional programs to complement what you already know.

Pretty Pictures

At one time, brides carried their cameras around with them, snapping photos at the florist, at the dressmaker, at the venue. Now things have been streamlined. With your smartphone, iPhone, or tablet you can snap photos of all things wedding and non-wedding that inspire you or that you want to remember. There are quite a few ways to catalog the gorgeous images and ideas you find online too. Look at these very cool tools that can help:

- **Pinterest:** Pinterest is a virtual online bulletin board. You create different boards (flowers, gowns, favors, etc.) and as you scan the Internet or Pinterest itself you "pin" the image with its corresponding URL/web address. When you are ready to revisit that particular element, you know where to find it. Pinterest has only been around since 2010, but its impact is huge and the number of users grows each day.

- **Flickr:** Flickr allows you to upload photos from just about any digital or mobile device or photo application to its service. Once uploaded, your photos are open for comments and conversation with other users. Should you decide to, you can easily share these photos via other social media sites as well.

- **Instagram:** Instagram is one of the most popular social media apps for weddings on your phone. You simply take a photo, crop it, add some quick lighting effects to it, make a comment on it, and post it. Your friends and followers can see what you posted and comment as well as like the photo. This can be a lot of fun when you are shopping for décor and dresses for your big day. Your mom and the best friend who lives in a different state can see what you are talking about instantly! Instagram has options for you to share the photo as well to Facebook, Twitter, e-mail, Tumblr, Flickr, and Foursquare. You can also look up ideas for your wedding by searching hashtags that are relevant to your wedding theme.

FACT

You should be careful what you say and post on social media. It can be shared and manipulated by hackers, thieves, frenemies, and unseemly characters. Good rule of thumb—don't post anything online you wouldn't want your mom to know!

How Social Media Can Hurt

For all the good social media can do, it can become too much . . . *you* can rely too much on your social media outlets. Weddings are fun and fabulous and your best friend and mom may want to know every detail, but that does not mean all of your friends and connections do. Brides tend to overshare and with the ease social media provides, oversharing is quite the issue. Here are some ways to avoid using social media:

You may want to post your engagement on Facebook. You might want to share all of the details of your event. In fact, a countdown to the big day sounds divine, but hold it right there. Unless every single one of your "Friends" is invited there will be some hurt feelings. Even though these "Friends" may be happy for you, seeing and hearing about all the amazing things happening in your life when they are not included can hurt.

Even for those who are invited and a part of the festivities, if you post wedding updates every hour, they are going to get tired of it really quickly. There *can* be too much of a good thing. If you become obsessed and narrow-minded with your wedding planning people are going to tune you out.

ALERT

If you share every last detail of your wedding on social media channels, what are you leaving the guests to be wowed with on the wedding day? Show or share too much of your wedding plans and you may end up with unsolicited advice before the big day and really miss that wow factor with your guests on the wedding day.

Being obsessed with anything is not pretty. Brides tend to be an obsessive group anyway and with the mobile devices available now, a bride can take obsession to new levels. Spending your days with your eyes glued to a screen, scrolling through wedding ideas, tweeting vendors, liking Facebook pages, and uploading photos to Instagram and Flickr, well, let's just say your fiancé may not even want to be near you.

Time for a Status Update

A ring. A magical question. A need to tell everyone! Easy, right? Just grab your mobile device, snap a photo, and let the world know you are engaged . . . right? *Wrong!* It may be tempting to announce the news to almost everyone with a few clicks, but that is not the right way to do it. Read on to find out how to gracefully use social media to plan and communicate.

The Right Way

You may be one half of a modern tweeting, texting, sharing couple, but that does not mean all of your guests are. Or, even if they are, seeing a status update or getting an e-mail may not be the way they want to hear the news of an engagement. With so many options, how do you make it all work? No matter what the inner social media maven inside you says, you must use the telephone if not have a face-to-face meeting to tell those closest to you that you are engaged. Your parents, then your fiancé's parents, especially need to be told before you tell the world. But don't stop there. Be sure to tell other close friends and relatives the news before you post it online.

There is really no official timeframe or waiting period before you post any updates on your marital status. Most important, you need to make sure that those closest to you have been told in person or via telephone (yes, the old-fashioned way!). After that, whether or not you announce your engagement on social media is up to you, but do it subtlety and tastefully. And if you do, be warned there will be those who, after following the news of your planning, will be hurt when they never receive an invitation.

QUESTION

Can I post a photo of my ring on Facebook?
Again, you must make sure that all of those important people in your life know the news first. Posting a photo of the ring on social media can seem ostentatious, so be careful if you do this. Perhaps a single shot of the two of you with the ring showing is a better idea than creating an album with multiple different angles of the ring.

The Wrong Way

As social media etiquette is just coming into play, you can actually get away with a lot of things as everyone learns what the rules are, but posting a gift-giving link on any social media site might seem a little greedy. Such links are best left to the wedding website where people expect them to be. If someone asks you this question directly (even if it is in a public forum, like on your Facebook wall), send him or her a private message with the information.

Wedding planning can be hard work. Dealing with logistics and money and family can take their toll, but keep the negativity off social media channels. Dealing with frustrations and airing dirty laundry are best left offline.

Use It!

If you are planning on using social media to its fullest extent, there are several ways to do it. On Twitter you can create a list that includes all of those invited to the wedding, but realize your Twitter feed is still public. If you feel the need to tweet, consider setting up a wedding Twitter account with protected tweets, meaning those friends and family members who know about it need to be approved (by you) to follow you. You can do the same with all of your social media accounts, especially Pinterest and Instagram.

The most subtle way to announce your engagement on Facebook or any other social media site with marital status as an option is to simply change that status on your profile page to "Engaged." It is simple, "quiet," and won't leave anyone thinking you are just showing off.

But you may be thinking, "I'm on Facebook all the time and so are all of my friends. Why can't I just post everything there?" Well, no one is stopping you, but one hopes your better judgment will. Consider setting up a private group on Facebook. You can create a private page and invite only those who are invited to the wedding. Then you have a private forum to share away and post wedding updates. Anyone who accepts the invitation for the page should be fully aware of what it is for. You can also create multiple groups to accommodate different needs, for example, one for your wedding party, and another for your mother, sister, and maid of honor.

Guest Considerations

There are a lot of ways to make social media work in your wedding plans, but you need to remember that not all guests are social media pros. Grandma may not be into checking a blog or Facebook. For that matter your parents may not choose to access these tools either. You need to find ways to use social media, but not exclude those who do not use it.

Oh No, You Didn't!

It used to be that even for the most casual weddings, e-mailing an invitation would not be considered proper. However, times have changed and so has our culture. For a formal wedding this might confuse the guests, as the invitation should match the tone and style of the event. For a casual affair, most wedding experts agree that you can e-mail invitations to your friends and family that are e-mail savvy and close to you. Business connections and some guests from older generations might still need paper invitations for practical and traditional etiquette purposes. Some people just simply do not communicate via e-mail— so you need to create a balance for you and your guests. Traditional etiquette experts say different things. You know all of your guests best and it may be that you hope to throw etiquette to the wind to show your individual personality!

QUESTION

A very distant friend continues to post somewhat negative things about me and my wedding on social media. Can I make her stop? If you have not already, contacting this friend is the first thing to do. Explain the situation and ask her to please stop this behavior. She may think she is being funny . . . even if you, or anyone else, are not getting the joke. Chances are she just may be immature enough to think that this is a good way to lash out for not being invited. Most social media avenues have ways to block or moderate comments from particular users, which can prevent them from being able to post anything on "your space." If the behavior continues, you can also report her to whichever platform she is posting the offensive comments on.

Info to Go

How you use social media is what determines if it is tacky or not. Blasts of information such as "Engagement party is in two days. Don't forget we are registered at . . ." is tacky. Anything that announces major invite-only events to masses of people who are not invited or is a post disguised as a "don't forget to bring a gift" statement is in bad taste. Using social media to privately communicate with only those who are invited is perfectly acceptable. Private groups and e-mailed newsletters in conjunction with your blog or website are how information can and should be conveyed.

Even if you are utilizing social media to disseminate information quickly, you still need to provide certain information in printed/mailed form to those who do not use social media. Until the day comes (and it surely will) when everyone is connected to social media somehow, passing on information such as accommodations, travel, attractions, and directions will need to be done via regular postal services for most of your guests as mentioned earlier in the chapter.

Social Media and the Bride

Unless you are the royal couple and can request (require) that everyone turn off their phones as they arrive at the wedding, you are going to need to contend with social media at your wedding. There is a time and place for it, if you want it there. Someone is going to take a photo and share it online. Someone will tweet. You just need to decide if you want to encourage it. If you do, here are some ideas:

Acceptable Behavior

When is it acceptable to use social media at a wedding? There is not one set answer to this question. Really it depends on the couple and their take on wedding traditions. Most experts agree that texting and tweeting during a ceremony should be off limits. No guest should stand up mid-ceremony to get a better photo so they can Instagram it. It is just common sense. However common sense seems to be disappearing quickly. If the guests are involved in social media interactions when they should be attentive and part of the larger event, it is considered rude. However, if you are trying to trend on Twitter, you will want the guests to be tweeting at any and all other convenient times. Making social media a part of your wedding can be fun, but it can also be a distraction.

Head Tweeter

If you dream of trending on Twitter on your wedding day but know that you will be too busy on the day, you can assign a head tweeter or a "Tweet of Honor" (or whatever name you want to use). You may even want more than one! Create a hashtag for the event and ask these tweeters to tweet before, during, and after the wedding. They need to ask or remind their followers to pass the word around and use the hashtag. They may even tweet celebrities asking them to send out the tweet as well (no guarantees!). This can ultimately be their job on the wedding day. If you are truly making this a social media event, ask the tweeters to visit guests and ask them to tweet or even ask for the words and tweet for them. If you really want to take it over the top, have one of the tweeters read some of the well wishes (at some point) during the reception.

FACT

Some couples are tech savvy and cannot imagine their wedding without social media. In fact trending on Twitter sounds like a dream come true and for some the ultimate gift—a gift you cannot buy. Be sure to spread the word of the hashtag in your private groups before the big day too, and then take a shot at being a Twitter superstar for a day.

Social Media Manager

If you're a fan of social media but aren't sure how to manage it for your wedding you can look for a social media manager. Surely you have a tech savvy friend—a social media master of sorts. Ask this person if they will be a community manager on the wedding day. This person would be in charge of setting up the laptop and photo/video station for the photo booth, making sure the guests know what the hashtag is on Twitter, relaying user and groups names for other social media outlets, and compiling the posted information after the wedding. Perhaps this is the person responsible for creating a display of the photos and tweets that happened during the wedding and presenting them at the reception.

Social Media Station

Social media stations are an up and coming trend. It is not quite commonplace yet, but if you are interested in really incorporating social media into the wedding, this is for you. A social media station needs a few basic things: a person to run it, a laptop, and an Internet connection. You can set up your station in a few ways: have guests take photos—think the photo booth trend—and upload the photos directly to Flickr for an instant visual guestbook. You can also ask the guests to tweet at the station, thus having a record of the 140-character (or less) well wishes from the guests—a social media guestbook!

We're on the Air

With today's technology everyone can attend your wedding . . . sort of. Some guests may be unable to travel for health or myriad other reasons, but they can still get a peek at your nuptials! Once upon a time you would buy DVDs or copies of photos and send them to guests who could not attend your wedding. Now, a live streaming feed of your wedding is a way to share with those who cannot attend. You can DIY it (with your Internet connection, a video streaming service, and a camera), or you can hire a company that can come in with a professional videographer and set it all up.

You Cannot Hide

With the easy access to phones, computers, tablets, and social media, you must realize you cannot control the flow of everything. If you have taken the steps to invite social media into your wedding day, some guests may have a hard time realizing that there is a line that should not be crossed. Someone may make an insensitive comment or post an unflattering photo—that is their downfall, don't let it be yours. You hope it won't happen, but you should be prepared.

Just Say No!

If you are serious about social media just for the wedding planning process and want social media to stop on your wedding day, you have a couple of creative and interesting ways to make this happen. When guests arrive, have a pretty sign asking all of them to have a social media–free day. Another creative way to do this is to have a message on your insert in your invitations as well as on your programs. You might be surprised that even your most tech savvy guests might see it as a welcome break from social media to just enjoy the day!

ESSENTIAL

Don't let social media overpower the real-time moments of the wedding. Have the ushers or your community manager pass out cards to the guests with the wedding hashtag, but also with a few notes such as: "Please refrain from tweeting during the ceremony and please do not post wedding photos until the couple has."

Control the Flow

You may notice that your photographer posts other couples' photos on his Facebook page. You need to think about whether or not you are comfortable with your pictures being there as well. And then have a talk with your photographer. Ultimately he should not post anything until you have agreed to it and given your approval. Just have a talk with him and explain your concerns, and add a clause to the contract.

CHAPTER 5

Planning Your Ceremony

Your ceremony is really the reason for all of the fuss! Everything from the legal details to the recessional takes careful thought and planning. The type of ceremony and the actual location of the ceremony set the stage for your reception. Whether you are having a large elaborate ceremony at your local cathedral or a small intimate family ceremony in your backyard, there are several details that require attention.

Legalities

Legalities are not the most exciting details of a wedding but they are inevitable and necessary. Certain minor details, such as what your married name will be and obtaining your marriage license in time, will need to be addressed. There is also that pesky little thing called a prenuptial agreement. Legal matters may not be your first or favorite place to start, however, taking care of them sooner rather than later will relieve stress.

Keeping Your Maiden Name?

As a bride, you may be unsure about which name you would prefer after you get married. You will undoubtedly be given all sorts of advice from friends and family to make this decision. In the end you have to decide what is appropriate for you and your fiancé.

A few things to think about if you decide to keep your maiden name:

- **His family**—For traditional marriages, if you decide to keep your maiden name, you need to be sensitive to how your in-laws may react. Keep the explanation short and be sure you have your fiancé's support.
- **The world's view**—You will always have to explain your reason to people who barely know you, like your husband's business associates or your future children's teachers. Social traditions have taught people to address you by your husband's surname. Try not to be offended and make things more awkward by barking your maiden name at them. Simply take the initiative and introduce yourself first or quickly correct them in a gracious matter.
- **The government**—One point to consider when keeping your maiden name is: taxes. If you plan to file jointly with your fiancé, but you use your maiden name, the government may ask for proof of your marriage. Whatever you do, always use your legal name when dealing with the government. Always have at least two copies of your marriage certificate handy for instances such as this one.

Changing Your Last Name?

If you do decide to change your name, you will need to fill out appropriate paperwork for your city and state. The easiest place to find information on how to change your name is either your state's website or your local courthouse. Wait until you have received a copy of your marriage certificate before you attempt to change your name anywhere. In many cases you will need proof of your marriage before anything can be changed. The most common things that a marriage certificate will be needed for are your Social Security card, driver's license, passport, bank accounts, car registration, insurance, and credit cards.

ALERT

When booking your honeymoon plane tickets, use your maiden name. You will need a valid photo ID before you can board a plane and the name on your ID must match the name on your ticket. If you can't produce an ID that matches the name on your ticket, you will not be allowed on the plane.

Some brides will choose to take their husband's name legally but continue to use their maiden name for business. In everyday social situations, you should use your married name, but in the office and in business situations you can continue to use your maiden name.

License to Marry

The criteria for obtaining a marriage license vary not only from state to state, but also sometimes from county to county within a single state. Before you head off to get your marriage license, find out how long the license is valid for. In some areas, the license is valid for several weeks, while in other areas it never expires.

Most information about marriage licenses can be found on your state or local governments' websites. The information that you should be looking for is:

- **Paperwork**—You will need some form of valid ID (a birth certificate or driver's license). You will also need to provide proof of divorce or an annulment on the form, if you or your fiancé were previously married.

- **Fee**—Every state charges a fee for a marriage license. Before going to the courthouse, be sure you know what forms of payment they accept. Don't be surprised if they only accept cash or money order.
- **Age requirement**—In most states you need to be at least eighteen years of age. Each state is different. If you are under the minimum age requirement, one of your parents will have to sign a consent form or other legal proceedings will have to take place depending on which state you live in.
- **Waiting period**—Some states require a waiting period of several days before obtaining a license. In other states, you can get the license and get married on the same day. Check your state's requirements.

FACT

Most states no longer require a blood test for marriage, but some still do. The purpose of the test is to determine if you have any sexually transmitted diseases. Be sure to research your state's requirements.

Even though you have a marriage license, it doesn't mean you are legally married. A marriage license is simply the state's permission to get married. For a marriage license to be valid and binding, the license has to be signed by a religious or civil officiant. Once you have your license, don't lose it. After the completion of the ceremony, your officiant will simply sign the license and send it back to the proper state office and then you will be legally married.

ESSENTIAL

When the time comes for you to sign the license, you should already have decided on your married name. In most states, the license is the first legal document containing your married name, so don't wait until the last minute to decide.

Prenuptial Agreements

The issue of prenuptial agreements (or "prenups") is normally an uncomfortable topic among couples. Some feel that prenups are depressing, while other couples feel they are incredibly necessary.

Prenups aren't just for couples that are trying to protect their financial assets. The most common reason for having a prenup is to protect the interests of any children from a previous marriage. Most parents want to make sure that their children's inheritances are not an issue in the event of their death or divorce. Each state has its own laws governing prenups, so consult a lawyer who understands prenup law within your state.

ALERT

Whether or not the prenuptial agreement is fair is up to you and your attorney. Before you sign anything, the recommendation is for each party to obtain separate counsel.

A prenuptial agreement includes the following elements:

- Full written disclosure of assets and liabilities of each party
- Reasonable terms
- Adequate time for the parties to review the terms with their own lawyers

Religious versus Nonreligious Ceremonies

The specifics of what type of wedding ceremony you will have will really depend on your beliefs. Whether you have a ceremony in your grandmother's church or a small government office, be sure the ceremony reflects the two of you.

Religious Ceremonies

The specifics of religious ceremonies vary widely between religions and denominations. Your officiant will be able to explain in more detail what is involved. A religious ceremony does not necessarily mean that you must have this rite performed in a religious edifice (such as a church, synagogue, or temple). A religious ceremony simply means that you are performing the requirements of the religious rite of marriage in accordance to the laws or traditions of your specific religious denomination. The most common religious ceremonies are Roman Catholic, Protestant, Jewish, Muslim, and Hindu. Following are a few guidelines for each of these popular religions.

Roman Catholic

If you are getting married in the Roman Catholic Church, you probably know that you will have extensive premarital requirements. First, there is Pre-Cana, which is the Roman Catholic Church's premarital course that every engaged couple must complete. Pre-Cana covers topics such as sex, finances, and children (within the context of Catholicism). Once you have completed Pre-Cana, you will then be given the option to go with an entire Catholic Mass complete with the Liturgy of the Word and Eucharist, or a shorter version that includes readings, a short message on marriage, prayers, exchange of rings, and vows.

ALERT

If you are a divorced Catholic, there are certain procedures that you will have to go through in order to be eligible for Catholic remarriage. You will have to go through a long annulment process (involving a Church investigation and possible trial) to prove that your first marriage was not valid in the eyes of the Church. Talk to your priest about the specifics and be prepared for a lengthy process.

Protestant

Protestant marriages, regardless of denomination, do not require premarital counseling. Normally a short informational meeting with the pastor is required to gather information about you as a couple and to tell you about the typical procedures of your denomination. The Protestant ceremony includes prayers, readings, ring exchange, celebration of the Lord's Supper (normally for the couple only), a message about marriage, and the benediction.

Jewish

Judaism has different divisions that adhere to different rules. Jewish weddings within the Orthodox and Conservative branches have a few stipulations that require rigid adherence. Weddings cannot take place on the Sabbath or any time that is considered holy. Both Orthodox and Conservative ceremonies are recited in Hebrew or Aramaic only and neither branch will conduct interfaith ceremonies. Men must wear yarmulkes and the bride wears her wedding ring on her right hand. However, in most Jewish traditions, the elements of the actual wedding ceremony are as follows:

- The *Bedeken* (veiling of the bride)
- Signing of the *Ketubah* (Jewish marriage contract)
- The *Kiddushin* (betrothal ceremony), which takes place under a chuppah (ornamental canopy)
- Seven Blessings are recited
- Blessed wine is taken from a *Kiddush* cup
- Glass is smashed by the groom (to symbolize the destruction of the Temple in Jerusalem in A.D. 70) usually followed by congratulatory shouts of "Mazel Tov!"
- Yichud—Bride and groom retreat to a private room alone after the ceremony for about fifteen minutes

Muslim

The only requirement of a Muslim marriage is the signing of a marriage contract. The *Nikah* is the ceremony where the bride and the groom sign the marriage contract, which normally includes:

- The couple's consent to marry
- The approval of the bride's guardian called a *Wali* or *Wakeel*
- The presence of two Muslim witnesses and a *Meher* (or *Mehr*), which is a monetary value of what the groom will give to the bride

Depending on the Islamic sect you are associated with, all sorts of various cultural traditions and customs can be included in the actual ceremony. There are some Islamic sects where there is a separation of genders throughout the ceremony and reception. Blessings are normally included in the ceremony, which are recited from the Koran. An *imam* (religious leader) typically will oversee the ceremony but according to the Koran and Islamic traditions, any trusted Muslim may officiate the *Nikah*.

Hindu

There are traditional Hindu wedding traditions and specific Bengali wedding traditions. Since there are many wedding traditions for Indian and Hindu ceremonies, you and your fiancé will need to consult your families in order to make sure your ceremony reflects your family's traditions and heritage. The topic of the elements of Southeast Asian weddings is covered in Chapter 6. Hindu weddings are based on three essential values: happiness, harmony, and growth. Hindu ceremonies are normally performed by a Brahmin or a *Purohit* (priest).

Nonreligious Ceremonies

Some couples faced with tension and potential family problems due to interfaith ceremonies choose civil ceremonies. Other couples choose to go the nonreligious, civil ceremony route because they are not particularly religious people. Another common reason to have a nonreligious ceremony is simply to avoid expenses and time constraints of a traditional church or temple wedding. Civil ceremonies are usually easier to plan than a traditional religious ceremony.

The officiant in a civil ceremony is a judge or other civic official legally able to perform a marriage. Where will you find your officiant? Contact your local city hall or courthouse in person, or online, to find specific information for your city. Each officiant will have his or her own specific fees, unless you get married at the courthouse.

A civil ceremony does not mean that you cannot have the ceremony of your dreams. A civic official, nonreligious officiant, or celebrant (a nondenominational officiant trained to create a personal and meaningful ceremony) can perform a marriage anywhere.

Interfaith Ceremonies

If you and your fiancé come from two different faith backgrounds, your ceremony should reflect both your religions. The most important aspect of an interfaith ceremony that you will need to consider is whether or not you will have officiants from both religions present. Consult your clergy to find out what is allowed within your religion.

Many couples choose to have officiants from both religions present at an interfaith ceremony. However, some officiants may not be comfortable with this situation. If both religious leaders are willing to perform the ceremony together, a meeting of the minds needs to be facilitated. If for some reason both officiants are not in the same city, ask them what their requirements are, and find the best way possible to help them communicate with each other. A phone conference will typically suffice.

If one of the officiants is unable to perform the ceremony, you may want to consider a nondenominational officiant who specializes in weddings. This becomes important if religious affiliations start heated debates with extended family. Your wedding should not be argued over, and should be a time of great joy. A nondenominational officiant will be able to perform a ceremony that declares both your values and can help you incorporate religious elements from both of your religions into the ceremony in simple (but meaningful) ways.

Another important issue to keep in mind when planning an interfaith ceremony is the setting. You will most likely want the ceremony to be held in a neutral and nonreligious building or space.

No matter where you have your ceremony and which elements from both religions you plan to include, always remember that this is *your* wedding ceremony. It is easy to get mixed up in the politics of each religion and family culture. If you truly combine both sets of values and beliefs in a setting that is beautiful, it can really create a unique and memorable experience for everyone involved.

Same-Sex Ceremonies

Same-sex weddings are not a new subject. With more states starting to recognize same-sex marriages, it is important for same-sex couples to know how to plan their ceremonies in a way that reflects their style and honors their beliefs and heritages.

Choosing Your Attendants and Officiant

When planning your same-sex wedding, there tend to be no traditional roles in regard to attendants. In general, same-sex weddings tend to have fewer attendants, but you have free reign to choose who you would like to stand beside you at the ceremony. Don't feel trapped into having all male attendants or all female attendants as it is perfectly acceptable to have both male and female attendants on both sides. If you don't want any attendants, don't have them!

Choose an officiant that is supportive and has experience performing same-sex ceremonies. Some same-sex couples choose to have a friend marry them, while others go a more formal route with a state-recognized officiant. Many religions do not allow for gay marriage, so be sure to consult your religious officiant and family on how to incorporate your religious beliefs.

FACT

Celebrants are nondenominational officiants that are trained to create a personal and meaningful ceremony. If you are concerned that a Justice of the Peace is too informal or a minister is too religious, consider a celebrant.

Same-Sex Wedding Traditions

The first year same-sex weddings were recognized legally in the United States on a state level was in May 2004 in Massachusetts. Essentially before this date, all same-sex weddings were considered *Commitment Ceremonies*. Since that time, same-sex wedding traditions have rapidly changed and grown. Here are some simple and authentic gay wedding traditions that stand out:

- Many same-sex couples choose to walk down two separate aisles or from two separate directions. Why? Since the ceremony is not focused on one person coming down the aisle, it is widely practiced that the couple walk down two separate aisles and meet in the middle (with respective attendants and families). If there is only one central aisle, you can of course choose to walk down the aisle together or in any other fashion you prefer.

- Many same-sex ceremonies will start off with champagne or a special cocktail prior to the ceremony.
- Many same-sex ceremonies start (after the processional) with a *Validation and Affirmation*, which is similar to an introductory blessing.
- Following the Validation and Affirmation, a history of the couple generally follows with an exchange of vows and rings. Typically there is not a receiving line at a gay wedding.
- At many same-sex wedding receptions, the couple will often toast the guests for coming.

ESSENTIAL

Some officiants of same-sex weddings will ask the couple to sign a *Foundation Covenant*. This covenant is based on principles similar to those found in a Jewish *Ketubah*, Quaker wedding certificates, and other sacred literature and texts. While the Foundation Covenant is not required, it is a great symbol of your commitment to each other that can also be displayed in your home for years to come.

In addition to those traditions, there are some general trends that have been seen in many same-sex weddings across the United States. These include the lack of wedding registries, engagement parties, showers, and typically, there are no garters or bouquet tosses. Even though these are trends, it does not mean you cannot have any or all of the above. The key is to make sure your wedding reflects the two of you as a couple.

Legality of Same-Sex Ceremonies

Same-sex ceremonies will differ from state to state, depending on your state's law concerning the legality of gay marriage. If your state does not recognize gay marriage, your legal rights as a married couple are hindered. If you want to be legally married and your state does not recognize same-sex marriage, consider eloping to one of the states that does perform legal same-sex weddings. The trend shows that some states are starting to consider the recognition of legal same-sex marriages from other states, even if they are not performing them in their own state. Progress in this regard has happened slowly, however, so you may want to be legally married in one state and follow up with a fantastic party in your state to celebrate! If you decide to elope to another state that performs same-sex ceremonies, it is wise to invest in a wedding planner who can help you navigate the ins and outs of the court system, waiting period, and local wedding vendors to help the day go off without a hitch.

FACT

In regard to the legality of your marriage, some states offer domestic partnership and legal marriage options. Be sure to check with your state government's website. Even though some states do not recognize same-sex marriages, the federal government does.
You can file your federal income tax return as a married couple if you become legally married in one of the states that recognizes same-sex marriage.

A few great resources for same-sex weddings are:

- 14 Stories (*www.14stories.com*)
- Gay Rites (*www.gayrites.net*)
- Human Rights Campaign (*www.hrc.org*)

The unfortunate reality is that not every vendor is gay-friendly. In order to save you some time and serious frustration, always call your potential vendors to see if they are providing services to the gay community before making appointments with them.

Choosing Your Officiant

In today's fast-paced global economy, the rise of interfaith and multicultural weddings has increased. Choosing your officiant may be as easy as calling your childhood pastor or as complicated as hiring two officiants from two different religions.

Your Religious Officiant

To some, hiring an officiant is nothing more than calling their childhood pastor and setting a date. To others, this may be extremely complicated if you now live in a different city and your family is scattered all over the world. In most cultures, marriage is a very specific, religious rite and therefore should be handled with care. Consult your parents, family, and friends to be sure to find the best religious officiant for you and your fiancé's religious ceremony.

ESSENTIAL

Although the Internet may seem like the last place to find your officiant, it really can be quite helpful in regard to locating the right officiant. If you do not have a regular place of worship and your family does not have contacts, do a web search based on your religion and type in the word *officiant* along with your city's name. You will be surprised at the amount of relevant search results that can point you in the right direction.

Selecting a Venue for Your Ceremony

Depending on your religion and culture, your ceremony location will vary. If you and your fiancé are of the same religion and want a religious ceremony, you might want to consider having your ceremony at your place of worship. Interfaith ceremonies can take place in varied locales such as gardens or your reception site.

If you are planning to have your ceremony in your place of worship, be sure you know their rules for photography, candles, flowers, and maximum occupancy. Many places of worship have specific rules that you will need to adhere to.

If neither one of you is religious or you are planning an interfaith wedding, the possibilities are endless as to where you can have your ceremony. A few examples are:

- **Parks or gardens**—Most public parks have certain available locations that are for rent (or free) for all sorts of occasions. Find as much information as possible when booking a park or garden for your ceremony.

94

You will need to know if they have a backup plan for weather purposes and how private the space will be if it is a public park or garden.
- **Hotel ballrooms**—If your wedding will be held at a hotel, many have options for having your ceremony in either the same or an adjacent ballroom from where your reception will be held.
- **Private or historic home**—A popular place for receptions is a historic home. Many historic homes are large enough with space inside or outdoors for your ceremony.

ALERT

Be advised that if you decide to have your ceremony at your reception site because it has a beautiful garden, you must have a backup indoor location for the ceremony. Any outdoor ceremony is susceptible to rain and other weather elements. Make sure your reception site has an indoor space available for you in a worst-case scenario.

Ceremony Basics

No matter what your religion or cultural background is, you will have some very basic ceremony issues to deal with. Who sits where and who will walk whom down the aisle are both very important concerns for you and your family. The following information is based on traditional Western etiquette.

Seating of the Guests

If your ceremony does not include groomsmen, you will need to have at least one usher per fifty guests to help seat them. Typically the bride's family sits on the left side of the aisle while the groom's family sits on the right side of the aisle in a Christian ceremony. The opposite is true for Reform or Conservative Jewish weddings. In Orthodox Jewish ceremonies, men and women are usually segregated. If adhering to religious mandates isn't an issue and one side has more guests than the other, you may dispense with these customs and seat everyone together. This way, you won't end up seating some people way in the back when there are much closer seats on the other side.

Your siblings and immediate family should sit in the first and second rows, either beside your mother and father (who are always in the front row) or behind them. Grandparents should never sit farther than the third row and close friends and other relatives sit behind the first three rows of relatives. Of course, if your family is much larger, make the appropriate decisions on where family members should sit based on seating restrictions at the location of the ceremony. In some ceremonies, the first few rows of pews (or chairs) are sectioned off by ribbons (or signs) that indicate they are reserved for family only.

FACT

Guests are seated at the ceremony as they arrive (often front to back). The mothers of the bride and groom should be seated just before the ceremony beings. Late guests are not escorted to their seats. They should take their seats near the back of the ceremony seating area, preferably via a side aisle.

The Processional

For Christian ceremonies, processionals can vary. What is allowed in the processional in your particular church is up to you and your officiant. Some churches encourage the bridesmaids and groomsmen to walk down the aisle together, while others prefer to have the bridesmaids walk alone. If the bridesmaids are walking alone down the aisle, the groomsmen will stand at the altar with the groom just in front of the officiant. Other couples choose to have the bridesmaids start out by themselves and have the groomsmen meet them halfway down the aisle to escort them to the altar. Your officiant or site coordinator will instruct your attendants on which is preferred at your particular church.

Typical order of your bridal party is: bridesmaids, maid of honor, ring bearer, and flower girl. For large weddings with many bridesmaids, you can send them down the aisle in pairs. Which bridesmaid starts first? The order of bridesmaids is completely up to you unless your officiant prefers that you line them up according to height.

ESSENTIAL

If your church or temple has two side aisles instead of a single center aisle, your officiant will most likely advise you to use the left aisle for the processional and the right aisle for the recessional.

After the flower girl has made her way down the aisle, it is now your turn! You can either walk down on the arm of the man or woman who is giving you away or by yourself. Some brides choose to be escorted by both their parents or a close relative if both parents are deceased. It is also perfectly normal (and romantic) to have your fiancé meet you halfway down the aisle!

Jewish Orthodox, Conservative, and Reform processionals vary according to the family's preferences, devoutness, and local customs. The traditional religious Jewish processional may begin with the rabbi and cantor, with the cantor on the rabbi's right. The grandparents (first the bride's and then the groom's) are then escorted in. The groomsmen will walk down one by one, followed by the best man. The groom then walks between his mother, on his right, and his father on his left. The bridesmaids then walk one by one, followed by the maid of honor, ring bearer, and flower girl. The bride is the last to enter, with her mother on her right and her father on her left.

Traditional Muslim ceremony processionals tend to be focused on the bride and the groom's separate entrances into the ceremony. However, many American Muslim and Hindu ceremonies tend to have processionals similar to Christian weddings due to Western influences.

FACT

If you are having your ceremony at your reception site or a venue other than a church or temple, you will have a little more flexibility about how you want the processional to flow. If you are not religious, keep your parents' requests in mind as to what they might like to see at the ceremony and go from there. Your processional can be as simple or as elaborate as you want!

Giving the Bride Away

In traditional Western ceremonies, the father of the bride gives the bride away. But sometimes death or divorce changes people's circumstances. When faced with the loss of a father, many brides wonder who will give them away at their wedding.

If your father has passed away, do whatever feels most comfortable for you. If your mother has remarried and you are close to your stepfather, he may be a good choice. Otherwise, a sibling, a grandfather, a special friend, or an uncle can do the honors. Some brides walk down the aisle with their mothers, a special aunt, or the groom, while others choose to walk without an escort. Keep in mind that whomever you choose will sit in the front pew with your mother during the ceremony (unless you choose your groom, of course).

If your parents are divorced and both parents are remarried, your decision will depend on your preference and family situation. To avoid tension, take care to somehow include both men in the proceedings. If you have remained close to your father, you may prefer that he fulfill his traditional role, while your stepfather does the reading. Or perhaps you will ask them both to escort you down the aisle. Often in Jewish ceremonies both parents, even when divorced, walk the bride down the aisle.

ESSENTIAL

Is your fiancé in the military? Then you should definitely think about a military wedding. Typically military weddings are formal affairs and look quite impressive. A military ceremony always concludes underneath a stunning archway of crossed swords! Keep in mind that if your groom decides to wear his sword or saber, you will stand on his right.

You may decide to do away with this tradition altogether. If so, there are options that you should discuss with your officiant. Instead of asking "Who gives this woman in marriage?" he or she may ask, "Who blesses this union?" Your father may respond "Her mother and I do." and take a seat next to your mother. It is also entirely appropriate for both parents to respond,

"We do." In this case your mother should also stand up when the officiant presents the question.

The Recessional

You've kissed, you've been pronounced husband and wife . . . now how do you get from the altar to your limousine (or cocktail hour)? In most Western and Christian ceremonies, you and your new husband lead the recessional followed by your child attendants (if they are able and old enough). Your maid of honor and best man are next, followed by the bridesmaids escorted by their respective groomsmen.

FACT

If you plan to have a receiving line, the order is as follows: mother of the bride, father of the bride, bride, groom, mother of the groom, father of the groom. If one or both sets of parents are divorced, (and there are lingering bad feelings), consider shuffling the parents or having just the mothers in the receiving line. You can also have the bridal party or (for simplicity purposes) just the maid of honor and best man.

The order of the Jewish recession is as follows: bride and groom, bride's parents, groom's parents, child attendants, honor attendants, and bridesmaids paired with groomsmen. Your cantor and rabbi walk at the end of the recession. Recessionals for Muslim and Hindu ceremonies are similar to Christian recessionals.

Writing Your Vows

You may want to formalize your commitment with something unique—something specific to your relationship or situation. If you want to write your own vows, check with your minister first to make sure that personalized vows are permitted during the ceremony. If, on the other hand, you're thinking, "*I'm* not writing any vows!" give it another thought.

You get to stand at the altar once with your fiancé, and what better way to pledge your love than to do it in your own words? Get your laptop out, and let yourself go with the flow.

Start at the Very Beginning . . .

Where to start? Think about your relationship and the things that have the most meaning for each of you. For example:

- How do you, as a couple, define the following terms: *love*, *trust*, *marriage*, *family*, *commitment*, and *togetherness*?
- How did the two of you first meet? What was the first thing you noticed about your partner?
- What was the single most important event in your relationship? (Or, what was the event that you feel says the most about your development as a couple?)
- Is there a song, poem, or book that is meaningful in your relationship?
- If you share common religious beliefs, is there a particular passage of religious text that you as a couple find especially meaningful?
- Do you and your partner have a common vision of what your life as older people will be like? Will it include children and grandchildren?

Take this opportunity to put into words the vision you and your partner share of what it will be like to grow old together. If you're particularly creative and/or expressive, the possibilities are endless.

Most officiants have a plethora of information and books surrounding the subject of their traditional wedding vows. If you want to use religious vows and also insert your own words, be sure to ask your religious leaders for guidelines—as some religions are stricter than others.

FACT

Remember, the right way to compose your own wedding vows is your way. The examples in this section are offered as general guidelines only. Let your imagination be your guide to developing vows that are meaningful to both you and your partner.

Love Letters

Maybe this material isn't enough to get across the full meaning of what you want to say, or maybe you simply can't find the right words. Is it time to panic? Nope. Chances are someone else has said it already. You may just need to find the perfect quote, poem, or song lyric to complete the mood (think William Shakespeare, Elizabeth Barrett Browning, and John Lennon).

The Second Time Around

Although certain celebrities may be experts at the remarriage game, there are some things you may have questions about if you're heading into your second (or third, or fourth) marriage. There are a few rules of protocol to follow.

Clean Slate

If this is not the first marriage for either you or your fiancé, the main thing to avoid is the appearance of duplicating (or competing with) your previous wedding. You certainly don't want your fiancé to think you're trying to live in the past by recreating your first wedding. You want to start fresh.

If there was something you did at your first wedding that was particularly meaningful to you—if you wrote your own vows, for example, or if you carried roses because you and your mother grew them together in her garden—it's all right to include them in the second wedding. (*New* vows will be written with your future husband in mind, of course, and the roses are a lovely personal touch.)

Things you should avoid recycling include music, readings, the dress (or any part of the bridal ensemble), the rings, and the reception site. Do things as differently as you can without crossing into foreign, this-is-not-the-wedding-I-want territory. Your fiancé should be a great help to you in this regard.

You Don't Have to Scale Back

Many people believe that if they had a large wedding the first time around, they must keep things very quiet and subdued for a subsequent wedding. That's not the case, particularly if either member of the marrying couple has never been married before.

In the past, second weddings were hush-hush, but these days they can include the same grandeur as a first wedding. The bride may still have a big wedding party and a big wedding dress, her father might walk her down the aisle, and there might be a slew of limos waiting for you and your attendants after the ceremony. You might also want to have the big reception with all the trimmings.

On the other hand, if you want to have a smaller second wedding, that's perfectly acceptable and not the sort of thing that will raise any eyebrows. It's up to you and your fiancé to decide what's appropriate for the two of you.

Gifts or No Gifts?

Another point of concern for some remarrying couples is the issue of shower and wedding gifts. They feel that if family and friends have already given gifts, it's not fair to ask them to do so again.

ESSENTIAL

As far as the ceremony itself goes, you should consult with your officiant about any restrictions or requirements surrounding the marriage of a divorced person. Once you've handled those issues, the ceremony can pretty much proceed as if it were a first marriage.

The answer to this dilemma is completely up to you and your fiancé. If the two of you are older and established in your lives, you might want to include a "no gifts, please" clause on your invitations. But if this is a first marriage for one of you, or if the two of you really would appreciate some help in starting your new life together, it's perfectly acceptable to have a shower and for guests to bring gifts to the wedding. (Of course, guests are never obligated to bring a gift—even to a first wedding—but many may want to anyway.)

If you're a real stickler for etiquette, you can consult any number of books dedicated solely to the issue of remarriage. But these days, it doesn't need to be that complicated. You and your fiancé should handle a remarriage in a way that makes both of you feel comfortable. If that means finding a middle ground somewhere between the big wedding he wants and the tiny wedding you want, then you'll have to play the game of compromise very carefully.

Ceremony Worksheet

Location of ceremony: _____ Address: _____

Date of ceremony: _____ Time of ceremony: _____

Officiant's name: _____ Location fee: _____

Officiant's fee: _____ Recommended church donation: _____

Wedding program available? _____ Fee: _____

Part of Ceremony	Description	Notes
Processional		
Opening words		
Giving away or blessing		
Reading		
Prayers		
Marriage vows		
Exchange of rings		
Pronouncement of marriage		
Lighting of unity candle		
Benediction		
Closing words		
Recessional		
Other		

CHAPTER 6

Multicultural Weddings

With the world changing so quickly and the global economy in which we live, more and more couples are finding the love of their lives in different countries, cities, and states. The mixing of cultures naturally leads to the mixing of love and marriage. It is important to make sure that both of you are able to incorporate both of your cultures on your wedding day. You may also find certain elements from countries where you have traveled together to be important to you as well.

Incorporating Your Cultures

Even within cultures, there are subcultures. It will be important for you and your fiancé to figure out which elements of culture you will incorporate into your wedding day.

Your research on what to include on your wedding day and in your ceremony needs to start with your family. Ask your parents and grandparents if they have photos from past generations to see what you can pull from your family's wedding traditions. Older family members typically love to tell stories of how it used to be, and may even have items from their weddings that you can incorporate into your own wedding. There are some traditions that you might have researched on your own that may or may not need to be incorporated into your ceremony. Some families are adamant about certain elements of a particular culture and some may not be as important to your family. Asking questions is key to incorporating family culture in both your ceremony and reception.

Some of the most common places where culture is infused throughout a wedding are in music, readings, clothing, favors, and food. Some of the traditions that you incorporate into both your ceremony and reception could be something as sentimental and simple as wearing your great-grandmother's pearls or incorporating the *Kiddush* cup your family has used for centuries. Culture can be pulled from your heritage or simply be a family tradition that has become a part of your family's heritage.

Once you know the basic facts on where your families are from and some of the basic wedding traditions they have practiced in the past, you will have to decide which traditions you want to incorporate, and then move on to more extensive research on the Internet or in books.

African Culture

Since Africa comprises so many countries, cultures, and languages, it would be difficult to list every wedding tradition that the continent celebrates in just one chapter. The single most important element of almost every African tradition is the importance of family. There is also a heavy emphasis on symbolism found throughout Africa.

African Family Traditions

Going back centuries in various different African cultures, girls have been taught from childhood about how to be a good wife, while boys are taught similar ideas on how to provide for the family. No matter which country your family is tied to in Africa, family is the center of marriage and the wedding day is no different. Most African ceremonies are festive and colorful events that can last for days with song, dance, and music being central to the actual wedding ceremony. Wedding ceremonies are also thought of as an entry into adulthood from childhood.

ESSENTIAL

In some African cultures, a particular color is vitally important in representing a particular tribe or particular value. Be sure to ask your relatives about how you can incorporate these colors to honor your family's past traditions.

African Symbolism

While there are over a thousand different cultures in Africa, there are several African cultures that incorporate the Twelve Symbols of Life in their wedding ceremonies. The symbols and their meanings are:

1. **Wine**—The mixing of the blood of the two families
2. **Wheat**—Fertility and the giving of life and land
3. **Pepper**—Represents the heated moments the families will have
4. **Salt**—The healing and preservation of marriage
5. **Bitter herbs**—The growing pains of marriage
6. **Water**—Purity and dissolution of bitterness
7. **Broom**—Cleanliness and well-being
8. **Honey**—Sweet love
9. **Spear**—Protection of the sanctity of the home and community
10. **Shield**—The honor and pride of the home
11. **Spoon and pot**—Healthy food that builds strong families
12. **Bible or Koran**—Symbol of God's truth

Another popular African symbol is the cowrie shell. Cowrie shells were used as currency for centuries in Africa. Due to the shell being used as currency, it symbolizes wealth, power of destiny, and prosperity. Over time the shell has also come to symbolize womanhood, fertility, and birth. However you interpret the symbolism of the cowrie shell, it has become a powerful and beautiful accessory in African fashion. Incorporating cowrie shells in your wedding wardrobe is a great way to incorporate an African tradition used for centuries.

African-American Traditions

It is traditional for newly married African couples to jump the broom. The broom, as mentioned, is a symbol of cleanliness and well-being. However, when it comes to jumping the broom at an African-American ceremony, the broom has a different set of meanings. Traditionally, jumping the broom represents the joining of two families. It is symbolic of sweeping away the old and welcoming the new. In essence, the broom is a symbol of welcoming a new beginning between two families. *Double brooms*, where the bristles of a broom are on both sides of the stick, help to better represent both sides of the family being joined together.

The symbolism of the broom takes on much deeper meaning for many African-Americans. Since slaves were not allowed to marry legally in the United States during the time of slavery, African-American slaves sought legitimacy of marriage by jumping over a broom. The simple act of jumping over the broom brought strength to their union with dignity. The jumping of the broom also represented that God sanctioned their ceremony. No matter which meaning you decide to place on the broom, be sure you let your guests know either through words that are spoken by your officiant or in your program.

FACT

While embarking on planning your African or African-American ceremony, be sure to do your research. With over a thousand cultures represented in Africa, it is easy to mistake customs or traditions from one culture to the next. Ask your family and take your time reading both online and in books.

A few popular resources online include:

- *www.munaluchibridal.com*
- *www.blackbridalbliss.com*
- *http://wednoir.com*
- *www.blackbride.com*

Asian Culture

No matter which Asian culture you or your fiancé belong to, all traditional wedding ceremonies are centered on the basic concept of *a new beginning*. You are starting a new journey down a path of life together. There are all sorts of symbols, most of which represent a new commitment of two hearts and hands joined together as one.

Japanese

In Japan, the land of the rising sun, purple is typically the color of love and a bride may choose to wear (at one point in her ceremony or reception) a beautifully embroidered silk kimono covered in either lavender or purple flowers. You can, of course, incorporate the color purple in other aspects of your wedding through flowers and other décor, too. There is also the tradition of painting the bride pure white from head to toe to symbolize her maiden status to the gods and also to proclaim her purity before marriage. The bride will normally wear a white hood to "hide her horns of jealousy, ego, and selfishness" (which are obviously unbecoming of a bride the day of her wedding); by covering these "horns," she also acknowledges her submission to her mother-in-law and her determination to become an obedient and docile wife. Of course, this is based on Japanese lore and customs, and most Western Japanese weddings do not incorporate these customs.

Part of the Japanese wedding ceremony requires both the bride and the groom to take nine sips of sake (Japanese rice wine). The couple is considered married after the first sip. Families and guests are also encouraged to drink sake to symbolize the bonding of the couple and the two families. During the Japanese ceremonies, the bride leaves to change clothes three or four times. (And you thought finding one wedding gown was a chore!) The first of her kimonos is white, typically to symbolize purity. At the wedding reception she will then typically change into a red kimono and later into a white or ivory Western-style gown (both red and white are thought to be auspicious colors). Typically the groom wears one wedding outfit consisting of a *hakama* (outer garment) over a full-length kimono. The traditional color of the hakama is black, gray, brown, or white pinstripe. However, modern couples can choose colors to suit their styles and tastes.

FACT

The kimonos that both the bride and groom wear are not only valuable monetarily but sentimentally as well. The kimonos are passed down through the generations. When they can no longer be worn, they are reused for other household uses to keep the fabric in the family.

Japanese weddings are traditionally Shinto or Buddhist. During a Shinto wedding, the natural spirits known as the *kami*, are called to bring blessings upon the couple. In a typical Buddhist ceremony, two strings of beads are interwoven, symbolizing the two families becoming one. Both of these ceremonies can be as simple or as elaborate as the couple chooses.

The guests are invited to play games, be involved in fun wedding skits, and perform karaoke throughout the wedding reception. The guests are expected to offer the couple *Goshugi* (money) normally in beautifully decorated envelopes either before or after the ceremony.

The Japanese art of origami can be incorporated in your wedding as well. Many couples choose to add origami to their centerpieces and other reception décor items such as escort card table arrangements and favors.

Some brides choose to add a bit of whimsy to their bouquets with a few origami accents.

The crane traditionally symbolizes honor and loyalty; both are largely associated with Japanese wedding ceremonies. The crane has been thought of by many cultures as a majestic bird that mates for life and is extremely loyal to its partner.

Again, find out your family's specific tradition over the generations and make them part of your ceremony and reception. Beauty, purity, and colors tend to play a major role in Japanese wedding ceremonies and elaborate accessories are often passed down from generations and borrowed from close family members and cousins. You never know what treasures you might find in your aunt's dresser!

Chinese

The Chinese wedding is typically rich in symbolism, décor, and rituals. Depending on which part of China you are from, there are different wedding customs. However, there are some very traditional Chinese wedding customs that are used in almost every part of China.

First and foremost, there are three letters and six items of etiquette. The three letters consist of:

- **The request letter**—The confirmation of an arrangement of marriage letter
- **The gift letter**—An actual list of gifts that will be given to the bride's family
- **The wedding letter**—The letter of confirmation of the bride entering the groom's family, given on the wedding day

The six items of etiquette include:

- **The request to marry the bride**
- **Request for birth dates**—The dates will help determine if the two match each other. This is based on a fortuneteller's predictions and on the Chinese calendar.
- **Initial gifts for the bride's family**—These are based upon an "acceptable" bride's birth date.

- **Formal gifts for the bride's family**—The groom's family will send gifts, cash, cakes, food, and sacrifices for worshipping ancestors.
- **Selecting the wedding date**—The fortuneteller master will select the most auspicious date for them to marry based on birth dates and astrology.
- **Wedding date**—The various traditions of a wedding ceremony typically performed at the groom's home.

ESSENTIAL

Typically the three letters and six items of etiquette are a nod to culture and heritage with most modern brides today. You can interpret the traditions and find ways with your family to incorporate them into your modern wedding celebrations (or pick and choose).

In a Chinese wedding ceremony, a goblet of honey and a goblet of wine are tied together with a red ribbon. Red is the color of love, luck, happiness, and prosperity, and the ribbon stands for unity. Honey has been a large part of Chinese history. Dating back to the Eastern Zhou Dynasty, honey and the larvae of bees were rare foods served mainly to royal families. Ancient Chinese poetry sings about red wine and honey; later friends and lovers would send honey as gifts to each other. Honey also represents the color gold, which is the color of wealth. The bride and the groom drink from the goblets to symbolize their union of love. A modern way to incorporate honey is to find a local honey maker or distributor and give small jars of it away as your favors. You can use the color gold as well in your reception décor or for bridesmaids dresses.

A traditional Chinese custom is for the bride to have at least three different outfits during the reception. Intricate brocades will feature Chinese symbols including the *Shuang XI*, the "double happiness" symbol. Typically the Shuang XI is represented with the dragon and phoenix symbols. Dragon and phoenix symbols are auspicious symbols representing the perfect balance of male and female forces. Together, the dragon and phoenix represent marital happiness and harmony for the bride and groom. This symbolism stems from ancient Chinese traditions of treating the bride and groom as "Empress and Emperor" for a day. This is rooted in ancient mythology where the dragon represents the emperor and his majestic powerful phoenix by his side. Many couples choose to use the double happiness symbol on favors and on their programs. As many Chinese brides change their clothes throughout their wedding day; see if you can incorporate the phoenix and the dragon in one of your dress designs!

Another popular Chinese custom is that the bride and groom will serve tea to their elders in the family, and the elders will give the couple red packages (*lai see*) with monetary gifts, and will wish them well.

All sorts of fanciful décor are used and fun activities take place, such as playing mahjong or having Lion Dancers perform special ceremonial dances for the newlyweds. Instead of a receiving line, the couple will have a retreating line to say goodbye to all of the guests.

Korean

Koreans go through a similar process that Chinese couples do. Again, most modern Korean couples do not consult a fortuneteller for their match, but older Korean-Americans still appreciate the custom. The tradition of finding a match based on astrological signs is called *kung-hap* which is "read" through a matchmaker. A matchmaker is most commonly used for arranged marriages in South Korea. Typically, a fortuneteller or matchmaker is found through family contacts and connections. The traditional wedding outfit worn by a Korean bride is a beautiful silk topcoat with flowing sleeves normally embroidered with flowers or butterflies. Underneath her topcoat, a bride will wear the *hanbok*, which is a doll-like dress. The bride will normally wear a white sash tied with a *Korum* or *Maedup* bow. A groom will typically wear a *sangbok*, which is also called a *turumagi*. This overcoat has loose sleeves and typically he wears black silk trousers (called *paji*) with the overcoat.

One of the most common elements of the actual Korean wedding ceremony is the sharing of special rice white wine called *jung jong*. At most Korean receptions, *jung jong* is normally available to all of the guests during the toast. A typical noodle dish called *kook soo* is served. This noodle soup is considered to bring the bride and groom a long and happy life together. Finally, desserts are served to represent playfulness in marriage and hope for children. Typical wedding desserts will include *dok* (sticky rice cakes filled with bean paste) and *yak* (sticky rice balls speckled with nuts and raisins).

Another fun tradition found in traditional Korean weddings is called the *peh beck*. Only immediate family and close friends normally attend the *peh bek* ceremony. The new wife will traditionally bring chestnuts and figs (symbols of boys and girls, respectively). There might also be wooden geese or ducks (symbols of fidelity) present at this ceremony. The bride and groom will sit together while family members take turns sitting in front of them. The bride and groom bow and touch their heads to the floor to honor and respect their elders. Typically the bride and groom will offer tea and, in exchange, the various elder members of the family will offer advice, wisdom, and cash gifts. At the end of this ceremony, the family members will toss the figs and the chestnuts at the bride and groom to see how many they catch. The number of the figs and chestnuts caught are supposed to represent the number of children each family member would like the couple to have. Maybe you won't want to catch them all! In some Korean-American weddings, the *peh bek* elements are incorporated into a Western ceremony, while others may choose to have a private *peh beck* ceremony before or after the Western ceremony. The choice is up to you on how to incorporate your Korean traditions.

If you don't plan on having a *peh beck* ceremony, you can incorporate some of the elements from the ceremony into your reception. For example, fill small favor bags with chestnuts and figs, or incorporate a beautiful goose design logo or symbol on your programs, invitations, or menus.

Filipino

The Filipino wedding is rich in family traditions that have taken shape over centuries. Unlike Japanese, Chinese, and Korean cultures, Filipino weddings take many of their traditions from Spanish culture and Catholic Church traditions.

QUESTION

Why do Filipino traditions have Spanish influences?
In 1521, Magellan claimed the Philippines for Spain. The Spanish colonized the Philippines in 1565; it continued to be governed by Spain until the country declared independence from Spain on June 12, 1898.

Typically, the groom's family will pay for the entire wedding. The bride and groom both wear white. While the bride will wear a typical Western white wedding gown, the groom will wear a *barong* (hand-embroidered long shirt). Many symbols are used in the actual ceremony. The most important part of planning a traditional Filipino ceremony is choosing sponsors (godparents) for the wedding. These sponsors are thought of as witnesses to the ceremony. These sponsors will be in charge of wedding candles, the veil, and cord. The candle, veil, and cord are used in ceremonies during a traditional Catholic Mass. The candles that are lit represent God's presence in the marriage. The veil symbolizes two people who are clothed as one. The cord symbolizes the infinite bond in marriage. The couple can also choose to incorporate the *arrhae*, which is a monetary gift to the bride of thirteen gold or silver coins. The person carrying these coins is typically called a coin bearer who will walk alongside or in front of the ring bearer. The coins represent the groom's commitment to provide for the welfare of his bride and future children.

Even though the couple chooses sponsors for the actual processional to carry various symbolic items, guests are also considered to be witnesses to the ceremony and are considered very important. The wedding ceremony is traditionally about bringing two families together and all guests are considered family on the day of the wedding.

A popular way to incorporate Filipino traditions into your reception is to see if you can find traditional Filipino dancers traced back to your ancestors from the Philippines. This is typically pretty easy if your family is well connected in your community. If not, you may want to consult with a talent agency to help. You may need to do a little research on which tribe your family came from.

A common celebratory dish is a roasted pig on a pit. If your reception won't allow such a thing, see if roasted pork can be one of your entrée items. All sorts of pastries and sweets are made for weddings, and a common item found during cocktail hours are empanadas made with sweet meat and raisin filling.

For favors, you may want to consider items made out of palm leaves, such as handheld fans or small boxes that you can fill with candy. Another idea is to fill up sinamay bags with candy or a favor of your choice. *Sinamay* is a plant-based material that is used to make anything from clothing to tea bags.

Southeast Asian (Hindu/Indian) Traditions

A typical Indian wedding will be at least a three-day elaborate and colorful affair. Typical Southeast Asian weddings are deeply rooted in Hindu, Sikh, Jain, and Muslim religious customs. Depending on your religion, the actual ceremony can vary widely. Not only will religion be the center of your ceremony, but also traditional family and city customs will play a major role depending on where your family is from.

ESSENTIAL

Since wedding traditions will vary greatly depending on your religion, ethnicity, language, and region from which your family is from, you will need to figure out between each family which wedding customs you want to include, in addition to the wedding day festivities.

An Indian bride will wear a *sari*, intricately embroidered fabric, which is draped around the body in various styles. Typically, the *sari* is wrapped around the waist and then draped over the shoulder. An Indian groom will wear a *sherwani* or *Nehru* jacket with trousers to match. The sherwani or *Nehru* jacket is normally embroidered and can be quite colorful and even match the bride's *sari*.

The most widely used aspects of typical Indian wedding ceremonies are:

- The *Mehndi* **ceremony**—This is typically a private affair held by the bride's family the day before the wedding. This ceremony is an exciting tradition of applying turmeric (commonly known as henna) paste in the form of intricate and beautiful designs on the bride's face, feet, and hands. Most modern Indian-American brides typically do not apply the designs to their faces.
- The *Baraat*—The entrance or welcoming of the groom
- *Jaimala* **ceremony**—The exchange of wedding garlands
- *Saat Phere*—The portion of the ceremony where the couple says their vows which typically consists of seven steps:

1. Prayer for provisions
2. Happiness and health
3. Wealth and prosperity
4. Love, trust, and the preservation of family ties
5. Welfare of universe
6. Long life and togetherness
7. Relationship of sacrifice for love's sake

A few other possible rituals that may be seen in an Indian wedding ceremony are:

- The bride and groom will sit side by side with their hands tied in union.
- As the bride and groom say their vows, they will walk around a sacred fire.
- The groom will present a *mangalsutra* (necklace or garland) to the bride.
- *Sindoor* (red vermilion powder) will be placed by the groom on the bride's hair parting-line or forehead as a visual symbol of their marriage.
- The groom will announce his desire for a lasting friendship with his wife.
- The father of the bride will say prayers for the new couple.
- The *purohit* (priest) will offer prayers and pronounce the couple husband and wife.

From the *Saat phere* to the pronouncement of marriage, the couple is typically seated underneath a canopy called a *mandap*. The *mandap* is typically elaborately decorated with fabric and flowers with large, decorated chairs underneath the mandap for the couple, parents, and (sometimes) other selected family members. Typically the priest will be seated on the floor (on a pillow).

Traditional Indian colors are deep reds, golds, and oranges. Marigolds, roses, and carnations are used widely in the *mandap* décor along with the floral garlands that are exchanged. Normally, the fabrics used for a *mandap* are made with the traditional colors, but you should always feel free to change up the colors to match your modern style (if your parents will allow it). Make sure if you are a wearing a *sari* that it matches (or coordinates with) the colors of your *mandap*.

Latino Fiestas

Depending on the country from which your family originates, Latino wedding traditions will vary almost as much as they do with Indian weddings. The most important element of any Latino wedding is to make sure your family is involved. Family is always central and the vast majority of Central and South American weddings are Catholic. Most Latino weddings also take some of their traditions from Spain. For instance, the mantilla veil is a classic Spanish tradition used in most Latin American weddings. The mantilla veil is typically a cathedral length veil that rests around the forehead of the bride with beautiful Spanish lace around the edge of it. Many mantillas are passed down from one generation to the next.

Most countries will have a typical wedding feast and almost all will have lots of dancing all night long! The dollar or money dance is very common at most Latino weddings where guests will pin dollars (or the local currency) on to the bride or groom for a dance. Like Filipino weddings, many Latino weddings will incorporate the tradition of the gold coin *arrhae* ceremony as described in the Filipino wedding tradition section.

Some typical wedding traditions from specific Latino countries include:

- **Mexico**—Calla lilies are traditional wedding flowers.
- **Puerto Rico**—The bridal doll is a unique wedding tradition; the doll is typically dressed exactly like the bride with beautiful charm souvenirs attached to the doll. The charms are given to guests and the guests will typically pin dollars to the doll in return.
- **Cuba**—Since Cuba is a communist country, the wedding ceremony is a simple and short civil service. In Cuba, the wedding is all about the procession in the streets on the way to the wedding ceremony, as well as the reception.
- **El Salvador**—The bride and her family must wait for seven white cars to escort her to the church.

- **Dominican Republic**—The wedding cake is typically the central décor item at the wedding reception. Most formal wedding portraits and photos with the guests are taken with the cake. It's tradition for the guests to take cake home instead of eating it at the reception.

One of the best places online to find more information about Latino wedding traditions, customs, and ideas is Bodaclick (*www.bodaclick.com*), which is in Spanish only.

Persian *Sofrehs*

The customs and traditions of Persian weddings are extensive and require the assistance of the family. There are two stages in a Persian wedding ceremony. The first stage is the *aghd*, which is the legal process of a bride and groom becoming married. The second stage is the *Jashn-e Aroosi*. The *Jashn-e Aroosi* is the wedding reception, which can last anywhere from three to seven days consisting of various family activities.

The actual wedding ceremony takes place in front of what is called a *Sofreh-ye Aghd*. The *Sofreh-ye Agdh* is a complicated, elaborate, and beautiful display, which is spread on the floor facing east. There are various elements placed on the *Sofreh-ye Agdh* including (but not limited to):

- **Mirror**—Represents fate
- **Two candelabras**—Represent brightness in marriage
- **Tray of seven multicolored herbs and spices**—To ward off evil and witchcraft: The herbs and spices include: poppy seeds, salt, wild rice, frankincense, black tea, angelica, and nigella seeds
- **Decorated flatbread**—Represents prosperity; the bread that is sometimes shared with the guests
- **Basket of eggs and separate vessels for almonds, walnuts, and hazelnuts—** All representing fertility
- **Cup of rose water**—Said to perfume the air of the ceremony
- **Incense**—Believed to ward off the evil eye and bring health
- **Bowl of gold coins**—Represents wealth and prosperity

- **A beautifully decorated shawl**—This fabric is held over the bride and groom by married female relatives, which in turn is said to bring happiness in marriage
- **Two crystallized sugar cones**—These cones are typically covered in tulle and ground together above the bride and groom's head (on the scarf) to literally "shower" them in sweetness and happiness
- **Pomegranates or red apples**—Represent a joyous marriage together
- **Goblet of honey**—Said to sweeten life. After the couple is declared married, the couple should dip one pinky finger each into the honey and feed it to each other.
- **One needle and seven strands of colored thread**—Representing sewing up the mother-in-law's lips from speaking unpleasantly to the bride! These threads are typically sewn in one corner of the shawl.
- **Holy book**—Depending on the couple's religion, their particular holy book is placed on the *Sofreh-ye Aghd* with a red rose laid in the center of it while the book is open. If a couple if not religious, a book of poems or the *Avesta* is used for tradition purposes.
- **Sweets and pastries**—These are shared with guests right after the ceremony; Jordan almonds and baklava are Persian favorites.

European Influences

North America tends to have a mix of influences from all over the world, many leading back to Europe. Here are a few key traditions taken from various European cultures:

French Traditions

In some French towns, the groom calls for his bride at her home and the couple will walk to the church together. While walking to the church, children will run alongside the couple and throw white ribbons. A couple will typically stand beneath a silk canopy, which is said to ward off evil spirits. In Southern France, guests leaving the church will throw coins to children. At the reception, the guests will partake in eating the *croquembouche*, which is a French cream puff tower normally in the shape of a cone.

Polish Weddings

At the reception, the parents of the couple may offer the newlyweds the bread and salt blessing. The couple is given lightly salted bread and a glass of wine. The bread symbolizes the parents' hopes that their children will never know hunger; the salt is to remind the couple that life is full of difficulties and they will have to work hard when faced with tough times. The wine symbolizes the parents' hopes that the newlyweds never know thirst; it is also a wish for health and happiness.

Polish weddings will also use the money dance. Unlike Latino weddings, the money is not pinned to the bride's dress but rather to an apron. Sometimes the maid of honor will wear the apron and money is collected by the maid of honor and pinned to the bride's dress depending on the number of guests. When the Polish bride enters the reception hall, her veil is removed during the *oczepiny* ceremony as a symbol of her exit from the single life and her entrance into marriage. The groom, meanwhile, is sometimes asked to don a hat, as a wish for the happiness and levity in the marriage.

Italian Celebrations

An Italian groom will sometimes carry a piece of iron in his pocket for luck. The bride's veil is torn for good luck as well. Confetti (Jordan almonds) bundles wrapped in tulle are given as favors as a sign of fertility. A traditional Italian wedding reception is filled with many courses and followed up with a Venetian Hour. The Venetian Hour is an Italian tradition during which cakes and pastries are served in large quantities and displayed in elaborate style.

FACT

At the reception of an Italian wedding, the bride and the groom often break a glass. The number of shards will be equal to the number of happy years the couple will share together.

Irish Customs

Many Irish couples believe there is a lucky day for weddings, one that only comes but once a year: New Year's Day. For good luck, a swatch of Irish lace may be sewn into the bride's gown and then used later for a baby bonnet. The couple also receives a horseshoe to display in their new home. A couple will traditionally exchange *claddagh* rings. The heart, crown, and hands found on the *claddagh* ring symbolize love, loyalty, and friendship.

There is nothing to stop you from using various traditions from several cultures for your wedding day. Make your ceremony unique and honor traditions at the same time, to leave you and your guests with lasting memories.

CHAPTER 7

Showers and Other Parties

With the excitement of being engaged comes the excitement of all the partying you get to do as a bride or groom! Should you decide that the wedding day is enough to plan for, feel free to keep it at just that. But if you're up for celebrating, your friends and families will love sharing the joy of your love, so let them chip in on the planning of all the other fun parties that can come along with being engaged. Soak it all in and enjoy yourself!

Engagement Parties

It is customary for the family of the bride to host some sort of engagement party. It is, however, perfectly acceptable for the family of the groom (or anyone else) to host such an affair. On the other hand, it is also acceptable to go without an engagement party altogether, if you prefer.

ESSENTIAL

Some guests of all of your wedding-related parties might feel the need to bring a gift. Whether it is a classic bottle of wine or a silly gift, be prepared to write a handwritten note or e-mail to thank them. Take note that your wedding party should be invited to all wedding-related parties (gender appropriate).

Most engagement parties nowadays are informal. Invitations can be made via phone, e-mail, online invitations, handwritten notes, or traditional mailed invitations. The party is typically held at either the host's home or in a restaurant. Guests typically do not bring gifts to engagement parties (but be prepared that some guests might).

Bridal Showers

There are typically only two real rules that you, your friends, coworkers, or family need to keep in mind when hosting a shower. First and foremost, any guest who is invited to your bridal shower must be invited to the wedding (this includes children). This is a hard and fast rule that *cannot be broken*! The second rule is that you should not have your shower less than two months prior to your wedding. This rule can be broken depending on the circumstances surrounding your wedding and scheduling. It is better to have the shower two to three months prior to the wedding only due to the fact that a shower so close to the wedding might be stressful (as opposed to something that should be fun)!

When making a guest list for your bridal shower, be sure to check with your host(s) about budget and space. You and your host(s) should work together on what would be an appropriate number of guests for the budget and space in which the shower will be held.

QUESTION

What if I do not want guests to bring gifts to my bridal shower?
Typically a shower is centered on "showering" the bride with gifts. However, you can ask your host to make it clear on the invitations that gifts are not necessary. You should consider making the shower centered on a theme (discussed later in the chapter) or telling your guests you have made a donation to a nonprofit organization in lieu of a gift.

The guest list should really dictate the type of shower that you plan to have. If you and your guests hate bridal shower games, do away with them! You can have anything from a classic food, drink, game, and present shower to a themed shower!

Who's Hosting?

In the past, etiquette dictated that a bridal shower could only be hosted by your friends, and not by family. Today, as with almost all things wedding, this has changed. Family, friends, coworkers, or anyone else who is so inclined can throw a shower for you. The most common hosts are your bridal party, in combination with your mother and other close family members—but who's to say which other generous (and ambitious) people might have a party up their sleeves?

ESSENTIAL

If someone offers to throw a shower for you, don't look a gift horse in the mouth. You should only decline in the most bizarre circumstances (say, if your former boyfriend's new girlfriend wants to throw a party for you, and up to this point, you and she have only hurled accusations at one another).

Typically a shower is held either at a small function hall or in someone's home, depending on the size of the guest list. The guests are usually women, but your fiancé can come along for the ride if he wants. He probably won't be nearly as excited as you are about the pots and pans and measuring spoons and placemats—but you never know.

Feeling Overwhelmed?

No matter how much society wants to make weddings into the most fantastic day of anyone's life, there are some brides-to-be who simply hate being the center of attention. If you get overwhelmed in crowds and cringe at the thought of attending a shower with 100 of your mom's closest friends, here are a few pointers to help you navigate!

- **Keep cool**—Even if you're completely overwhelmed, every guest wants to see you looking happy. Try to breathe and smile as much as possible.
- **Mingle**—All of these women have come to celebrate your impending marriage, and they brought you gifts. Say hello to every single one of them and make them feel welcome.
- **Feed yourself**—You're going to have a long afternoon. If you know that you become easily irritated when you feel crowded or hungry, don't turn a potentially bad situation into a disaster.
- **Fudge it**—Every gift deserves a sincere (or at least sincere *sounding*) "ooh" and/or "ahh," even if you find you're losing steam when you're only halfway through the pile.

Some brides are on edge during pre-wedding parties. Unfortunately, these are the same brides who earn the labels "difficult" or "Bridezilla." Don't act as though someone forced you to come to this shower and collect all the goodies. Go into each party with a good attitude and it will go by faster than you think!

The In-Law Shower

How can you possibly attend a shower where you don't know anyone and act as though it's perfectly natural to be opening expensive gifts given to you by complete strangers?

If your future in-laws host a shower for you, you may be meeting many of your husband's relatives for the first time—and you may feel incredibly awkward about accepting gifts from them. Don't. For starters, no one is forcing these women to come to your shower. For another thing, it's a sure bet that your mother-in-law has gone to bridal showers hosted by these ladies (and given for brides your mother-in-law didn't know yet) and that they're returning the favor.

ESSENTIAL

If you are not the biggest fan of your future in-laws, don't despair! Typically the maid of honor and your mother are always invited to every single shower. So just cling on to them for support throughout and breathe!

The best thing you can do (when you're surrounded by strangers) at your own bridal shower is to smile and say thank you, and make as much polite conversation as you can. You'll leave those ladies saying, "Wow! We could use more of *her* type in this family!"

Co-Ed Showers

Many couples opt for the co-ed shower. Why should the bride have all the fun? Some brides are shy and simply do not like being the center of attention. The co-ed shower is the best way to make sure your groom is there to take some of that attention off of you. Some couples share the same friends and a co-ed shower is a great way to make sure everyone can be involved.

ALERT

Since co-ed showers tend to be more inclusive (and can be in lieu of multiple showers), be sure you have the right host(s) and space available. Co-ed showers are typically larger showers than bridal showers and you don't want your guests to be cramped in a smaller space.

Typically the groom will invite his groomsmen along with any of his other best friends and their dates. As a bride, feel free to invite your best friends and your wedding party as well. Be sure to serve foods that everyone can enjoy, as opposed to tea sandwiches and iced tea! A barbecue is the perfect setting for a co-ed shower. You might even be able to fit in some fun games like volleyball and a potato sack race! Keep the atmosphere fun and light.

Themed Showers

Themed showers are the norm these days with brides having multiple bridal showers. Each host of each shower should be made aware of any particular theme that may be on the horizon at another shower. Most themed showers are centered on a particular room in your home, such as your kitchen or bathroom. Here are a few ideas for you and your host:

- **Stock the Shelves Shower**—Have your host say in the invitation that they want to stock the shelves in your kitchen! This would include finding items on your wedding registry having to do with your kitchen from china to salt and pepper shakers.
- **Lingerie Shower**—Make sure you don't have the shy ladies on your guest list for this one! Let your host know your measurements so your guests can bring the right size bras, panties, and other fun lingerie items for your honeymoon (and beyond). You will most likely receive something that may not be your particular style. Don't worry; most lingerie stores will take back anything unworn and with tags (so don't ask for the receipt)!
- **Baking Shower**—This shower is to help you get your bake on! No matter where you are in life, baking will happen—from celebration cakes to cookie making with your children or nieces or nephews. This is a shower that helps you get ready for all of those celebrations! Have your host(s) go all out and either buy a festive cake or have a cake or cookie-making shower! What is a shower without cake anyway?
- **Wine Shower**—What better way to celebrate than with wine? From table wines to sparkling wines, you can keep those bottles stashed away for years and wait for the right occasion for each bottle. Your host can get creative and ask each guest to bring a specific year of wine or type of wine. Have plenty of cheese, chocolate, and palate cleansers available for this party!

- **Linen Shower**—This shower is for stocking the shelves with pillow-cases, guest towels, beach towels, sheets, and blankets. Your host(s) can ask one guest to bring the laundry detergent too!

FACT

Whichever type of shower you end up with, don't forget to say thank you after the event! Make sure you thank the host(s) with a kind letter or a gift. If gifts were given at the shower, a handwritten note to each guest is important. Make sure you have someone at the shower taking notes of who gave which gift!

Keeping Track

During the gift-opening part of the shower, put someone you trust (an organized bridesmaid, your mother, a friend—but not your six-year-old niece) in charge of recording each gift and who gave it. Choose someone who can keep things organized even if the party gets hectic, so that when you sit down to write your thank-you notes, you won't come off sounding like a confused bride. (You don't want to thank your Aunt Marion for the gift that Aunt Mary gave you, and vice versa.)

Make sure the person charged with keeping track of who gave you which gift understands the importance of the task. You *don't* want to see this person chit-chatting or hitting the buffet while you're working your way through the stack of presents.

Shower Games

Everyone has a definite opinion on shower games: You either love 'em or you hate 'em. Unfortunately, your personal feelings and the opinions of your guests (and most important, your host or hostess) may be different, so in the interest of keeping everyone amused and happy, showers often include games. If you hate them, and your hostess wants to have them—try to be courteous!

Think of this as a way to liven things up a bit for your guests. Alas, even the most engaging party games can encounter some initial resistance from a party pooper or two. If you offer prizes for the winners of these games, though, even the biggest wet blankets may be encouraged to play! Following are some ideas for fun shower games.

- **Guess the Goodies**—Fill a large decorative jar with white or colored candies. Ask the guests to guess how many candies are in the jar. They can take as long as they want to hazard a guess; at the end of the shower, they hand in their answers on a slip of paper. The person who comes closest to the number without going over wins the jar and the candy (and maybe an additional prize).
- **Famous Couple Trivia**—Try developing some trivia questions with a love theme for your shower. Sample questions include these:

  - Who was Tom Cruise's first wife? (Mimi Rogers)
  - Who did Prince Rainier marry? (Grace Kelly)
  - Who dies first in *Romeo and Juliet*? (Romeo)

- **Make up your own questions**—It's a fun game and most of the guests will have an equal chance of winning if you include questions about couples from every generation represented at your shower. Set a time limit for answers, and give a prize to the winner. The person with the most correct answers wins.
- **Knowing Your Groom**—Have the hostess of the party interrogate your groom to come up with fun and interesting facts about your husband-to-be. See who gets the most answers. Naturally, the bride should know all the answers!

ESSENTIAL

A word to the wise: Keep it clean, especially if you're in mixed company. It's one thing to play rowdy games when you're sitting around with your girlfriends—it's quite another to include Grandma and Great Aunt Ruth. You'll send them packing, and they won't look back.

Prizes

Prizes are the bribe you'll need to get some of your guests to play these games. For others, game playing is nothing less than an expectation. But what kind of prizes? New cars? Small appliances? An all-expense-paid tropical vacation for two? Nope!

Winners of shower games expect something useful, but not something that's incredibly cheap. When your hosts (or you) are out looking for prizes, think middle-of-the-road. You don't want anything too expensive, but nothing should look like it came from a dollar store, either. Some suggestions include books, note cards or stationery, coffee/tea mugs, candy, bubble bath/bath oils, decorative magnets, coasters, houseplants, etc.

To guard against the possibility of a riot, prepared hosts will have more than one prize on hand for each game, just in case there's a tie.

ESSENTIAL

The prizes should be wrapped if possible to ensure maximum suspense for the guests ("Ooh, I wonder what she'll get!") and the prize winner as she makes her blind choice ("This one looks like it might be a magnet, but I *really* want some note cards").

If there are no ties, or if your hosts are particularly generous, or in the event that the "No Games" opinion wins out, the prizes can be door prizes. When the ladies enter, hand them a number (or a ticket—you can buy rolls of them at your huge warehouse/grocery/household goods store or online). If the tables have place cards, you can write small numbers in the corner of each guest's card. One of the hosts chooses a number, and whoever has the number chooses a prize.

Bachelor Parties

As a bride, you have heard all about the infamous bachelor party. The groom has been looking forward to this party all engagement long. In the past, this party was held the night before the wedding. Too many hung-over grooms and headache-prone groomsmen have led to more rational, earlier dates for a bachelor party! Not to mention that most rehearsal dinners take place the night before the wedding. A week before the big day is the closest your groom should try to have his "last night on the town." Don't let all the hoopla fool you. Many men are not into going to topless bars and becoming ragingly drunk. Here are few great ways for your groom to spend his bachelor party or weekend:

- **Golf and more golf**—Many grooms have opted for a weekend with the boys at their favorite golf course! Whether it is just eighteen holes at the local country club or a weekend at a golf resort on some island, this is a great way for the guys to hang out just before the big day!
- **A ski retreat**—If your man's favorite sport is skiing, why not a lodge weekend where skiing and drinking (hot chocolate, of course) are typically intertwined?
- **Weekend in Vegas**—Okay, this may not be the bride's first choice. However, a weekend in Vegas does not always mean debauchery. You probably do not want your man gambling up a storm while you are trying to save up for your dream home. Let his buddies gamble it all out of him the week before the wedding on their dime! Plus drinks and food tend to be pretty cheap.

Bachelorette Parties

Maybe this particular get-together is something you have been looking forward to as well. Or perhaps you have been trying to talk your bridesmaids out of doing it altogether! No matter what kind of bride you are, make sure that if you are going to have a bachelorette party you tell the organizer what you do not want. The same timeframe for the bachelor party applies; a hung-over bride typically will not glow on her wedding day! This party can be one night or a themed weekend just like the guys get to have. Here are a few examples:

- A few popular *weekend bachelorette getaways* include—Las Vegas, nearby beaches, a slumber party at your house, ski retreat, or a weekend at a spa in the mountains.
- If you can't get away for an entire weekend, try a *night out on the town*—Go to your favorite bar/club, or find the best restaurant in town to have a multicourse meal complete with wine tasting. The possibilities are endless when it comes to a night out on the town!

- *Spa day with the girls*—This always tends to be the favorite for women who are just not into a drunken night on the streets. A full day at the spa including massages, pedicures, and manicures is the perfect girl time!

Pampering Parties

A pampering party typically has nothing to do with actual presents like showers do. This is a time to pamper you and your bridesmaids. Here are a few ideas to get you started:

- **Massage party**—What better way to relax than having a massage party! This type of party can be done at a spa, on the beach, at your house, or really anywhere a masseuse can kick up her massage table or chair! With massages being incorporated into so many health insurance programs and holistic healing centers, many therapists now have the ability to travel. Don't let hefty spa prices scare you. Many massage therapists have reasonable rates (even when traveling). You can even have this party the day before or the day of the wedding, depending what your schedule is like.
- **Makeup, hair, and nails party**—Let's face it, every bride needs to have her hair, makeup, and nails done for her wedding day. Whether you have a professional do your hair and makeup on your wedding day or not, you should have a trial run-through, so why not invite the bridesmaids to the salon or makeup counter? This is the perfect time to throw out the old lipstick and try something new.

Rehearsal Dinner

After the rehearsal at the ceremony location, you will want to consider having a dinner. Rehearsal dinners can be small, intimate affairs or can end up like a wedding reception all their own! Some couples do not have ceremony rehearsals at all, in which case they simply call this dinner the welcome dinner.

The Host and the Guests

Traditionally, the expense of the rehearsal dinner is borne by the groom's parents. But anyone can be the host of this party. In modern society, many brides and grooms can feel uncomfortable asking either set of parents to host this particular affair. So feel free to host this event yourselves.

Who should come to this party? Etiquette states that the minimum guest list should include the wedding party (along with their spouses or significant others), immediate family (including parents, stepparents, and siblings), grandparents, godparents, and the ceremony officiant with his/her spouse.

ALERT

The parents of child attendants should also be invited to the rehearsal dinner. Make sure that the dinner starts early enough that if the parents need to leave to get an overtired child to bed, they can. You should also consider hiring a professional nanny service to take care of not only children attendants but also children of your wedding party.

If you have the budget, the space, and the time to plan, this dinner can include anyone you would like who is invited to the wedding the next day. Many couples feel the need to include out-of-town guests for this event. This way you will be able to spend more time with your guests. This also helps to welcome those guests to your city instead of them trying to find the closest restaurant for dinner or just hanging out in the hotel room the night before your wedding. So in essence, you can invite anyone from just family and your bridal party to all of your wedding day guests.

Location, Location, Location!

The rehearsal dinner can be as formal or as informal as you or your host wants to make it. The only thing you should really keep in consideration is that it should not be grander than or have the same décor as the wedding day. This event can be held at someone's home, a restaurant, hotel, park, beach—really anywhere at all! Make sure your guests know about the location and what the appropriate attire should be. Invitations can be handwritten, by phone, by e-mail, or specialty printed. An online invitation is also completely appropriate for an informal rehearsal dinner. The formality of your rehearsal dinner will dictate what kind of invitation should be sent. If you are having a potluck dinner at the church just after the rehearsal, a quick phone call or e-mail should suffice. If you are having a semi-formal dinner at the hotel where your guests are staying, a formal invitation should be sent. Make sure the invitations for this particular event are sent out at least two to four weeks prior to the dinner.

One for You, and One for You . . .

The rehearsal dinner is usually when an engaged couple hands out their gifts to the attendants (and parents, if you're feeling very generous). You might also choose to give your fiancé(e) a wedding gift at this time, and he or she may have a little something wrapped up for you.

However, if the two of you would rather hold off on giving each other your wedding gifts until the honeymoon, that's not a horrible idea, especially if one or both of you is just too exhausted or nervous to appreciate another gift at this point. After all, each of you has put a lot of thought into the gift you've chosen. You want your fiancé(e) to be able to take the time to really take note of the significance of what you've given to him or her, and you want to be able to do the same with the gift that is given to you.

Speech! Speech!

If you follow the traditional rehearsal dinner route, toasts will be a part of the evening. If the groom's parents are hosting, the father of the groom offers up a toast to the bride and groom and to the bride's parents. The father of the bride responds with a toast to the hosts and to the almost-newlyweds. The groom then toasts the bride and her family, and the bride responds with a toast to the groom and his family.

Of course, you're not being watched by the etiquette police, so if someone *else* wants to make a toast (or someone on that list of toasters would rather not speak publicly), you're not bound to follow the traditional order. And if you prefer to skip the toasts altogether, that's fine, too. Remember, there'll be enough formality on the wedding day.

The After Party

You said "I Do," kissed, danced, cut the cake, tossed the bouquet, and now the caterer is breaking down. It is only 11 P.M. and you are thinking, "I am still wide awake and so are my guests!" What is a married couple to do? Have an after party! This party is one of the easiest of all the parties to plan. Why? You can make big elaborate plans complete with a funky bar and DJ or simply gather a bunch of your friends and tell them to meet you at your local bar. Typically an after party should be planned ahead of time if you have a large amount of out-of-town guests coming to your wedding. The most ideal place to have this after party is the hotel where the majority of your guests are staying. This way, if they are drunk afterward, they can simply go upstairs to their hotel rooms. Always make sure that wherever this after party is, your guests can easily find their way back home or to their hotels by taxi or by some other pre-arranged shuttle service to ensure their safety.

The other great news about this particular party is that you do not necessarily have to pay for it. If you wait to plan it on the spot at the reception the night of your wedding, your friends and family will pick up the tab of what they are drinking on their own. Even if you do have a pre-planned after party, you should really only worry about beverages, music, and some basic snack foods.

Day-After Brunch

Having a light breakfast or brunch served for your guests the day after the wedding is quite popular. Typically the morning-after-the-wedding brunch can be hosted by anyone. Many parents of a bride or groom will either host the brunch at their homes or at a room pre-selected at the hotel where the majority of the guests are staying. A brunch is appropriate for larger weddings that have a lot of out-of-town guests who will be leaving at various times during the day or week after your wedding. This is another great time to spend with guests. The bride and groom are not obligated to come to this event and typically the parents of the bride and groom are present to wish the guests well. Again, anyone can host this brunch and some brides and grooms will host the event themselves! A brunch is not something that is obligatory and should only be done if there is enough room in your budget for it.

Bridal Shower Guest List

Name: _____ Address: _____

Telephone: _____ RSVP Number in Party: _____

Name: _____ Address: _____

Telephone: _____ RSVP Number in Party: _____

Name: _____ Address: _____

Telephone: _____ RSVP Number in Party: _____

Name: _____ Address: _____

Telephone: _____ RSVP Number in Party: _____

Name: _____ Address: _____

Telephone: _____ RSVP Number in Party: _____

Name: _____ Address: _____

Telephone: _____ RSVP Number in Party: _____

Name: _____ Address: _____

Telephone: _____ RSVP Number in Party: _____

Name: _____ Address: _____

Telephone: _____ RSVP Number in Party: _____

Name: _____ Address: _____

Telephone: _____ RSVP Number in Party: _____

Name: _____ Address: _____

Telephone: _____ RSVP Number in Party: _____

Name: _____ Address: _____

Telephone: _____ RSVP Number in Party: _____

Name: _____ Address: _____

Telephone: _____ RSVP Number in Party: _____

Name: _____ Address: _____

Telephone: _____ RSVP Number in Party: _____

Name: _____ Address: _____

Telephone: _____ RSVP Number in Party: _____

Bridal Shower Guest List (continued)

Name: _____ Address: _____

Telephone: _____ RSVP Number in Party: _____

Name: _____ Address: _____

Telephone: _____ RSVP Number in Party: _____

Name: _____ Address: _____

Telephone: _____ RSVP Number in Party: _____

Name: _____ Address: _____

Telephone: _____ RSVP Number in Party: _____

Name: _____ Address: _____

Telephone: _____ RSVP Number in Party: _____

Name: _____ Address: _____

Telephone: _____ RSVP Number in Party: _____

Name: _____ Address: _____

Telephone: _____ RSVP Number in Party: _____

Name: _____ Address: _____

Telephone: _____ RSVP Number in Party: _____

Name: _____ Address: _____

Telephone: _____ RSVP Number in Party: _____

Name: _____ Address: _____

Telephone: _____ RSVP Number in Party: _____

Name: _____ Address: _____

Telephone: _____ RSVP Number in Party: _____

Name: _____ Address: _____

Telephone: _____ RSVP Number in Party: _____

Name: _____ Address: _____

Telephone: _____ RSVP Number in Party: _____

Name: _____ Address: _____

Telephone: _____ RSVP Number in Party: _____

Shower Gift Recorder

Name	Description of Gift	Thank-you note sent?
		☐
		☐
		☐
		☐
		☐
		☐
		☐
		☐
		☐
		☐
		☐
		☐
		☐
		☐
		☐
		☐
		☐
		☐
		☐
		☐
		☐
		☐
		☐
		☐

The Party Checklist

The Engagement Party

- Where?_____
- When?_____
- Who will be the host(s) or hostess(es)?_____
- Contact person telephone number_____
- Contact person e-mail address_____
- Guest List completed?_____
- Food and beverage_____
- Invitations_____
- Website/Directions_____

Shower

- Where?_____
- When?_____
- Who will be the host(s) or hostess(es)?_____
- Contact person telephone number_____
- Contact person e-mail address_____
- Theme?_____
- Guest List completed?_____
- Food and beverage_____
- Invitations_____
- Website/Directions_____

Bachelor Party

- Where?_____
- When?_____
- Who will be the host?_____
- Contact person telephone number_____
- Contact person e-mail address_____
- Theme?_____

- Guest List completed?_____
- Food and beverage_____
- Invitations_____
- Transportation needed?_____
- Website/Directions_____

Bachelorette Party

- Where?_____
- When?_____
- Who will be the host(s) or hostess(es)?_____
- Contact person telephone number_____
- Contact person e-mail address_____
- Theme?_____
- Guest List completed?_____
- Food and beverage_____
- Invitations_____
- Website/Directions_____

Rehearsal Dinner

- Where?_____
- When?_____
- Who will be the host(s) or hostess(es)?_____
- Host contact telephone number_____
- Contact person e-mail address_____
- Contact person for rented space_____
- Contact person telephone number_____
- Contact person e-mail address_____
- Guest List completed?_____
- Food and beverage_____
- Invitations_____
- Transportation needed?_____
- Website/Directions_____

After Party

- Where?_____
- When?_____
- Who will be the host(s) or hostess(es)?_____
- Contact person telephone number_____
- Contact person e-mail address_____
- Guest List completed?_____
- Food and beverage_____
- Invitations_____
- Transportation needed?_____
- Website/Directions_____

Brunch

- Where?_____
- When?_____
- Who will be the host(s) or hostess(es)?_____
- Contact person telephone number_____
- Contact person e-mail address_____
- Guest List completed?_____
- Food and beverage_____
- Invitations_____
- Website/Directions_____

CHAPTER 8

Your Reception

Your wedding day is more than just saying "I Do!" Going down the aisle is generally the easy part of the wedding day. When it comes to your wedding day, the reception is where the bulk of your decisions are made and where most of your budget is allocated. Finding the right reception space, which dictates the flow of the day, is what the party is all about!

Interesting Spaces

Once you know your guest count, the next step is to find a place to have your reception. Some experts say you should find your ceremony space first while others say you should find your reception space or location first. Whichever camp you belong to, you want to find the right space that is interesting for both you and your guests. Some reception spaces, in any town, will be the first to be booked simply due to popularity. So if you have your heart set on a particular space, find out their availability first. Then again, many places have the capability of having both your ceremony and reception all in one. You will know which reception space is right for you when you see the space and the price tag.

ESSENTIAL

During the peak wedding months of late March through early November, competition for popular wedding reception spaces can be cutthroat. If you are marrying within this peak timeframe, plan on looking for your ceremony and/or reception sites at least one year in advance. However, people cancel or reschedule events all the time, so get on a waiting list if they have one!

Modern Spaces

When dreaming about your wedding, do you think of dinner surrounded by funky architecture or a place that has fun art everywhere? Then a modern space might be the right space for you. There are all sorts of fun, funky, and modern spaces in most metropolitan cities. Some museums that focus on architecture, archaeology, and nature tend to be fun, interesting, and modern. Many museums have interesting exhibits that last for months at a time. You can even center your reception around the theme of the exhibit.

The main thing you should be thinking about when it comes to a modern space is its fashion-forward aesthetic or clean, cool lines. You might also be interested in a modern space if it is a nonprofit that supports the local community. Forward-, modern-thinking may not always be a loft in New York City overlooking Manhattan; it can be an interesting mansion that is revamped to be eco-friendly using solar panels and filtered rainwater.

Finding a modern space for your wedding reception (simply put) is finding a space that is the last place people think a wedding should be! You will be surprised how your favorite ice cream parlor becomes a fabulous, whimsical wedding space!

ALERT

Be advised that while you and your fiancé may dream of a fun and modern reception space, your parents may not. Try to find a space that is both modern and piques the interest of your parents. If your father loves boats, find your modern space near the water where he can paddle you in to the reception! Being creative will be your best selling point.

Artsy Spaces

How is an artsy space different from a modern space? Well, the answer is that not all modern spaces have art in them and not all art is modern! An artsy space is for the couple that loves being surrounded by paintings, sculpture, music, and other fine arts. Castles, estates, museums, and art galleries may be what are dancing in your head.

Most old buildings, mansions, and castles are typically filled with interesting artwork, stained glass, carpentry, and interesting, decorative architectural elements. The buildings themselves are pieces of art. The tapestries hung in the main entrance of the castle, or the beautiful greenhouse filled with orchids attached to the main dining room, can delight your guests.

FACT

The availability of some art galleries and museums may be limited. Most small art galleries are privately owned and will not rent out the space or will not have enough space for entertaining with seated dining guests. Some museums and art galleries are government owned and may not allow for social occasions (such as weddings) to take place. Be sure you know their availability before you get your heart set on that corner gallery!

Of course, certain museums and art galleries go way beyond art and sometimes on to pomp and circumstance. Finding the perfect art gallery and giving each guest a postcard of your favorite painting is a lovely way to share your interests.

Another perk of some of the public and nonprofit museums, galleries, and other spaces is that some of their fees may be tax-deductible. Even if you are forced to pay a higher fee for the upscale gallery in your city, you may be surprised when you read your contract that a certain amount is tax-deductible. Always ask!

Swanky Spaces

A swanky space can be any space that is hip, glamorous, posh, and modern. Think of the new nightclub downtown that has three different dance floors! With a little lighting and fabric draping, that dance club can turn into the most glamorous wedding location of the season! Other swanky places could include:

- Newly renovated old theatres
- Five-star restaurants
- Uptown lofts and penthouse spaces
- Exclusive resorts (whether it be the ski lodge or the beautiful covered terrace in the Caribbean)
- Jewelry stores. Some jewelry stores will let you rent their space for a cocktail hour or even your reception depending on the type of store. Would it not be perfect to have the cocktails where your fiancé bought your ring? It may require some extra insurance and some careful planning, but could be worth it in the end!

ALERT

Keep in mind that some of the swankier places know they are swanky. Where there is swank, there is money to be had. Be prepared to pay a higher price for these spaces, especially if they are typically open to the public on a Saturday night, when they make the most money. If you are a posh kind of girl, you probably already knew this!

You get the point. A swanky space is the place that everyone in town is talking about—the places that get written up in the Style section of your local newspaper and pop up on TV. If you have an uptown style, then have an uptown reception space!

Traditional Spaces

Just because you want to have your wedding in a traditional space, it does not mean it is not an interesting space! Traditional wedding spaces are the classic cream of the crop wedding venues that everyone places their bets on first. They are typically the easiest spaces to have weddings and places where your best wedding professionals will be able to give you the most advice and ideas.

Hotels

Hotels are the easiest place for a couple to plan their wedding. Most hotels are set up not only for housing your guests, but for entertaining them as well. Your larger hotels and chain hotels typically have their own catering department for their salon spaces.

Hotels work best for couples who plan to have a lot of out-of-town guests. Hotel spaces normally have wedding packages that are easier on the budget as well.

ALERT

While most hotels will offer package pricing, don't assume that the price is going to be the lowest you can get for what they are offering. Some hotels are extremely popular (and they know it) and can get away with higher prices on their packages. If you find another space near your favorite hotel, be advised to price shop the difference between catering at the outside venue space versus the in-house catering at the hotel.

The other great advantage of a larger hotel is that you can almost always have your ceremony onsite as well. Religious officiants can come to a hotel to marry you in their outside garden and their backup ballroom space!

Gardens

One of the most classic and romantic places to get married is in a garden. There are so many wonderful venues all over the country that have spectacular gardens attached to interesting mansions, conservatories, greenhouses, and other types of reception spaces.

ESSENTIAL

While falling in love with the garden space of your choice, make sure you love, or at least like, the backup space for your ceremony if it rains the day of your wedding. Most couples get so caught up in the garden space for their ceremony that they forget about Mother Nature and how she can turn on you!

Don't always assume that the most fabulous gardens will cost you thousands of dollars. While there are some garden venues that are expensive, there are so many public gardens maintained by state and federal funding as well (some that also have a tax-deductible part of their fee). Many local parks and gardens have facilities for educational purposes that are rented out for all occasions. You not only get to have the wedding of your dreams but you support your local community and get the most out of your tax dollars at the same time!

Weddings at Home

For many couples, the perfect solution to a reception dilemma is having their wedding at someone's home. If you are lucky, you, your parents, or someone you know will have a house and a yard big enough to accommodate your reception. What better way to celebrate the most important day of your life than in the house where you grew up or the backyard where you used to play? Placed in a unique context, and surrounded by family and friends, you will have an incredible reception experience.

Depending on the type of wedding you want, a home reception really gives you a lot of flexibility as to what you can do. If you want a formal wedding in the backyard with a tent and a band, you can do that! If you want a good ole' fashioned barbecue, you can do that too! Flexibility is the main draw for couples that want to have their weddings at home.

ALERT

Don't assume that having a home reception means your parents have to sweat in the kitchen. Hire a caterer to take care of the cuisine. At the same time, don't expect that a home reception will save you a lot of money either. Some home receptions can cost more due to the amount of equipment that has to be rented. Be sure to review the checklist at the end of this chapter!

All in a Day's Reception

Most weddings have a lot of the same elements that can be varied. For example, almost every wedding has a toast of some kind. How many you have and when you have them differ from one wedding to another. Here are a few main reception elements that you should consider for your big day.

Toasts

After the guests have been seated for dinner, everyone is served a glass of champagne or a sparkling beverage of choice for the toast. Toasts, of course, are an important part of the wedding reception, and, like every other wedding ritual, toasting has its own etiquette.

ESSENTIAL

You and your fiancé should know that the recipient of a toast does not drink at the end of the salute. You should simply smile at the person who is offering the kind words. If the person who is toasting is close to you, it would also be appropriate to hug or shake hands with them.

Fathers and best men are typically the first in line when it comes to toasts. A welcome toast can be done by anyone; however, the most common is the father of the bride. Since the parents of the bride are considered the hosts of the reception, a welcome toast by the host is always appropriate. The best man can also give the welcome toast or a toast right after the welcome toast. If toasts at dinner are not to your liking, a toast after the cake cutting is appropriate as you will have everyone's attention again.

If you have a long list of attendants and family wanting to toast you, make sure parents, siblings, and attendants get first dibs.

Important Dances

The couple's first dance is often one of the most romantic parts of your reception. You want to make sure that your guests are aware that it is about to happen! You and your new spouse will dance to a song the two of you have carefully chosen for its message of love that reflects your relationship while onlookers swoon!

For traditional weddings, after the first dance, the bride dances with her father and then the groom dances with his mother. Afterward, the bride and groom's parents dance, the bride dances with her father-in-law, the groom dances with his mother-in-law, and finally the attendants dance with their accompanying significant others.

FACT

If you have your first dance before the dinner is served for a formal reception, you want to make sure that the dances with mothers and fathers take place directly after the dinner. This will get your guests out on the dance floor and help them transition into the dancing portion of the evening.

At this point you must be exhausted just thinking about all the dancing you have to do just after eating a pretty heavy meal! You should not feel obligated to do all of this dancing. Most weddings will have at least just the first dance. Some brides are not close with their fathers and some grooms are not comfortable dancing at all, let alone with their mother. There is always an exception to every rule, and while dancing is fun for most people, some people would rather not!

The Cake-Cutting Ceremony

Aside from being the most beautiful and delicious concoction at your wedding, the wedding cake performs a very important function as the centerpiece of the cake-cutting ceremony. The cake-cutting ceremony is when the newlyweds cut the first piece of cake together and feed it to each other. In some cultures there is not an actual cake involved but fruits and/or other types of sweets. The tradition dates back centuries symbolizing the couple's desire to provide for each other.

The Bouquet and Garter Toss

Once widely accepted traditions, these two elements have recently started to lose favor in the United States. Here is how the tradition usually goes: The bride will toss her bouquet (or a smaller toss bouquet) to a group of single women. The woman who catches it is said to be the next to get married. The groom then removes the garter from the bride's leg and tosses it into a crowd of single men. The two winners come together in the middle of the dance floor, where the woman is seated, and the man with the garter slides it as far as he can up her leg. Supposedly the further the garter goes up her leg, the longer the marriage of the couple.

Today, some brides find this tradition degrading and dreadful, especially to the women involved. As a result, most brides have decided to eliminate at least the garter portion or do away with the tradition altogether.

Table Layouts

Unless you are planning a cocktail reception with hors d'oeuvres or an informal buffet with partial seating, you will need to have a table layout. Guests (especially those who do not know many people at your reception) often feel uncomfortable without assigned seating.

It is best to realize early on that no matter how hard you try, someone is bound to be unhappy with some aspect of your seating plan. The easiest way to approach this project is to get input from both sets of parents. Parents will know the ins and outs of who feels comfortable with whom within your family and their friends. Your friends are typically the easier part of the equation.

Placing People

If you're planning a formal wedding, escort cards and sometimes place cards are necessary for guests. What is the difference?

- **Escort cards**—These cards are placed at a table outside the reception area. They are placed in alphabetical order. Each card shows guests which table they are assigned to. Etiquette calls for married couples to be listed on the same card and all others to be written individually (even if unmarried couples are living together).
- **Place cards**—This type of card is important if your guests have chosen their entrée prior to the wedding. Every guest is placed individually at each table. Typically the cards are marked slightly for the catering staff to know which entrée goes to each individual. Typically the marks or variations in the cards can be in the color of the card, ink, or with a sticker, ribbon, or some other small decoration.

Another option is to set up a large seating diagram with all of your guests' names in alphabetical order. This type of diagram works well if the diagram is made available during the entire cocktail hour.

ESSENTIAL

If you do not want to number your tables and want something more creative, consider naming your tables. You can name your tables after places you have been together or the types of candy you both like. The more creative you are with naming your tables, the more conversations you will spark!

Save Me a Seat!

The head table is wherever the newlyweds sit and tends to be the focus of the reception. This table can either be a long table facing the other tables or the same type of table that the guests are seated at. As long as you place your head table in the center of the reception, your guests will be able to find you easily.

Traditionally, the two of you along with honor attendants, bridesmaids, and groomsmen sit at the head table. The two of you will sit in the middle of the table if it is a rectangular table. The best man typically sits next to the groom (followed by the rest of the groomsmen) and the maid of honor next to the bride (followed by the rest of the bridesmaids).

You may also choose to have a table just for the two of you. This is typically called a *sweetheart table*. Some couples feel that it makes more sense for them to sit with their parents and siblings, leaving the attendants with the ability to sit with their spouses, significant others, and dates. This last option also makes the most sense when you have a large wedding party.

FACT

Child attendants should sit at a regular table with their parents. Spouses of attendants also typically do not sit at the rectangular long head tables. If the spouses or significant others don't really know anyone else at the reception, try to seat them with someone they might have something in common with.

Parents

Depending on the type of family you have, many parents end up having to have their own table with extended family. Entertaining family who come from out of town is extremely important during the reception. The officiant from the ceremony should always be invited to the reception and should have a place of honor at one of the tables near the head table. Be sure to invite the officiant's spouse if he or she is married.

Make sure that after you have made out all the escort cards and place cards and have properly placed table markers for your guests to find their way that your wedding party knows where they are supposed to sit. This point is especially important if your wedding party is being announced into the reception. If not all of them are sitting at a head table per se, be sure to let them know where their tables are in proximity to the head table before they are to be announced. The best way to do this is to have a printed layout with marked tables. This is extremely helpful for your wedding professionals as well. Most venues will provide you with a general layout of the space and you can draw tables on it or recreate it in a presentation worksheet. All of your planning will pay off as you are announced for the first time as the newlyweds into the reception!

QUESTION

Where do I sit my divorced parents?
Your divorced parents should obviously not sit together at the same table and neither should they sit far away from you as the couple. Separate tables at opposite sides of the head table tend to work the best. The trick here is to place each of them at tables where they don't actually have to hear each other's voices.

Reception Site Worksheet

Reception site:

Address:

Telephone:

Contact: Hours:

Appointments:

Date: Time:

Date: Time:

Date: Time:

Date: Time:

Total amount due: Date:

Amount of deposit: Date:

Balance due: Date:

Sales tax included? ☐ Yes ☐ No

Room reserved:

Date: Time: Number of hours:

Overtime cost:

Occupancy:

Final head count due date:

Reception location includes the following services:

Reception location includes the following equipment:

Terms of cancellation:

Other:

Reception Site Worksheet (continued)

Item	Description	Cost	Notes

Reception Site

Site rental

Overtime fee

Other

Rented Reception Space Selection

Amount of fee that is tax-deductible

Backup space in case of rain

Equipment

Tent

Chairs

Tables

Linens

Other

Service

Servers

Bartenders

Valet parking attendants

Coat checkers

Other (list below)

Total of All Expenses:

Home Wedding Checklist

Maximum number of guests

Backup space in case of rain

Tent needed?

Catering tent needed?

Heaters, fans, or A/C units needed?

Dance floor needed?

Ground need leveling for guest dinner tables?

Lighting needed?

Stage for band needed?

Caterer contracted

Additional bathrooms needed?

Wedding planner needed?

Landscaper contacted?

Home Owners Association contacted?

Is there a noise ordinance?

Homeowners insurance contacted for wedding coverage?

Neighbors' contact information

Valet hired?

Equipment rental (tables, chairs, linens, etc.)

Other

Reception Events Worksheet

Give a copy of this checklist to your reception site coordinator and band leader or disc jockey.

Introduce entire bridal party? ☐ Yes ☐ No Music:

Introduce only bride and groom? ☐ Yes ☐ No Music:

Parent(s) of bride:

Parent(s) of groom:

Grandparent(s) of bride:

Grandparent(s) of groom:

Flower girl(s):

Ring bearer(s):

Bridesmaids: Ushers:

Maid of honor: Best man:

Matron of honor:

Bride's first name: Groom's first name:

Bride and groom as they are to be introduced:

Receiving line at reception? ☐ Yes ☐ No When:

Music:

Blessing? ☐ Yes ☐ No By whom:

First toast? ☐ Yes ☐ No By whom:

Other toasts? ☐ Yes ☐ No By whom:

By whom:

By whom:

Reception Events Worksheet (continued)

First dance: ☐ Yes ☐ No When:

Music:

To join in first dance:

Maid of honor and best man? ☐ Yes ☐ No

Parents of bride and groom? ☐ Yes ☐ No

Bridesmaids and ushers? ☐ Yes ☐ No

Guests? ☐ Yes ☐ No

Father-daughter dance? ☐ Yes ☐ No Music:

Mother-son dance? ☐ Yes ☐ No Music:

Open dance floor for guests after first dance? ☐ Yes ☐ No

Cake-cutting? ☐ Yes ☐ No Music:

Bouquet toss? ☐ Yes ☐ No

Garter toss? ☐ Yes ☐ No

Last dance? ☐ Yes ☐ No Music:

Other event:

When: Music:

Other event:

When: Music:

Special requests and dedications:

Notes:

CHAPTER 9

Transportation and Accommodations

If most of your guests will be coming from out of town to be part of your wedding, be prepared to arrange for all sorts of logistical amenities. Everything from directing your guests to the right airports to finding their way to the reception is your job, in order to make sure the day runs smoothly. While arranging transportation for your guests, you need to be sure you arrive in style too. Take care of your guests and knock out a few logistical items for you and your wedding party at the same time.

Guest Travel

No matter the size or location of your wedding, there will be some sort of travel involved in order to get to and fro. Whether it is a destination wedding in Hawaii with only ten of your closest friends and family or a local wedding for 200, travel is always going to be an integral part of making sure the day goes smoothly.

Planes, Trains, and Automobiles

From the moment your guests open that Save the Date card, they will start to think about how they are going to get to your wedding. If your guests are local, they may even think about catching cabs versus driving their own vehicles. Whether your guests live in a city nearby, across the country, or in another country, they will all have to start thinking about how they will travel to your wedding. Making this decision easy for your guests shows real hospitality and how much you want them to share the day with you.

If you know you will have guests traveling from out of the area, make sure you let them know which airport is the closest to your wedding site. Some cities have multiple airports; saving a few dollars on a taxi is always appreciated! If you know your city is train accessible, let them know which subway or train station is closest to your hotel accommodations.

Finally, if the majority of your guests will be driving, it never hurts to include a small map with your invitation, along with some general driving directions from various points due east, west, north, and south (depending on where your wedding city is).

Local Flair

If the large majority of your guests live locally, make sure you spice up your invitation and be creative to entice them to see something new in your city. A quirky invitation with a hand-drawn map is a welcome alternative to the boring GPS directions that they are used to. Show your guests why you picked your particular venue and talk about what surrounds your wedding venue. Who knows, some guests may have never been to that part of town!

Accommodations for Your Guests

With out-of-town guests comes the need for accommodations. You will need to make sure that those who are coming from afar know where to stay and how much it will cost. A happy and informed wedding guest is always better than a grumpy, tired, and broke guest!

Hotel Room Blocks

Some hotels will offer lower rates for a group of rooms. Grouping your out-of-town guests in one hotel has several advantages in additional to possible lower rates:

- Your guests can mingle with the other guests during the downtime between weekend-wedding events.
- Guests staying at the same hotel can make carpooling to and from the festivities easier.
- It will be easier for you to provide transportation with a limo or shuttle company, especially if you are fearful of guests becoming too inebriated.

FACT

While it is true that some hotels provide great rates for blocking rooms, some guests may find better rates online. Some websites may provide lower pricing at the same hotel. Your wedding block typically will make sure the rooms are available up to thirty days prior to your wedding. Check your wedding block contract carefully!

Grouping everyone at the same hotel is preferable; however, some guests may not be able to afford the hotels you've chosen. Be sure to provide at least three price points for your guests at hotels that surround your ceremony and reception sites. Other guests may have specific preferences based on mileage points they have received through their credit cards. Whatever accommodations you offer your guests, some may simply want their privacy.

Friends and Family

Weddings are the best times for family reunions. If your family is scattered all over the country, be prepared for some of them to stay with you locally if you have the space in your homes. Some parents would not dare ask grandparents to stay in a hotel (or even an uncle for that matter). Feel fortunate if your families have homes large enough to house several out-of-town guests. Be wise and utilize the space accordingly. Not only will this save time and money for your guests, but it will also give them an opportunity to spend more time together.

If you have friends that will be coming in from out of town as well, also be prepared for budget issues. If your best friend is unable to attend due to the cost of hotel expenses and airplane tickets, be prepared to take on the expense yourself, especially if you have asked her to be your maid of honor. Most brides and their families are unable to afford the expense of hotel rooms for all their guests. Get creative and rent out homes for the weekend or ask friends locally to open their homes to relatives and friends. Don't expect everyone to be able to lend a helping hand. You know your friends and family the best. If a family member or a friend offers help, this is probably not the time to say "no thanks"!

Hospitality Gifts

Nothing says "gracious host" more than a nice hospitality gift bag at the hotel upon arrival. Whether you have a small bag filled with a water bottle, mints, and snacks or a large gift basket filled with local fruits, cheeses, and wines, your guests will be thrilled that you even took the time. Most hotel rooms are stocked with overpriced snacks and drinks. Get your guests excited about the event by adding a short note letting them know the sequence of events for the weekend and some local restaurants and hot spots they might want to check out while they are in town.

Getting There

Your guests and your wedding party have all made it to town and are safe and snug in their hotel rooms. What next? They have to get to the rehearsal dinner and then to the ceremony and the reception. There are all sorts of ways to make sure your guests get to the chapel on time, along with you and your wedding party.

One-Way Transfers

Since many of your guests may be at the same hotel with your brides-maids, you may want to consider one-way transfer shuttles for everyone. This will typically save you money, but it is also hard to organize. Your guests all have to be at the same pick-up location at the same time, which means there is not a rotating shuttle that comes every fifteen minutes to pick up your guests. This allows the shuttle company to be able to conduct other business in between the time your ceremony starts and the end of the reception. If you have a wedding of fewer than 100 guests (and a large portion of the guests are local), this form of transportation can work well with a small gathering of guests coming from one location. Then the same bunch can gather together at the end of the night to get back to the hotel.

One-way transfers can also be done with sedans and limousines for parents, grandparents, and your wedding party, especially if you only want the nice vehicle for their grand arrival at the hotel or your place of worship.

Shuttle and Valet Services

When you have a large quantity of guests that are going to need transportation to and from the wedding, shuttle services are really your best bet. There are many factors that lead to making the decision for a shuttle bus service for your guests. Typically the most common reason is simple: getting everyone to one place on time. With venue contracts becoming stricter (with every hour comes a higher price tag), shuttles will ensure that your guests will arrive safely and on time.

ESSENTIAL

While it is important for your guests to arrive on time and in safe transportation, keep in mind your guests have their own schedules as well. Not everyone plans everything down to the last minute. Make sure you schedule your shuttle reservation with at least two times to pick up guests prior to the ceremony to make sure your slower guests still have a chance to see you walk down the aisle!

Another common reason for getting shuttle bus transportation is simply due to the large amount of alcohol that will be consumed at the reception. There is always that certain pesky amount of liability that goes with having a reception with alcohol. The last thing you want to be associated with is a drunken guest driving back to his or her hotel.

Finally, another reason to have a shuttle is that it can just be plain fun for your guests. If you plan it right you can rent interesting trolley cars that have informed tour guides that know the downtown area through to your venue. This will give your guests some interesting trivia and make your wedding feel like a vacation!

FACT

While shuttles and trolleys may seem like a lot of work and a lot of planning, they are typically the most efficient and cost saving hospitality choice you can offer for your guests. You could be saving tons of carbon emissions and money for your guests by providing transportation and having fewer cars and less traffic on the road to your wedding—a bonus for you, your guests, and the environment!

Another way to make sure your wedding starts on time is to hire a valet service. If your wedding is taking place in a congested part of the city (or at a hotel), your local guests will appreciate a professional valet service. Typically valet services will help your guests park their cars and keep their cars safe. This type of service is typically another huge cost savings for your guests, as they are not spending $5–$30 on just parking their cars for your wedding.

Taxis

When shuttles, sedans, and limousines are just not in the cards in regard to your budget, make sure you have taxi information available. Some taxi services will arrange for several of their drivers to be available at your hotel, ceremony, and reception if you contact them ahead of time. Ask your hotel concierge for the best taxi service in your area and enlist their help in ensuring that the number of taxis you will need will be available at the appropriate time.

Limousines and Luxury Cars

Limousines are the most common mode of wedding transportation. Though it may not be as original or exciting as arriving in a helicopter, showing up in a limousine has its real perks. You can seat anywhere from seven to twenty people in limousines depending on the type of limousine you reserve. Not only can you transport you and your wedding party, but they can watch television, take turns pouring champagne at the bar, and have a chauffer that can open and close doors and help stow away and transport large items in the spacious trunk. A big shiny limousine is also impressive enough to inspire awe in the occupants of those boring regular cars that are sitting next to you in traffic.

Reserving Your Limousine(s)

One thing to realize is that you should not wait until the last minute to reserve limousines. If you are getting married during prom season or you have a particular limousine model in mind, get your reservation done sooner rather than later! As soon as you start thinking about your wedding-day transportation, get moving on booking those various vehicles.

ALERT

Even with advance reservations, it is easy for everything to go south if your driver does not have the right directions or a GPS to find his way to your venues. To ensure the least amount of problems the day of the wedding, call your limousine company the day before to get the driver's name and cell phone number. A friendly reminder call two hours prior to pickup will ensure a smooth ride!

Finding a reputable limousine company can be tricky at times. The best place to look for recommendations is on the Internet. Many websites, such as *www.weddingwire.com*, *www.weddingbee.com*, *www.weddingchannel.com*, *www.yelp.com*, and local wedding blogs will be extremely helpful. Try to take all comments on message boards with a grain of salt though. If one company has a lot of people that are raving and they have a couple that might have a rant or two, more than likely the company is reputable. Take a look at their website, make sure they have photos, and ask questions about their vehicles and their company. Here is a great list to start with:

- How old is their fleet?
- Do their drivers smoke?
- How many events do they take per day for one vehicle?

How Much?

Most limousine services charge by the transfer, hour, or in three-to-four–hour timeframes. Unfortunately for you, the clock starts running the second the driver arrives at the location for pickup. If you specify a 3:00 P.M. pickup and your bridesmaids are not ready until 3:30 P.M., you have lost those thirty minutes. Some companies have package deals with a specific number of hours included. Make sure you plan accordingly. For example, if your ceremony is at 4:00 P.M. and your limo is picking you up at 3:00 P.M. and the ceremony ends at 5:00 P.M., with a three-hour contract you will have the limo until 6:00 P.M. If photos are going to be taking place for forty-five minutes and the reception site is thirty minutes away, be prepared to pay for those extra fifteen minutes. Typically, most transportation companies automatically include gratuity in their contracts. In most cities it can be anywhere from 15–20 percent. However, if you see that it is not included, you should always tip your driver anywhere between 10–20 percent for a job well done.

FACT

Your driver is very important to you and your wedding party arriving on time. It is paramount that you treat your driver with respect. He is a professional driver, hired to provide a service. Don't become the diva or let a drunk groomsman treat the driver like a slave. It is your wedding day; it is not a throw back to your prom night when you did not know any better!

Also, depending on the laws in your state, some limo companies are not allowed to provide a fully stocked bar. You may have to supply the alcohol yourself. Some limo companies, even if they cannot supply alcohol, might provide water and ice for you and your entourage. The most important thing is to carefully look over your contracts and see what they are providing in their packages and how much, if anything, the extras will cost.

ALERT

Some limo companies will provide a red carpet service for their brides. Don't be fooled. Sometimes you will get charged for the extra red carpeting that is folded up nicely in the trunk for all of their passengers. If the red carpet is included, great! If you are being charged for it, just make sure you know.

Always ask about their contingency plan. If something should happen to your specific limo on the way to the hotel or, even worse, while you are in the limo, what happens then? Will you get refunded? How do you get a backup vehicle? Make sure that this is not just based on a phone conversation but included in your written contract.

The Getaway Car

If limousines are not your thing, there are a whole host of other types of cars that can be used as your getaway car. Why not get something special and out of the ordinary? A classic Bentley or Rolls Royce tends to fit the bill for traditional luxury. Some like it sporty with fun convertibles and fancy sports cars. With all sorts of companies providing rental transportation, almost any car can be rented for a day (especially if you live in a large metro area).

Other Forms of Transportation

Some other forms of fun transportation that are used for weddings are:

- **Pedicabs**—What a fun, economical, and eco-friendly way to make your way to the reception—a cab made with a bike!

- **Horse and carriage**—Like in the movies, there is something about a horse pulling a beautiful sleigh in the winter or a fun wooden carriage clip-clopping across cobblestones that pulls the heartstrings!
- **Public transportation**—Believe it or not, brides and grooms have been known to hop on the subway, jump in a cab, or on the local bus. What a fun and whimsical way to end your wedding day. Don't laugh; maybe that is how the couple met! (It's also an eco-friendly alternative!)
- **Walking**—Some hotels are right next door to venues where the ceremony and reception take place. If your reception is four blocks away, walking could be the thrill of your wedding day as strangers congratulate you and your new spouse on your way!
- **Boat**—Some weddings take place on the water. Why not have the ceremony near the water and have someone paddle both you and your father to the shore or dock? Who knows, your wedding could be on an island where all the guests have to take a boat to the reception!

The important thing to note when it comes to any form of transportation the day of the wedding is: Enjoy every minute of it. If renting vehicles sounds like a lot of hype created by the wedding industry to you, then have your dad take you to the church in the pick-up truck you grew up with, decorated with flowers. If you just bought a brand new car for your new life together and love that fresh new car smell, have your friend drive you to the reception in it. Whether you rent a huge SUV limo with all your friends or bike to the reception, have fun and revel in it.

Travel Services Worksheet

Travel Agency:

Address: Telephone:

Fax number: Contact:

Hours: Directions:

Notes:

Car Rental Agency:

Address: Telephone:

Fax number: Contact:

Hours:

Description of reserved vehicle (make/model):

Terms:

Notes:

Transportation:

Destination:	Destination:
Carrier:	Carrier:
Flight/Route:	Flight/Route:
Departure date:	Departure date:
Time:	Time:
Arrival date:	Arrival date:
Time:	Time:
Confirmation number:	Confirmation number:
Date:	Date:
Notes:	Notes:

Travel Services Worksheet (continued)

Accommodations:

Hotel: Address:

Telephone: Fax number:

Check-in date: Time:

Check-out date: Time:

Type of room: Daily rate:

Total cost: Confirmation number:

Date:

Notes:

Hotel: Address:

Telephone: Fax number:

Check-in date: Time:

Check-out date: Time:

Type of room: Daily rate:

Total cost: Confirmation number:

Date:

Notes:

Hotel: Address:

Telephone: Fax number:

Check-in date: Time:

Check-out date: Time:

Type of room: Daily rate:

Total cost: Confirmation number:

Date:

Notes:

Guest Accommodations Worksheet

Be sure to give a copy of this to your mother, maid/matron of honor, and anyone else guests may contact for information about accommodations.

Blocks of Rooms Reserved for Wedding at:

Hotel:

Address:

Directions:

Approximate distance from ceremony site: Reception site:

Telephone:

Toll-free reservations number:

Fax number:

Contact:

Number of single rooms reserved in block: Daily rate:

Number of double rooms reserved in block: Daily rate:

Total number of rooms reserved in block:

Date(s) reserved:

Cut-off/Last-day reservations accepted:

Terms of agreement:

Payment procedure:

Notes:

Hotel:

Address:

Directions:

Approximate distance from ceremony site: Reception site:

Telephone:

Toll-free reservations number:

Fax number:

Contact:

Transportation Worksheet

Name of company: ....   Address: ....

Telephone: ....   Contact: ....

Hours: ....   Directions: ....

Services provided: ....

....

....

....

....

....

....

....

....

....

....

....

....

Number of vehicles rented: ....

Description: ....   Cost per hour: ....

Minimum number of hours: ....   Overtime cost: ....

Hours of rental: ....   Name of driver(s): ....

Cost: ....

Total amount due: ....   Date: ....

Amount of deposit: ....   Date: ....

Balance due: ....   Date: ....

Sales tax included? ☐ Yes ☐ No

Terms of cancellation: ....

....

PART II

Details for the Big Day

CHAPTER 10

Style for the Aisle

Your wedding day is supposed to be the most beautiful and romantic day of your life. Part of the beauty and romance of any wedding is how you and your wedding party dress the part! Make sure you have everything you need to mesh your personal fashion with your aisle style.

The Dress

When shopping for your dress, just know you need to set aside time and shore up your patience. Here are a few key points that you will need to keep in mind while shopping:

- **Informal versus formal gowns**—If you are having an informal wedding, you should have a relatively informal dress. The same rule applies if you are having a semi-formal or formal wedding. The gown should always be appropriate for the type of ceremony and reception you plan to have.
- **Sleeves**—Can you wear a sleeveless or strapless gown in the coldest months? Yes! Just be sure you have some sort of formal wrap in case you find yourself chilled. What about a long-sleeved gown in the hottest month? Maybe. In any type of hot weather, most people do not wear long sleeves, however, beautiful lace and organza (along with other breathable fabrics) can be a perfect choice for long-sleeved gowns even on the haziest day!
- **Length**—If you are having an informal ceremony, a pretty suit or a simple tea-length dress is acceptable. If you are having a formal wedding, choose a floor-length dress with a very long train. For a semi-formal wedding, either a tea-length or floor-length gown is appropriate.

Trains

When dealing with trains, there are two things you will want to keep in mind: length and style. The three most common lengths are sweep, chapel, and cathedral. The sweep train just touches (or *sweeps*) the floor. The chapel train trails three to four feet behind the gown. A cathedral gown ranges from six to eight feet in length behind the gown.

Other train lengths include:

- **Royal/monarch**—Typically nine or more feet behind the gown
- **Semi-Cathedral**—Five to seven feet behind the gown
- **Mermaid**—This term is sometimes used interchangeably with a sweep train. However, most mermaid sweeps are slightly longer and require a bustle during your reception; most sweep trains do not require a bustle.
- **Watteau**—A beautiful alternative to the more familiar styles. This train falls from the shoulder area to the hem of the gown. This type of train is typically either a panel of fabric attached at shoulder length or two pieces of fabric coming together from the over the shoulder blades down to the floor. You can also find shorter and longer Watteau trains with different designers.

No matter what kind of train you end up with, be sure you have your seamstress create a bustle for you. A bustle helps to harness the extended amount of fabric that is falling behind your dress, tucked up or under your dress. You can have just a simple hook or button or something intricate hidden underneath your dress like colorful numbered ribbons to tie in order to create a new look with the same dress for the reception. A bustle is extremely important during your reception. The last thing you want is to trip over your gown during your first dance!

Finding or Making the Right One

You know the style of dress you want. Now what? Have you always been handy with a needle and thread? Hand-made dresses save loads of money and have an extra-sentimental feel to them. Make sure you have enough time and be prepared to have some help! If you hire a professional to make a gown from scratch, be sure you try on similar designer gowns. This way you can be sure that they see the design on you and the dress created will actually look good on you! Some dresses look better on paper than they will on you, unfortunately.

If you are like a majority of brides, you will be hitting the bridal salon circuit in your area in search of that perfect gown. Most reputable bridal salons require an appointment. Be prepared for at least an hour at each salon visit (if not more). Most salons offer hundreds (if not thousands) of dresses to choose from. Hence the need for an appointment! The sales reps at bridal salons will take an incredible amount of time to find that right dress for you. Even when you find the right dress, you will most likely have to make slight adjustments.

ALERT

Wedding apparel is twice as hard to buy than everyday apparel. Women typically wear a different size on top than they do on the bottom. Don't be surprised if they recommend you purchase one to two sizes larger than your typical dress size. Most gowns run small. However, if they suggest that you buy four or more sizes larger, note that this is an unfortunate wedding salon scam to make you need tons of alterations!

An important note to make here is that you must take the sufficient amount of time prior to your wedding date to order your gown. Your bridal salon cannot be held liable for your indecisiveness or late purchasing. Some gown designers only take a few weeks for delivery, while other designers can take six to twelve months to ship or design a dress. It really depends on the designer.

Alterations

When purchasing your gown, make sure you allot enough time for at least two fittings. When you first receive your gown, you might have to make a few minor or major adjustments to it. Then you will have your second fitting to see if those adjustments make the cut. Some brides may need four to five fittings depending on the amount of changes they want to make.

ALERT

Your engagement will bring out all sorts of emotions for you and your fiancé. Most couples find that they lose weight during engagement due to the stress of the planning while others gain weight due to all of the celebrating going on. Be sure to buy larger; you can always take in fabric but sometimes you can't let fabric out!

Bridal Bargains

Most brides start to feel overwhelmed with the amount of money being spent on their wedding day. When it comes to wedding gowns and your trousseau (wedding ensemble), there are all sorts of places to find a deal!

Used/Consignment Gowns

One way to get an inexpensive gown is to make an appointment at a bridal consignment shop. There are even some places online that team with brides who want to sell their worn-once gowns. A previously worn wedding gown can be yours for a fraction of the cost of a new dress and you can take it home with you the same day (or have it sent to you the same day).

Finding a quality wedding gown on consignment may require additional time as not all cities have great bridal consignment shops. Some online stores will let you try on the dress and return it if you are not satisfied, while a majority are final sales only (meaning no returns!). Make sure you always read the fine print. Some of the best places to find used gowns online are *www.tradesy.com* and *www.oncewed.com*.

FACT

With some online auctions, you may find communicating with the seller before you buy to be helpful. Some large websites (like *www.ebay.com* and *www.craigslist.org*) are filled with people who just want to clean out their closets. Find out as much as you can about the dress, then bid low and watch! If you win and you don't like the dress, you can re-auction it yourself (and possibly make money)!

Outlet/Warehouse Sales

Maybe you have seen TV news coverage of a local warehouse or department store's one-day wedding gown sale. Brides-to-be line up as early as the day before to camp out and get the first crack at wedding gowns. Some of these sales feature top designer dresses at a mere fraction of their original costs. When the doors open, the brides with their teams of friends and family rush in to grab all the dresses that they can. The goal is to grab as many as possible to have more bargaining power with other brides. Brides come prepared and very few go into the dressing room as time is of the essence! If a bride does not like a gown she tries on, she can trade with the girl at the next rack.

The obvious advantage of these sales is financial. You can get a new gown for the price of a previously worn one. However, you will have to hustle and negotiate with the other brides around you. Fortunately, most people have very different tastes and styles. If you get a dress that is slightly too big, remember you can always find a great seamstress to take it in and maybe add some lace to it. But it goes without saying that you will not get the pampering of a bridal salon. In fact, you will be lucky to get space at the mirror (some brides bring their own mirrors).

Wedding Party Style

When thinking of your wedding day, the style and color of your event will sometimes revolve around what you and your wedding party wears. Since most brides and grooms wear shades of white or ivory with black and blue, the bridesmaids' dresses all of a sudden become the center of attention.

Choose the formalwear for your wedding party wisely as it will stay with you throughout the planning process.

Bridesmaids

You have chosen your sister or your best friends to join you at the altar and witness your nuptials. Now what will they wear? Keep in mind that your bridesmaids will spend a lot of money on your wedding day (even though they are not the ones getting married). Finding one dress that suits three to ten different body types can be an impossible and daunting task. Choosing a color is typically easier. Decide on the color and then find the dress for your bridesmaids. Many dressmakers and designers have fantastic bridesmaids lines with flattering fabrics and different styles within the color. This way your bridesmaids can choose the styles that suit them with the color that you love.

ESSENTIAL

Even though your reception may be painted in hot pink and orange, not everyone looks great in those colors. Try to pick a third, neutral color that blends well. Typical neutral colors are champagne, green, brown, and black. More and more brides are choosing black gowns for their bridesmaids since black goes with almost any color.

Again, it goes without saying that the dresses your bridesmaids wear should reflect the formality of your wedding day. Don't have your bridesmaids buy long evening gowns if you are having an afternoon cocktail reception.

The Groom and His Groomsmen

The real issue of style for the men in your wedding party is suits versus tuxedos. Depending on the formality of your wedding suits with matching ties for your groomsmen will do the job. However, if you are having an evening wedding at a formal location, tuxedos really are in order. In regard to men's wedding style, you have to keep in mind the formality and time of year. Here is a quick guide:

- **Informal and semi-formal weddings (daytime)**—A light or dark formal suit, dress shirt, and dress shoes
- **Semi-formal wedding (evening)**—Formal suit or dinner jacket with matching trousers (preferably dark blue, charcoal gray, or black), dress shirt, cummerbund or vest, bow tie or regular tie, and cufflinks
- **Formal wedding (daytime)**—Cutaway or stroller jacket in gray or black, white high-collared (wing-collared) shirt, waistcoat, trousers, bow tie or ascot, studs, and cufflinks
- **Formal wedding (evening)**—Black dinner jacket and trousers, white tuxedo shirt, waistcoat, black bow tie, cummerbund or vest, and cufflinks

Some other formal accessories include gloves, tailcoats, and various types of shirts. Whichever choice you make, keep in mind that you and future generations will be looking at these photos for years to come. Timeless suits and tuxedos are always a safe bet.

Toddlers and Tots

When it comes to children, the best advice any wedding professional can give is to make sure you involve the parents of the child that you have asked to be in the wedding party. Although you are not obligated to buy outfits for the children in your wedding party, offering to do so is always polite. Children grow out of clothes so quickly. If you are dying to have your four nieces wear the same fabric from your designer gown, be prepared to foot the bill. Typically a cute little dress for girls and a nice pair of pants and button up shirt or rented mini tuxedo for boys will work for your little ones.

The Rings

While some couples focus only on the engagement ring, one must not forget the all-important wedding bands. Finding the right wedding band to match your beautiful engagement ring can be tough. The timing, types of metal, and stones will all play major roles when shopping for these significant marriage symbols.

Shopping Ahead of Time

Just like your wedding dress, be sure to shop for your wedding bands months in advance. Some weddings bands can take weeks for delivery. Then, once your wedding bands arrive, you will need to get them sized to fit and engraved. Don't be pressured into thinking you must buy your wedding bands from the same jeweler that sold you the engagement ring. Depending on how elaborate your engagement ring is, you will most likely need to have the wedding band customized to go with it (no matter where you buy it from). Any reputable jeweler will want to make sure it is done right as customization takes time.

Metals and Stones

Due to the overwhelming amount of fair-trade and ethical issues in regard to mining over the past few decades, brides and grooms are starting to take their time when finding the right engagement ring or wedding bands. By the time you buy this book, you probably already have your engagement ring. If not, be sure you do your homework about the ring you are about to buy. Not only will your rings be some of the most expensive pieces of jewelry you buy in your lifetime, but they could also be passed down from you to many future generations. Taking your time and finding something interesting, timeless, and humane all at the same time can be surprisingly difficult for couples.

Here are some key things to look out for when it comes to the most common metals and gemstones that are purchased for wedding jewelry:

- **Gold**—Tends to be the most malleable of metals and holds its value well. Since most gold is easily recycled and can easily be transformed into other objects, it has been the most widely used choice for wedding jewelry for centuries. When looking for bands, make sure your band is 18k gold as it is the most recommended karatage for jewelry (since it tends to be the strongest). Pure gold (24k) is too soft and a stronger metal is needed to alloy with it in order to withstand the heat that is given off from your body. Since many people leave their wedding rings on, it is important to have the strongest gold possible to make sure your rings do not lose shape and then eventually break.

- **Platinum**—Is known for its high level of durability and its pretty, shiny silver color. This particular metal is typically the strongest metal used in wedding jewelry. When looking at platinum bands, you should be looking for "950 Plat" or "Plat" marked inside the ring.
- **Diamonds**—It goes without saying that diamonds are the most popular stone used for wedding jewelry. You will most likely look for the cut and shape of your diamonds first, then move on to the carat weight (size) and then to color and clarity. Most consumers know about the cut and carat size but know less about color and clarity. Diamonds have a color grading system based on the letters D–Z, with D being the most colorless (and most valuable) to Z having the most color and being the least valuable. Your jeweler will tell you what color grade your diamond is, and then he should inform you about the clarity of your diamond. Clarity is based on number, position, and size of flaws that naturally occur inside diamonds. The Gemological Institute of America (GIA) has a specific grading system for clarity ranging from flawless to obvious-flaws-under-magnification that affect the brilliance and transparency of the diamond (such as cloudiness and knots). Every diamond is unique, so be sure you have an experienced jeweler when it comes to buying diamonds.

ALERT

While many jewelers are starting to offer titanium as a wedding band option (especially for men), be careful when making this choice. Titanium is stronger than platinum, and it cannot be cut with typical metal clippers that emergency personnel use. If something happens to your finger or hand and the band needs to be cut off in order to save the hand, emergency personnel may have no other choice than to cut your finger off!

- **Emeralds**—Many brides choose emeralds as side stones or the center stone for their engagement rings or wedding bands. Some brides love emeralds because they are their birthstone (May) or because they are getting married in May. Whatever the reason brides choose emeralds, there are a few things to consider. First, emeralds do not have a high resistance to breakage. Depending on the clarity of your emerald stone, you may have a higher chance of chipping the stone. Similar to diamonds, emeralds are graded on their color, cut, clarity, and crystal. Keep in mind that some emeralds are also color enhanced or produced synthetically. Be sure you know what you are buying!

- **Sapphires**—These beautiful stones can be any color but red. The most common color of sapphire is blue. The same grading system that is used for diamonds is typically used for sapphire stones and many sapphires are synthetically made. Sapphires are popular in wedding bands and some engagement rings since they incorporate the color blue (think: "something blue") and are very durable stones.

Accessories

You have found the dress and have the rings, now the accessorizing begins! You might want a veil or a pretty headpiece. Some bridal salons offer jewelry, corsets, and accessories galore. Make sure you shop around, as you might find something more unique at another store! The key in finding the right accessories is starting early enough so that you can find what you need without being pressured for time.

Tradition and Accessories

Brides are fairly particular about their wedding-day wear. Many brides will simply not leave the house until every last tradition has been followed. Sometimes brides do this without knowing why. Read on so that when your friends ask you why you're insisting on wearing blue panties under your wedding gown, you'll be able to tell them. Many base these necessities on a traditional English poem, as follows:

Something old, something new

Something borrowed, something blue,

And a lucky sixpence in your shoe.

The odds are pretty good that you'll be wearing all of these on your wedding day. But do you know why? The *old* is to stand for a bride's ties to her past; the *new* represents her hope for the future; the *borrowed* item is something that's dear to a close friend or family member—and must be returned to ensure good luck; and the *blue* is thought to come from an Israeli tradition, when brides wore blue ribbons to symbolize fidelity.

Here are a few popular ideas brides use to incorporate all aspects of the poem into their ensemble:

- Handkerchief
- Jewelry from family—rings, bracelets, earrings, anklets, and necklaces will all do the trick
- Your wedding gown
- A hair clip
- Garter
- Wrap/sweater/jacket
- Purse

But the possibilities are endless. Anything from gorgeous blue shoes to your grandmother's favorite brooch could fit the bill. Use your imagination!

ESSENTIAL

The coin in the shoe is to symbolize wealth in the coming years, and many brides still slip a coin into one of their shoes before they walk down the aisle. In the United States, a dime is the currency of choice, but a sixpence is easy to order online!

Headpieces and Veils

The symbolism of the veil, like many other wedding traditions, has many theories behind it. One theory suggests that the veil was used as a disguise to foil any evil spirits. (In this same theory, the bridesmaids are also used as decoys for the bride.) In other legends, veils were originally meant to symbolize the virgin bride's innocence and modesty. These days, society considers the veil a purely romantic custom. But in parts of the Middle East and Asia, the veil is still used to hide the bride's face completely.

ESSENTIAL

The first lace veil is said to have been worn by Nelly Curtis, George Washington's adopted daughter, who married one of his aides. Apparently, the first time the aide ever saw her, she was behind a lace curtain. He was mesmerized by her beauty. Nelly, the story goes, made herself a lace veil for the ceremony in an effort to duplicate the effect.

Your headpiece or veil should complement the style of your dress. Don't pick a veil that outshines your dress. On the other hand, don't pick a headpiece that does not match your style! You could always consider borrowing a veil, as it is one part of your wedding ensemble that is typically taken off after the ceremony. Did you hate the dress your mom wore but thought her veil was fantastic? Even if the fabric has faded some over the years, there are skilled tailors and dry cleaners that can work miracles.

If you are not a veil kind of girl, why not go for a simple headpiece, clip, or comb for your hair? Some brides are doing away with all headpieces and going for a beautiful "up-do" with a fantastic single floral bloom (either fresh or silk).

Jewelry

The rings have been covered; now on to all the other jewelry that you may or may not want to wear. First, most brides wear earrings. Your earrings should be classic and match the style of your dress (like pearls, gold, or diamonds). Then again, if you are having a rather informal or semi-formal wedding, there is nothing wrong with choosing dazzling colored gemstones if that is your style. Some multicultural weddings call for several bracelets and necklaces. Keeping in line with your family's heritage will always be your best bet. Jewelry is one of the best ways to check off the "something borrowed, something new, something blue" list. Borrowing your mom's blue sapphire ring would knock off borrowed and blue at once.

Don't forget your bridesmaids and groomsmen in the jewelry department. Matching bracelets or necklaces are always a wonderful way to thank your bridesmaids for being a part of your day. Buy your groomsmen traditional and classic cufflinks for their suits. Cufflinks that can be used again are always a hit, as most men hate to shop for them.

Footwear

When it comes to your feet, handle with care. You will be on your feet practically the entire wedding day. Whether you are at your altar or line dancing, you want to make sure you find the right shoes that will last. Some brides even buy two pairs of shoes! Consider buying one pair of shoes for the ceremony and dinner and then another pair to dance in. In the past, many brides would only dare choose white or ivory shoes to match their wedding gowns. Now, brides are all over the place when it comes to fancy footwear. Some brides have such large gowns that you barely ever see their feet . . . so why not have those fun, bright-pink pumps underneath all the white fluff? Some brides love to wear pale-blue shoes to bring in their "something blue." When it comes to shoes, most brides choose beauty before comfort for photo purposes and then end up in flip-flops while dancing.

You will also have to consider whether or not you will need hosiery. Your body type, time of year, and type of dress will dictate whether or not you need hosiery. Ask your stylist or bridal salon for their advice as well.

ESSENTIAL

Make sure you have bought your shoes for your dress by the time you have your first fitting. You will need to make sure that your hemline goes well with the height of your heels so that you will not trip over your dress.

Handbags

You won't be carrying a handbag during the ceremony, but you will need a bag to carry your personal items (lipstick, mirror, comb, mints, medicine, etc.) in. The purse should also complement your ensemble. Typically you want to think about a little evening purse. If you have a place to stash some of your items, consider asking your maid of honor to carry at least your lipstick if you don't want a handbag at all.

Intimate Apparel

You will want to purchase undergarments that work specifically with your gown. These may include a bra, corset, petticoat, control top underwear, hosiery, and a slip. Some seamstresses can actually sew your bra or corset right into the dress. Not all dresses can handle the amount of fabric and sewing for this, so be sure to ask your seamstress what would work best.

Wedding Beauty and Nutrition Regimen

By the time you get married, you have a pretty good idea as to what works for your body, skin, and hair. The only thing extra you should do now is maybe change your typical makeup colors and style, as well as exercise and eat differently to help reduce stress. There are some practical things that all brides can do to get ready for their big day.

Since every woman is different, basic bridal beauty can include:

- **Don't get a haircut or change your hairstyle right before the wedding—** you may not like it!
- **Don't get a facial for the first time the month before your wedding—** most skin can be sensitive to facials, so give yourself at least three months before the wedding if you've never had a facial.
- **Change up the color or style of your makeup** for your wedding day to make it special.
- **Consider waxing your eyebrows for your wedding.** If you have never done this before, make sure you try it at least two to three months prior to your wedding day. Then, if you don't like it, you will have time to let it grow back. Remember, there will be tons of people taking photos of you that day (in addition to your photographer)—you don't want to realize after the fact that one eyebrow looks thicker than the other!
- **Consider teeth whitening for your wedding.** You can either get this done professionally with your dentist or try any number of over-the-counter teeth whiteners. You will be smiling all day, so you will want your teeth to be sparkling white!

- **Get a manicure and pedicure the day before your wedding**—even if you have never had a manicure before, this is the day to do it! Everyone will be looking at your rings and at your shoes, so make sure your nails play the part of a blushing bride.

Healthy Eating and Exercise

Getting engaged can sometimes hurl a bride into a rigorous exercise and diet frenzy for the sake of fitting into a particular type of dress. It is important to note that your fiancé loves you the way you are and will not care if you are ten pounds thinner or twenty pounds thicker (hence the reason you have the engagement ring on your finger!). The best exercise and diet advice that a bride should use are the types that help reduce stress and anxiety. Always ask your doctor for recommendations as far as dieting and exercise are concerned, as every individual is different!

Here are a few simple ideas to possibly change your diet and exercise routine:

- If ever there was a time to **try to quit smoking**, this is it! Smoking not only affects your overall health, it also darkens your teeth and leaves bad odors on clothing. The last thing you want is it to be caught smoking in your wedding gown, let alone having the ashes fall on your dress!
- **Stop drinking soda!** Some brides feel they have to have their daily dose of soda. If you are drinking full-calorie sodas every day and are trying to lose weight, this is a surefire way to lose some! Even if you are drinking diet sodas, research has shown that the artificial sweeteners in diet sodas can actually help you gain weight. It's better to go cold turkey and turn to water for at least two months prior to your wedding. You will lose weight, feel better, and see your skin glow!
- **Reduce the amount of caffeine and salt you ingest.** This may sound like a no-brainer to you, but if you are addicted to your morning and afternoon coffee breaks, this may be the most difficult item on the list to consider. Everything in moderation typically makes the most sense. Salt is a bloating agent, so be careful about the amounts you consume (especially the week leading up to your wedding).

- **Exercise at least three times a week.** Again, this is something you probably already heard. If you hate exercise, try going for a walk for twenty minutes, three times a week. Or you may love all sorts of exercises. Many brides like to have arm workouts to help buff up biceps. Find a local gym and get a personal trainer. You may find that the exercise regimen a personal trainer develops for you during your wedding planning stays with you after the wedding is over!

Image and Style Consultants

A bridal stylist can make you and your attendants look like a million bucks on your wedding day (and beyond).

The Right Color

If you have no idea what the difference between stardust white and champagne ivory is, you are not alone. Many brides fall into a sea of ivory and white dresses at the bridal salon and have no idea where to start. Hiring a stylist who knows about bridal gowns will not only save you time and money but also your sanity!

Most brides wear white, or some variation of white (such as off-white, eggshell, or ivory). It wasn't always so easy to decide on a color, however. Brides used to wear their best dress for their wedding, whatever color it happened to be. Legend has it that Queen Victoria herself set the trend for marrying in a white gown, defying the royal tradition of marrying in silver.

The first thing your stylist will do for you is help you find what colors actually look great with your skin tone. Not every bride should wear stark white and some brides look dreadful in ivory. A stylist will not only find what shade of ivory or white suits you, but she typically will create a color palette designed specifically for you.

The Style Checklist

☐ Check out the prices of local image stylists

☐ Set-up color consultation with stylist

☐ Find out which stores have the types of designers and styles I love

☐ Make appointments at 2–3 bridal salons

☐ Consider consignment shops or online auction for similar gowns

☐ Buy wedding bands

☐ Consider purchasing accessories for bridesmaids and groomsmen:

    ☐ Jewelry for bridesmaids

    ☐ Wraps for bridesmaids

    ☐ Matching ties for groomsmen

    ☐ Cuff links for groomsmen

☐ Bring shoes to all fittings for wedding gown

☐ Ask seamstress or salon for a swatch of the bridesmaid gowns to match with reception linens and décor

Bridal Attire Worksheet

Bridal Salon:

Address: .... Telephone: ....

Salesperson: .... Store hours: ....

Directions: .... Notes: ....

....

....

Wedding gown: .... Description: ....

Manufacturer: .... Style number: ....

Color: .... Cost: ....

Order date: .... Deposit paid: .... Date: ....

Balance due: .... Date: .... Delivery date and time: ....

Delivery instructions/Pick-up date: ..... Notes: ....

....

....

....

Headpiece and veil: .... Description: ....

Manufacturer: .... Style number: ....

Color: .... Cost: ....

Order date: .... Deposit paid: .... Date: ....

Balance due: .... Date: .... Delivery date and time: ....

Delivery instructions/Pick-up date: ..... Notes: ....

....

....

....

Attendants' Attire Worksheet

Place of Purchase: Name:

Address: Telephone:

Salesperson: Store hours:

Directions: Notes:

Attendants' Attire:

Description of dress: Manufacturer:

Style number: Color:

Cost per dress: Number ordered:

Total cost of dresses: Order date:

Sizes ordered:

Deposit paid: Date:

Balance due: Date:

Delivery date and time:

Delivery instructions/Pick-up date:

Description of alterations: Alterations fee (**total**):

Description of accessories
(hosiery, shoes, jewelry, etc.):   Cost of accessories:

Cost of dyeing shoes (if applicable):   Color:

Notes:

Maid/Matron of Honor:

Name: Dress size:

Shoe size: Other sizes:

Fitting date #1:   Time:

Fitting date #2:   Time:

Fitting date #3:   Time:

Notes:

Attendants' Attire Worksheet (continued)

Bridesmaids:

Name: _____ Dress size: _____

Shoe size: _____ Other sizes: _____

Fitting date #1: _____ Time: _____

Fitting date #2: _____ Time: _____

Fitting date #3: _____ Time: _____

Notes: _____

Name: _____ Dress size: _____

Shoe size: _____ Other sizes: _____

Fitting date #1: _____ Time: _____

Fitting date #2: _____ Time: _____

Fitting date #3: _____ Time: _____

Notes: _____

Name: _____ Dress size: _____

Shoe size: _____ Other sizes: _____

Fitting date #1: _____ Time: _____

Fitting date #2: _____ Time: _____

Fitting date #3: _____ Time: _____

Notes: _____

Name: _____ Dress size: _____

Shoe size: _____ Other sizes: _____

Fitting date #1: _____ Time: _____

Fitting date #2: _____ Time: _____

Fitting date #3: _____ Time: _____

Notes: _____

Attendants' Attire Worksheet (continued)

Flower Girl's Attire:

Description of dress: Manufacturer:

Style number: Color:

Cost per dress: Number ordered:

Total cost of dresses: Order date:

Sizes ordered:

Deposit paid: Date:

Balance due: Date:

Delivery date and time:

Delivery instructions/Pick-up date:

Alterations fee (**total**):   Description of alterations:

Description of accessories (hosiery, shoes, jewelry, etc.):

Cost of accessories:

Cost of dyeing shoes (if applicable):   Color:

Notes:

Can You Afford a Stylist?

Make sure the stylist you are choosing has been certified and trained in image consulting. Some consultants charge by the hour and some have package pricing. Some brides choose just a color consultation while some hire stylists to pull dresses before they arrive at salon appointments. If you are planning a formal wedding and you typically have trouble just buying a pair of jeans at the mall, a stylist will become your new best friend!

Stylists will range in pricing depending on your city and the services you are asking of them. A trained stylist or image consultant can typically help your entire wedding party. Like all of your vendors, a reputable stylist will have a contract listing out the services you need. If you want help for your mom and your wedding party, that should also be on your contract. Talk through what your needs are with a stylist and they can make suggestions on which services will work best for your budget and style. For great tips on bridal styling, start with the experts at Polished Image and Style (*www.polishedimageandstyle.com*).

CHAPTER 11

Gift Registry

No matter what, all weddings bring gifts galore. Your guests will be so happy for you that they will feel the need to give gifts. Maybe you and your fiancé are just out of college and will need everything from forks to towels. Or you might be a successful couple that owns two households full of everything anyone can need. Whatever the case may be, you will need to register for some things and be prepared for things you may not actually want! At the end of the day, be sure you have a nice stack of thank-you notes ready at the helm.

Gift Registry 411

Though some of your closest friends and family members have probably already decided on the perfect gift for you, there are most likely others, outside your immediate circle of friends and relatives, who would love a few hints! This is where the gift registry comes in.

A *gift registry* is a free service provided by most retail stores. You and your fiancé register for a list of gifts you would like to receive. When friends and relatives go into these stores, pulling up your registry is as easy as finding the touch-screen computer and typing in your last names. Most registries are available on the store's website as well. As each item is bought, it is removed from the list, helping to prevent duplication.

Which Stores?

You and your fiancé should put some careful thought into which store or stores you will register with. Make sure each store has a variety of quality items in the colors and styles that you desire. You might consider registering with a department store and then with a specialty store. You should always keep in mind that the point of the registry is to make gift buying as convenient for your guests as possible.

ESSENTIAL

To prevent receiving gifts intended for another couple in another city, be sure you always include your and your fiancé's first and last names, wedding date, and city when registering. This way your friends and family will have a point of reference when looking up your last name (especially if you have a very popular first and last name).

Even though *you* don't mind making the trip down to your favorite little shop downtown, some of your guests might. What's more, smaller stores, though they may offer a wedding registry, may not be set up to offer the convenience of purchasing gifts online. While you may choose to register for a few household goodies in a small boutique, you may want to reserve the lion's share of your registry for a store that is easily accessible to the majority of your guests. However, don't rule out locally-owned businesses as they may be able to provide more personalized service to your guests.

It is best to register with at least one well-known department store that is sure to have almost everything you need. Your registry will be automatically available to all stores and online. The online option is key, especially for your out-of-town guests.

Top Wedding Registry Websites

Although most stores offer online wedding registries, some have joined together with larger wedding search engines to make it even easier for your guests. You can now register at multiple stores without ever stepping foot into a store to register. The most popular wedding registries are with stores that are found everywhere around the country. A few key websites for gift registries are:

- **Crate and Barrel (*www.crateandbarrel.com*)**—This store is filled with everything for your kitchen, bath, and style for your home. While there may not be a huge variety of linens, Crate and Barrel has become the staple store for tabletop items and kitchen gadgets such as stemware, plates, cooking utensils, and beyond. Crate and Barrel has some of the most knowledgeable customer service reps at their stores and they are very careful when recommending what you should register for when you are unsure of quantities.
- **Target (*www.target.com*)**—Has become one of the largest department stores that offers all sorts of items at lower prices for their clientele. They have one of the easiest registries to use but you will not have as informed customer service reps in their stores.
- **My Registry (*www.myregistry.com*)**—This website has brought together all sorts of stores from around the country and lets you meld all items onto one list. You can even register for your honeymoon, cash gifts, and eco-friendly specific items.
- **Newlywish (*www.newlywish.com*)**—This registry site is filled with all sorts of smaller brick and mortar stores supporting small businesses around the country. Based out of New York City, this registry site has everything from gifts for your bridesmaids to cool mixing bowls from the hip store around the corner.

Many online registries will offer services for you to e-mail your guests about your wedding registry. Whatever you do, do not fall victim to this concept; do not e-mail your guests or mention your registry on your wedding invitations or programs. A wedding gift is not obligatory and your guests have up to a year to send you a gift. Your other party hosts may, however, mention registry information on your shower invitations or your wedding website.

What to Register For

With so many types of registries out there, many couples can get overwhelmed about what to register for. This section is meant for the couple that is really starting from scratch and needs help selecting what to actually register for. Your wedding registry should be filled with things you need both now and for the future. Although you may not see a need for a soup tureen now, when you finally have that big family Thanksgiving dinner at your home you will be happy to see it in your cupboard.

A carefully assembled gift registry can help put you on the road to a beautiful, functional, and well-stocked home. It will also help ensure you don't get Art Deco pieces when you wanted that modern fondue set! A good registry list will also help ensure you don't end up with three blenders and ten spice racks.

Take your time and browse either through the store or online. Items you are most likely to register for are:

- Formal dinnerware
- Everyday plates
- Silverware and flatware patterns
- Glassware
- Pots and pans

- Linens
- Small appliances
- Kitchen gadgets
- Various household décor items

Many couples know exactly what they are looking for, while others have no idea what to do, and some just plain hate to shop! Fortunately, for the couple that has no idea what to do, most stores have easy-to-follow registration and guidelines online or at the kiosk at the store. Any store that has a comprehensive wedding registry (both in the store and online) will walk you through the process to help take away the guesswork.

QUESTION

How many place settings should we register for?
That depends on you! If you love to entertain, you will need a good number of formal place settings (ten or twelve sets). If you entertain rarely, however, you may want eight settings just for special occasions.

Other Items to Consider

When registering, make sure you give your guests options. You don't have to just register for all the formal stuff and everyday items. If you see a great vase or fantastic game of chess that matches the colors in your living room, add it to the list. People can get to see the fun side of you and a little more of your style that way. Go ahead and register for that flat screen HD television. A TV may be just the thing your fiancé's seven high school buddies would love to chip in together to buy for you two!

Gift Etiquette

Once you have your registry up (and all of your guests can happily shop or click away for your nuptial bliss), you need to be ready for the various issues that couples inevitably come across. There are certain elements of etiquette that you should be aware of ahead of time.

Gifts at the Reception

Contrary to popular belief, gifts should not be brought to a wedding at all. Etiquette states that gifts should be sent to the couple (or the parents of the bride) before the wedding. The guests will have up to one year after the wedding to send gifts as well. The reasoning behind this etiquette tip dates back for centuries. Typically, the newlyweds are off to their honeymoon the day after or even the night of the event. How will they keep track of and transport all those gifts?

However, since most guests are unaware of this element of etiquette (or they choose to ignore it as they feel obligated to bring a gift to the actual event), you will inevitably receive a few (if not a lot of) gifts at the wedding.

Gifts can get lost or damaged at the reception. Tell everyone who might be asked to pass the word that you would prefer things be sent directly to your home. Make sure that if you do have a gift table, that it is strategically placed away from dancing and where someone is watching it (like security or the venue manager).

For courtesy, etiquette, and breakage reasons, wait until you get home to open your gifts. Make sure you have someone designated to take your gifts at the end of the evening. You should, however, take any envelopes with you as they typically will hold money or checks that you do not want to get lost in the shuffle of packing mom's car with leftover cake, favors, and flowers.

Returning/Exchanging Gifts

What if someone sends you a duplicate gift or a gift that you know you will never use or have the ability to "re-gift" to another bride? The best thing you can do to avoid an awkward situation with the gift giver is to wait about a month after the wedding to exchange it. Some couples will display all of the gifts they received somewhere in their home in the days before and just after their wedding. Anyone who visits you at that time is likely to look for his or her gift and even ask your opinion of it.

If you received a damaged gift, try to track down the retailer who sold the item. If the item did not come from your registry, you may need to let the gift giver know that the gift was damaged. You may be directed to the store where the purchase was made, or the giver may offer to exchange the gift for you. He or she may even still have the receipt!

ALERT

If you do return an unwanted gift, do not let the gift giver know about it. Send a prompt thank-you note expressing your gratitude and make it sound as sincere as you possibly can. Not all of your guests have the same taste as you but the gift typically comes with the same amount of thought and well wishing as your best friend's gift to you.

No Gifts Please!

With more and more couples getting married later in life or getting married a second time around, gifts can be the last thing a couple is thinking about. When two established households are coming together, the thought of another vase and another set of glassware can seem ridiculous.

The only way you can tactfully make this announcement is through family and friends. Some couples have made a small statement on the direction insert card or talk briefly about it on their personal wedding website. Consider telling people to donate to your favorite nonprofit in lieu of a gift.

Some guests will want to bring you a gift no matter what you say. Be prepared with some thank-you notes and possibly a very small registry list at your favorite specialty store.

Thank-You Notes

As soon as you receive a gift, you should send out a thank-you note. As hard as it will be given the many notes you will be writing, try to be as warm and personal as possible. Always mention the gift and (if possible) how you and your fiancé plan on using it. This small touch will prevent people from feeling that you just sent them a form letter (which is completely unacceptable). When sending notes for gifts you receive before the wedding, sign with your maiden name.

ESSENTIAL

The gifts may start arriving as soon as you announce your engagement and can typically continue up until one year after you are married. Setting up a gift organizer will help you keep a record of what you receive and from whom and when. Organizing from the beginning will help when you sit down to write all of those thank-you notes.

When writing a thank-you note for gifts of cash, checks, or a gift toward your honeymoon registry, the amount of the gift should not be mentioned in the thank-you note.

Gift Registry Checklist

	Desired Quantity:	Quantity Received:	Manufacturer:	Pattern/Model:
FORMAL DINNERWARE				
Dinner plates				
Sandwich/lunch plates				
Salad/dessert plates				
Bread and butter plates				
Cups and saucers				
Rimmed soup bowls				
Soup/cereal bowls				
Fruit bowls				
Open vegetable dishes				
Covered vegetable dishes				
Gravy boat				
Sugar bowl				
Creamer				
Small platter				
Medium platter				
Large platter				
Salt and pepper shakers				
Coffeepot				
Teapot				
Butter dish				
Other:				
CASUAL DINNERWARE				
Dinner plates				
Sandwich/lunch plates				
Salad/dessert plates				

Gift Registry Checklist (continued)

	Desired Quantity:	Quantity Received:	Manufacturer:	Pattern/Model:
CASUAL DINNERWARE (cont.)				
Bread and butter plates				
Cups and saucers				
Rimmed soup bowls				
Soup/cereal bowls				
Fruit bowls				
Open vegetable dishes				
Covered vegetable dishes				
Gravy boat				
Sugar bowl				
Creamer				
Small platter				
Medium platter				
Large platter				
Salt and pepper shakers				
Coffeepot				
Butter dish				
Mugs				
Other:				
FORMAL FLATWARE				
Five-piece place setting				
Four-piece place setting				
Dinner forks				
Dinner knives				
Teaspoons				
Salad forks				

Gift Registry Checklist (continued)

	Desired Quantity:	Quantity Received:	Manufacturer:	Pattern/Model:
FORMAL FLATWARE (cont.)				
Soup spoons				
Butter spreader				
Butter knives				
Cold meat fork				
Sugar spoon				
Serving spoon				
Pierced spoon				
Gravy ladle				
Pie/cake server				
Hostess set				
Serve set				
Silver chest				
Other:				
CASUAL FLATWARE				
Five-piece setting				
Dinner forks				
Dinner knives				
Teaspoons				
Salad forks				
Soup spoons				
Hostess set				
Serve set				
Gravy ladle				
Cake/pie server				
Other:				

Gift Registry Checklist (continued)

	Desired Quantity:	Quantity Received:	Manufacturer:	Pattern/Model:
ADDT'L SERVING PIECES				
Sugar/creamer				
Coffee service				
Serving tray				
Relish tray				
Canapé tray				
Chip and dip server				
Cheese board				
Cake plate				
Large salad bowl				
Salad bowl set				
Salad tongs				
Gravy boat				
Butter dish				
Salt and pepper shakers				
Round baker				
Rectangular baker				
Demitasse set				
Other:				
HOME DÉCOR				
Vase				
Bud vase				
Bowl				
Candlesticks				
Picture frame				
Figurine				
Clock				

Gift Registry Checklist (continued)

	Desired Quantity:	Quantity Received:	Manufacturer:	Pattern/Model:
CRYSTAL				
Wine glasses				
Champagne flutes				
Water goblets				
Cordials				
Brandy snifters				
Decanters				
Pitchers				
Other:				
CASUAL GLASS/BARWARE				
Water glasses				
Juice glasses				
Beer mugs				
Pilsners				
Highball glasses				
Decanter				
Pitcher				
Punch bowl set				
Cocktail shaker				
Ice bucket				
Champagne cooler				
Irish coffee set				
Whiskey set				
Martini set				
Wine rack				
Bar utensils				
Other:				

Gift Registry Checklist (continued)

	Desired Quantity:	Quantity Received:	Manufacturer:	Pattern/Model:
HOME DÉCOR (cont.)				
Lamp				
Framed art				
Brass accessories				
Picnic basket				
Other:				
SMALL APPLIANCES				
Coffee maker				
Coffee grinder				
Espresso/cappuccino maker				
Food processor				
Mini processor				
Mini chopper				
Blender				
Hand mixer				
Stand mixer				
Bread baker				
Pasta machine				
Citrus juicer				
Juice extractor				
Toaster (two-slice or four-slice)				
Toaster oven				
Convection oven				
Microwave				
Electric fry pan				
Electric wok				
Electric griddle				

Gift Registry Checklist (continued)

	Desired Quantity:	Quantity Received:	Manufacturer:	Pattern/Model:
SMALL APPLIANCES (cont.)				
Sandwich maker				
Waffle maker				
Hot tray				
Indoor grill				
Crock-Pot				
Rice cooker				
Can opener				
Food slicer				
Electric knife				
Iron				
Vacuum cleaner				
Fan				
Humidifier				
Dehumidifier				
Space heater				
Other:				
CUTLERY				
Carving set				
Cutlery set				
Knife set				
Knife block				
Steel sharpener				
Boning knife (specify size)				
Paring knife (specify size)				
Chef knife (specify size)				
Bread knife (specify size)				

Gift Registry Checklist (continued)

	Desired Quantity:	Quantity Received:	Manufacturer:	Pattern/Model:
CUTLERY (cont.)				
Slicing knife (specify size)				
Carving fork				
Utility knife (specify size)				
Kitchen shears				
Cleaver				
Other:				
BAKEWARE				
Cake pan				
Cookie sheet				
Bread pan				
Muffin tin				
Cooling rack				
Bundt pan				
Springform cake pan				
Pie plate				
Roasting pan				
Pizza pan				
Covered casserole				
Soufflé dish				
Rectangular baker				
Lasagna pan				
Pizza pan				
Pizza stone				
Other:				

Gift Registry Checklist (continued)

	Desired Quantity:	Quantity Received:	Manufacturer:	Pattern/Model:
KITCHEN BASICS				
Kitchen tool set				
Canister set				
Spice rack				
Cutting board				
Salad bowl set				
Salt and pepper mill				
Kitchen towels				
Pot holders				
Apron				
Mixing bowl set				
Measuring cup set				
Rolling pin				
Cookie jar				
Tea kettle				
Coffee mugs				
Other:				
COOKWARE				
Saucepan (small)				
Saucepan (medium)				
Saucepan (large)				
Sauté pan (small)				
Sauté pan (large)				
Frying pan (small)				
Frying pan (medium)				
Frying pan (large)				

Gift Registry Checklist (continued)

	Desired Quantity:	Quantity Received:	Manufacturer:	Pattern/Model:
COOKWARE (cont.)				
Stockpot (small)				
Stockpot (large)				
Roasting pan				
Omelet pan (small)				
Omelet pan (large)				
Skillet				
Double boiler				
Steamer insert				
Wok				
Griddle				
Stir-fry pan				
Microwave cookware set				
Tea kettle				
Dutch oven				
Other:				
LUGGAGE				
Duffel bag				
Beauty case				
Carry-on tote				
Suitcases (specify quantity and sizes)				
Garment bag				
Luggage cart				
Other:				

Gift Registry Checklist (continued)

	Desired Quantity:	Quantity Received:	Manufacturer:	Pattern/Model:
HOME ELECTRONICS				
Stereo				
CD player				
Television				
DVD or Blu-ray Player				
Camera				
Other:				
TABLE LINENS				
Tablecloth				
Place mats				
Napkins				
Napkin rings				
Other:				
BED LINENS				
Flat sheets (specify full, queen, or king)				
Fitted sheets (specify full, queen, or king)				
Pillowcases (specify standard or king)				
Sets of sheets (specify full, queen, or king)				
Comforter				
Comforter set				
Dust ruffle				
Pillow shams				

Gift Registry Checklist (continued)

	Desired Quantity:	Quantity Received:	Manufacturer:	Pattern/Model:
BED LINENS (cont.)				
Window treatment				
Down comforter				
Duvet cover				
Bedspread				
Quilt				
Blanket				
Electric blanket				
Cotton blanket				
Decorative pillows				
Down pillows (standard, queen, or king)				
Pillows (standard, queen, or king)				
Mattress pad				
Other:				
Fingertip towels				
Shower curtain				
Bath mat				
BATH TOWELS AND ACCESSORIES				
Bath towels				
Bath sheets				
Hand towels				
Washcloths				

Gift Registry Checklist (continued)

	Desired Quantity:	Quantity Received:	Manufacturer:	Pattern/Model:
BATH TOWELS AND ACCESSORIES (cont.)				
Bath rug				
Lid cover				
Hamper				
Scale				
Wastebasket				
Other:				
OTHER				

CHAPTER 12

Stationery, Invitations, and Calligraphy

By the time you send off your wedding invitations, the majority of your guests will probably already know the date, the time, and the place of the big day. Even though we live in a wireless age, you may still find that some people *need* something to stick on their refrigerator as a reminder of the upcoming event. Whether you send your Save the Dates or invitations online or send traditional invitations in the mail, it is the only way to keep track of who's coming and who's not, providing that people pay attention to your request to RSVP.

Save the Dates

The Save the Date is a relatively new and Western concept stemming from the never-ending compulsion to be as informed as much as possible. Any engaged couple can send a Save the Date either via mail or e-mail. Some couples even send video Save the Dates that can be seen online. The Save the Date can be particularly helpful for brides and grooms who have a lot of out-of-town guests who will need to start planning for travel and transportation. If you decide to mail a Save the Date, here are some sample wording layouts.

Example Wording Layout #1

Save the Date
Kimberley & Jake
are getting hitched!
06.21.2014
Washington, DC
Invitation to follow

Example Wording Layout #2

We're Tying the Knot!
Kimberley & Jake
6.21.2014
Washington, DC
Invitation to follow

FACT

Since Save the Dates are generally informal correspondence, it is best to keep their message as simple as possible. If you have a lot of out-of-town guests, send a preliminary list of hotels that are near your ceremony and reception sites. Also, if you have created a wedding website, include that as well.

Save the Dates can be made into all sorts of keepsakes. You can include a photo or make it into a magnet or bookmark. How about a fun photo-booth strip of the two of you holding signs that say "Please"—"Save"—"the"—"Date" (with the actual date on the last photo) in the four different shots. Then place a detachable magnet on the back so it can be placed on the fridge or used as a bookmark!

Where to Find the Perfect Invite

There are several options available when it comes to choosing the style of your invitations. Whether you want paper options or online options, be sure you choose invitations that are appropriate for the occasion you are planning.

Paper Invitations

While there are several brick-and-mortar stationery stores, there are also many to choose from online. If you are unwilling to order online without knowing the feel of the paper's weight and texture (and quality), most online stores will send you samples. Always ask to avoid buyer's remorse. This is the reason why many engaged couples (and their parents) choose stationery stores instead of online stores.

The look of your invitation gives people their first hint as to the type of wedding you'll be having. If you are trying to have a party and not a formal affair, be sure your invitations reflect that. And conversely, an elegantly engraved invitation is always appropriate for the most formal of occasions.

FACT

If you normally have a hard time choosing among many options, take someone along who can help you narrow down the choices. Though the store employees will be of great assistance, your attendants (or mom) will be the voice of reason if you find yourself overwhelmed by all the options.

Online Options

Just like the online Save the Date option, there are options for online invitations as well. Keep in mind that not everyone is connected to the online world. If you choose to do an online invitation, you may want to purchase a small amount of actual printed invitations. You will need to mail an invitation to those who you know do not have e-mail addresses (or who rarely check their e-mail accounts). Most invitations have to be ordered in sets of twenty-five, so order accordingly. The most popular online invitation websites are *www.paperlesspost.com* and *www.evite.com*.

Printing Methods

When it comes to ordering your wedding invitations, the type of print you choose is a big factor in how much or how little they will cost.

Engraving and Letterpress

Engraving is the most elegant form of putting ink on paper. The paper is stamped from the back by metal plates (typically copper or steel) the printer creates, which raises the letters up from the paper as they're printed. Stationers all over the world will tell you that this is the best form of printing to produce exquisite detail. However, you'll pay extra for all that elegance, so unless you have a generous invitation budget, engraving may be off limits.

Similar quality printing (and in some cases price) is available with *letterpress*. This method uses firmly pressed inked letters from a polymer plate onto a single sheet of paper, the type sinks into the surface creating a dense image on paper.

Cost-Saving Methods

A great way to get the look of engraving without the cost is through a process called *thermography*. Most mass-produced invitations these days are done using this method. By using a special press that heats the ink, the printer creates a raised-letter effect that is almost indistinguishable from engraving. What is distinguishable, however, is the price. It's about half the cost of engraving. Offset printing, also called *lithography*, produces flat images and is the starting point for thermography.

ESSENTIAL

If you're inviting fifty people or fewer, etiquette states that you can write your invitations out by hand. That may not be good news for your hands, but a master calligrapher could take your elegant occasion to a different level. All you need to do is find the right paper, envelopes, and ink.

If you've always loved the look of calligraphy but didn't think you could afford to have a calligrapher write your invitations by hand, you are in luck. Printers are also able to reproduce calligraphy using software, a method considerably faster and cheaper than the human hand. If you're interested in hiring a *human* calligrapher, ask your local stationery store or your wedding planner for referrals or search for various calligraphers online.

Traditional Invitation Etiquette

Having trouble figuring out how to word your invitations? You're not alone. With all the mixed families in the world today, many couples find themselves wondering how to word invitations without offending anyone. Don't worry! There are as many options for styles of wording as there are for styles of invitation.

Note that in all cases you should spell everything out: names, the year, the time, and so on. It's all right to abbreviate common titles (such as Mr. and Mrs., for example), and it's also fine to use the numerical representations for the address of the church or synagogue, but only if you must. Generally, the address (including the street name) of the church can be omitted altogether, unless doing so will cause extreme amounts of anxiety for your guests (if, for example, you're getting married in New York City and no one would know which St. Andrew's you've chosen for your wedding site). If your entire guest list knows your smallish hometown area well, you can simply opt for the name of the ceremony site, followed by the town on the next line. Zip codes are never included.

Mr. and Mrs. Roger Parker
request the honor of your presence
at the marriage of their daughter
Elizabeth Elaine
to
Mr. Justin Clark
on Saturday, the ninth of August,
Two thousand and fourteen
at two o'clock in the afternoon
Fairview Baptist Church
Fairview, Pennsylvania

When the bride's parents host the wedding

Mr. and Mrs. Robert Clark
request the honor of your presence
at the marriage of
Miss Elizabeth Elaine Parker
to their son
Mr. Justin James Clark
on Saturday, the ninth of August,
Two thousand and fourteen
at two o'clock in the afternoon
Fairview Baptist Church
Fairview, Pennsylvania

When the groom's parents host the wedding

Mr. and Mrs. Roger Parker
and
Mr. and Mrs. Robert Clark
request the honor of your presence
at the marriage of their children
Elizabeth Elaine
and
Justin James
on Saturday, the ninth of August,
Two thousand and fourteen
at two o'clock in the afternoon
Fairview Baptist Church
Fairview, Pennsylvania

Mr. and Mrs. Roger Parker
request the honor of your presence
at the marriage of their daughter
Elizabeth Elaine Parker
to
Justin James Clark
son of Mr. and Mrs. Robert Clark
Saturday, the ninth of August,
Two thousand and fourteen
at two o'clock in the afternoon
Fairview Baptist Church
Fairview, Pennsylvania

When both the bride's and groom's parents host the wedding

The honor of your presence is requested
at the marriage of
Miss Elizabeth Elaine Parker
and
Mr. Justin Clark

Miss Elizabeth Elaine Parker
and
Mr. Justin James Clark
request the honor of your presence
at their marriage

When the bride and groom host their own wedding

QUESTION

If you are including the actual address of the church on the invitation for practical reasons, should you spell the street number out? You'll see invitations done both ways. If you're shooting for a more formal look, a good rule of thumb to follow is the one writers use: Spell out numbers under 100 and do not use abbreviations. Words like "Street" and "Road" are never abbreviated.

Divorced Hosts

Circumstances will probably vary when divorced parents host a wedding. Use these examples as general guidelines.

When the mother of the bride is hosting and is not remarried

Mrs. James Parker
requests the honor of your presence
at the marriage of her daughter
Elizabeth Elaine

Mrs. David C. Hayes
requests the honor of your presence
at the marriage of her daughter
Elizabeth Elaine Parker

Mr. and Mrs. David C. Hayes
request the honor of your presence
at the marriage of Mrs. Hayes' daughter
Elizabeth Elaine Parker

When the mother of the bride is hosting and has remarried

Mr. Roger Parker
requests the honor of your presence
at the marriage of his daughter
Elizabeth Elaine

Mr. and Mrs. Roger Parker
request the honor of your presence
at the marriage of Mr. Parker's daughter
Elizabeth Elaine

When the father of the bride is hosting and is not remarried

When the father of the bride is hosting and has remarried

Deceased Parents

Deceased parents are usually not mentioned on wedding invitations because only the hosts of the event are listed. However, if you want to mention your late mother or father, no one is going to fault you for it.

When one parent is deceased and the host has not remarried

Mrs. Ann Parker
requests the honor of your presence
at the marriage of
Elizabeth Elaine,
daughter of Mrs. Parker and the late
Roger Parker

> *Mr. and Mrs. David Spencer*
> *request the honor of your presence*
> *at the marriage of Mrs. Spencer's*
> *daughter*
> *Elizabeth Elaine*

When one parent is deceased and the host has remarried

> *Mr. and Mrs. Frederick Parker*
> *request the honor of your presence*
> *at the marriage of their granddaughter*
> *Elizabeth Elaine Parker*

When both parents are deceased, a close friend or relative may host

Military Ceremonies

In military weddings, rank determines the placement of names. If the person's rank is lower than sergeant, omit the rank, but list their branch of service. Junior officers' titles are placed below their names, followed by their branches of service. Titles are placed before names if the rank is higher than lieutenant, followed by their branches of service on the next line.

> *Mr. and Mrs. Roger Parker*
> *request the honor of your presence*
> *at the marriage of their daughter*
> *Beth Elaine*
> *United States Army*
> *to*
> *Justin James Clark*

When the person's rank is lower than sergeant

> *Mr. and Mrs. Roger Parker*
> *request the honor of your presence*
> *at the marriage of their daughter*
> *Beth Elaine*
> *to*
> *Justin James Clark*
> *First Lieutenant, United States Navy*

When the person has a junior officer's title

When the person's rank is higher than lieutenant

Mr. and Mrs. Roger Parker
request the honor of your presence
at the marriage of their daughter
Beth Elaine
to
Captain Justin James Clark
United States Navy

Invitation Extras

As if choosing the invitations and carefully wording them isn't enough, you'll also have choices to make about the envelopes, and how you want to alert your guests to the particulars of the reception.

Envelopes

Like the invitations themselves, the envelopes you choose can range from simple (with plain to high-quality paper) to elaborate (with ornate paper liners). Beautifully packaged invitations are a nice touch, but as you might expect, the more you add to the envelope, the greater the cost.

ALERT

Before you break the budget, keep in mind that the envelope is a throw-away item. Ask yourself if it really makes sense to spend extra on something most people rip to shreds and then toss in the recycle bin.

Preprinted Return Address

Plan to have the return address preprinted on the outer envelope and on the response cards. Whose address should it be? Traditionally, whoever is listed as the host for the wedding receives the RSVPs. If you are the one communicating with the reception site coordinator or caterer (even though your parents are the actual hosts) you might prefer to have the responses sent directly to you. That way, you don't have to bother your parents every week (or every day as the big event draws near) to see who has accepted and who hasn't. Before you make a decision to put yours as the return address, make sure you tell whoever is hosting the wedding, just so you don't step on any toes.

Reception Inserts

If the reception is at a different location than the ceremony, you have a couple of options. For formal invitations, you should include a reception card. For informal invitations, you can simply write out the reception site's name, city, and state at the bottom of the invitation (if there is room).

When you are including a reception card, be sure to write out the full address of the reception site for out-of-town guests. For all of your out-of-town guests, you many want to insert a directions card (explained later in this chapter), which will also have the address of the reception.

Mr. and Mrs. Roger Parker
request the pleasure of your company
Saturday, the ninth of August
at three o'clock in the afternoon
Fairview Country Club
1638 Eastview Lane
Brookdale, Illinois

Sample formal reception card

Reception
immediately following the ceremony
Fairview Country Club
1638 Eastview Lane
Brookdale, Illinois

Less formal reception card

Response Cards

You'll also need to include response cards. These are the cards that the guests send back to you so that you can add them to your final list of guests or scratch them from it.

Each response card also needs an envelope, unless you are providing a postcard as a response card. In either case, you will need to affix a postage stamp for your guests.

And for those oblivious souls who neglect to return your card . . . try not to be too hard on them. Make a simple phone call or send a personal e-mail (one that tactfully passes over their failure to RSVP), and ask whether they will be attending or not.

ESSENTIAL

If you decide to put your wedding website on your direction insert card, you still should never mention anything about the registry! Simply state: "For more information, please see our website: *www.yourwebsite.com*" at the bottom of the card. Remember, none of your guests are required to give you a gift.

M _____

_____*accepts*

_____*regrets*

Saturday, the ninth of August
Fairview Country Club

The favor of your reply is requested
by the twenty-second of July

M _____

_____ *will attend.*

Sample response cards

Direction Cards

As mentioned before, it will be important for you to send a direction card, especially for your out-of-town guests. These cards should not be as large as the invitations and should be similar in size to the other inserts. Your direction card should include general directions to the ceremony and the reception. The direction card is also typically the best place to remind your guests which hotels you have blocked rooms for (or recommend). Whatever you do, do not include your registry information anywhere on this page or on any other part of the invitation. You can, however, put your wedding website address (if you have one) for more information.

Addressing the Envelopes

Addressing the envelopes is a project of massive undertaking. Give yourself plenty of time, and be realistic. Don't think you're going to write out several hundred envelopes in one sitting. Remember that this is supposed to be fun and exciting—you're sending out your wedding invitations!

Handwriting versus Calligraphy

To address your invitations, you will need all of the following:

- Several pens (in the ink color of your choosing)
- A few friends and/or family members with good penmanship
- Stamps
- Invitations, inserts, and envelopes

Make sure the same person who writes the information on the inside of an invitation also addresses its outer envelope. This makes the invitation package look uniform and convey that it was put together with care.

Know how to address people of various professions and marital statuses. Examples are as follows:

- A judge is addressed as "The Honorable George Smith"
- A member of the clergy is "The Reverend George Smith"
- A lawyer is addressed as "George Smith, Esq."

- Medical doctors are addressed as "Dr." (but PhDs do not require any title)
- Everyone else is "Mr.," "Mrs.," or "Ms." These are the only abbreviations (aside from "Jr.") that are acceptable
- For unmarried same-sex couples, you would address the envelope as you would any other couple. On the outer envelope, each name should have its own separate line and in alpha order (by last name). For example:

Ms. Sarah Smith

Ms. Anne Thompson

- For married same-sex couples with different last names, you would address the envelope as you would any other couple. For example:

Mrs. Sarah Smith and Mrs. Anne Thompson

- For married same-sex couples sharing the same last name, you would address the envelope as follows:

Mrs. & Mrs. Anne & Sarah Thompson (first names are in alpha order)

Everything else (with the exception of street numbers) is written out.

Of course, you can always employ a calligrapher to take care of all of this for you! All well-trained calligraphers know the ins and outs of traditional addressing etiquette and will almost always ask you questions when you send information to them that is outside of normal etiquette (as the previous information is not an exhaustive list!).

ALERT

Never use a printed label to address a wedding invitation envelope—it looks as if you were too busy to take the time to personally invite your guests. You may *feel* that busy, but don't let your guests know it.

Formal or Informal

When addressing the outer envelope, include the full name of the person or persons you are inviting. On the inner envelope, you can be more casual. If you're addressing the outer envelope to Mr. and Mrs. Stephen McGill feel free to write "Steve and Linda" on the inner envelope, but only if they happen to be your close friends. Otherwise, drop the first name and simply address the inner envelope to Mr. and Mrs. McGill.

If you are inviting the whole family, the approach is pretty much the same. (Children's names should come after their parents'.)

Children who are over eighteen and are invited to the wedding should receive their own invitations, whether they're living at home or on their own.

One more note on those inner envelopes: Remember how careful you had to be when addressing members of various professions on the outer envelope? You're not off the hook yet. While you addressed the judge's outer envelope, "The Honorable George Smith," on the inner envelope, he is simply "Judge Smith." The Reverend George Smith is transformed into, simply, "Reverend Smith."

. . . And Guest

When you invite a single person with a guest, you're faced with two schools of etiquette: old school and actual world. Old-school etiquette soundly denounces the use of the phrase "and Guest" on the outer envelope of an invitation *or* on the inner one. In the actual world, however, invitations are addressed this way all the time—and everyone understands it.

Bottom line: If you want to toe the etiquette line, you'll address separate invitations—one to the guest you're inviting and one to his or her guest. This will require a considerable amount of effort, in that you'll have to track down your guest's address at a time when you're incredibly busy—which is why most brides shun this practice. If you just want to make things easier on yourself (because, after all, isn't it nice of you to allow your friend to invite a guest in the first place?), go ahead and address the outer envelope with the name of your friend or relative. Then add the phrase "and Guest" on the inner envelope following his or her name or write out the guest's name if you have it.

Additional Paper Items

Your business with printers and stationery suppliers may not end when you order your invitations. Depending on the type of wedding you are having (and where), you may need various cards for entrance to the ceremony, special seating, or weather-related contingencies. You'll need some thank-you notes, and you just might want to print some formal announcements. Announcements are discussed in Chapter 19.

Ceremony Cards

Ceremony cards guaranteeing entrance into the proceedings are not necessary for a traditional wedding site. However, if your wedding is being held at a public place where people other than your guests can enter, you may need some way to distinguish your guests from the tourists.

ESSENTIAL

So few couples include ceremony cards, as most wedding venues will only rent their spaces when the venue is already closed to the public. However, it is always wise to ask the events manager at your venue if ceremony cards are needed.

Pew Cards

You will need pew cards (also called "Within the Ribbon" cards) if you wish to reserve seats at the ceremony for any special family and friends. Have them sit as close as possible to where the action is. Your special guests can pass the pew cards to the usher at the ceremony, who then knows to seat the special guests in the sections marked as "Reserved."

Thank-You Notes

You can order thank-you notes that match your invitations, or you can choose something completely different. The note cards can be as formal or informal as you like. If you already have personal stationery, you might consider using that for your thank-you notes instead of ordering something new. It's perfectly proper as far as the rules of etiquette are concerned, and you might save some money.

When to Order

Order your invitations at least three to four months before the wedding, and always order more than you need. Don't fool yourself into believing you won't make mistakes while you're addressing all of those envelopes. The last thing you need is a fistfight with your maid of honor because she messed up the last one. Ordering at least twenty extra invitations will lessen the tensions among those writing them out and will save you the cost of having to place a second order. (The majority of charges for your invitation are for the initial start-up of the press and such; adding a few more to your initial order is much cheaper than ordering again.) Even if you don't make any mistakes, you'll probably want to have a few invitations as keepsakes (for you, both moms, grandmothers, etc.). When tallying up the number of invitations to order, don't forget to include all of the people who will be at the rehearsal. This includes attendants, siblings, parents, and the officiant, along with their respective significant others. Although a reply is not expected or required, these people may like to have the invitation as a memento.

ESSENTIAL

Plan to mail out invitations about six to eight weeks prior to the wedding, with an RSVP date of two to three weeks before the wedding. This will allow you time to give the caterer a final headcount.

Be sure to leave yourself plenty of time to address and stamp all those envelopes. If you're planning a wedding near a holiday, mail out your invitations a few weeks earlier to give your guests some extra time to plan. If you plan on inviting more guests as regrets come in, send your invitations out at least eight weeks in advance, with a response date of at least three weeks before the wedding. Pressed for time? Ask if your printer can provide you with the envelopes in advance. That way, you can write them out while the invitations are being printed.

Stationery Worksheet

Name of Stationer: Address:

Telephone: Contact:

Hours: Directions:

Appointments:

Time: Date:

Time: Date:

Time: Date:

Wedding Invitations:

Description: Manufacturer:

Style: Paper:

Paper color: Typeface:

Ink color: Printing process:

Tissue paper inserts: Printed outer envelopes:

Inner envelopes: Envelope liner:

Number ordered: Cost:

Reception Cards:

Description: Number ordered:

Cost:

Response Cards:

Description: Printed envelopes:

Envelope liner: Number ordered:

Cost:

Stationery Worksheet (continued)

Ceremony Cards:

Description: _____ Number ordered: _____

Cost: _____

Pew Cards:

Description: _____ Number ordered: _____

Cost: _____

Rain Cards:

Description: _____ Number ordered: _____

Cost: _____

Travel Cards/Maps:

Description: _____ Number ordered: _____

Cost: _____

Wedding Announcements:

Description: _____ Printed envelopes: _____

Envelope liner: _____ Number ordered: _____

Cost: _____

At-home Cards:

Description: _____ Printed envelopes: _____

Envelope liner: _____ Number ordered: _____

Cost: _____

Thank-you Notes:

Description: _____ Printed envelopes: _____

Envelope liner: _____ Number ordered: _____

Cost: _____

Stationery Worksheet (continued)

Ceremony Programs:

Description: Number ordered:

Cost:

Party Favors:

Description: Number ordered:

Cost:

Other:

Description: Number ordered:

Cost:

Order date: Ready date: Time:

Delivery/Pick-up instructions:

Description: Number ordered:

Cost:

Order date: Ready date: Time:

Delivery/Pick-up instructions:

Description: Number ordered:

Cost:

Order date: Ready date: Time:

Delivery/Pick-up instructions:

Cost:

Total amount due: Date:

Amount of deposit: Date:

Balance due: Date:

Sales tax included?   ☐ Yes   ☐ No

Terms of cancellation:

CHAPTER 13

Planning Your Menu

Although you and your fiancé will probably be too excited to eat much on your wedding day, it would be wrong to assume the same about your guests. The two of you will be running on the adrenaline created by love, excitement, and romance. Your guests, on the other hand, will probably be looking forward to the menu. Your goal is to find the right caterer to provide the cuisine to fit your budget, style, and taste!

The Basics of Catering

Catering can be basic or complex. It might involve two people in a kitchen making tea sandwiches and hors d'oeuvres for an at-home reception or a full-service caterer supplying cuisine, tables, chairs, linens, dinnerware, and a full bar. Along with your budget, the type of reception you want will help you determine the kind of caterer you need.

But most important, don't hire anyone without tasting their food first. If no samples are available for you in the initial consultation, ask if they have general tastings or if they can provide a sampling at a later date.

In-House Caterers

If you're lucky, the reception site will have an in-house caterer who fits your budget, serves great food, and knows how to work with you. Hotels offer these services, as do most country clubs. There are several advantages to using an in-house caterer, the biggest being that you don't have to go through the trouble of finding one yourself.

The in-house caterer is already familiar with the particulars of the room, which itself is a perk with many advantages. For instance, the wait staff already knows their serving routine and they will be able to answer any questions your guests may have.

Some reception places with onsite caterers may allow you the option of bringing in another catering service, but with most, it's their way or the highway. If the food is good and the price is reasonable, you might find this arrangement completely acceptable.

ALERT

If your reception site offers in-house catering *only*, and the food is not up to your standards, you'll have to make a very difficult choice. Serve your guests rubber chicken in the setting of your dreams, or find another caterer and site for your reception.

Off-Site Caterers

Before you go searching for an independent caterer, find out what your reception site provides and what it doesn't. Some sites offer linens, glass and dinnerware, tables, chairs—everything but the food. Others provide nothing but the space you'll be standing in. Know what you need before you go looking for an independent caterer.

Simple Catering

Some caterers specialize in keeping it simple. They provide food, period. Everything else—beverages, linens, dinnerware, glasses, even servers—is left up to you. Sometimes this can work out to your advantage. Caterers like these may offer great food at a low price. However, don't be fooled into thinking that this will always mean less money; it almost always doesn't. Contracting with a simple caterer only makes sense when you have a very specific type of food in mind that you feel no one else could provide. It could be your Aunt Mary because you love her amazing crab cakes or that favorite restaurant where you go every Saturday night. Either way, be prepared to take on extra work and allow for extra time for planning your wedding.

The disadvantage, of course, is that it is considerably more work for you. What you could be getting in one fell swoop from a complete catering service, you're going to have to go out and do yourself. If you're a savvy businesswoman who doesn't mind making lots of calls (and asking a lot of people to help you), this will be a project for you. If you absolutely abhor this type of thing, it could be a logistical mess.

There are businesses that specialize in renting party goods and equipment. If your reception site doesn't provide tables and chairs, for example, you'll have to do some research to find out what you'll need and to determine a fair price for the cost of these rentals. Then you'll have to orchestrate getting it all to the site on the day of your wedding and getting it back afterward. This is not impossible, but the job may require more work than is apparent at first glance.

You will also need to find a bunch of people who are willing to set things up for you the day of the wedding. You will need to get ready the day of and not be at the reception site hauling chafing dishes around. Of course, the best thing to do would be to hire a wait staff personnel company to provide the waiter staff and set-up crew that you need.

In the end, you may end up spending the same amount of money that you would with a full-service caterer (or more). If you are not a great negotiator and have not planned a large event before, your wedding is not the best place to start. Having relationships with other vendors are what caterers are all about.

ALERT

The average couple spends between 300–400 hours planning their wedding—even when they have a regular full-service caterer. Ask yourself if taking care of every single detail (down to the way the napkins will be folded) is what you want for your wedding day. Will you be able to enjoy your wedding day? Think about those extra hours of planning you will have to take on!

Full-Service Caterers

This type of caterer, which most people associate with a wedding reception, provides food, beverages, a wait staff, and bartenders. Most also offer linens and tabletop items. If you need tables and chairs, these caterers will usually do all the legwork for you and simply add that to the cost of your total bill. If you're lucky, they'll charge you exactly what the rental agency charged them, but it's not uncommon for them to add a fee for their trouble, so get a written estimate before you authorize anything.

FACT

Your best bet is to find a catering company that owns its own equipment. Typically this will save you more money as the caterer will have more flexibility in the menu pricing for you. They may still charge you for renting their equipment, but it will normally be less expensive than renting it outright.

Some of these caterers will let you supply the alcohol, but others prefer not to worry about the potential liability (or their loss of liquor revenue). The beauty of getting your own alcohol delivered—if allowed—is that you can return what is not used and take home the bottles that have been opened.

ALERT

If you're searching for a caterer for a wedding at home, make sure the catering service checks out the kitchen, the appliances, garage, and electrical capabilities to ensure that everything is adequate in size and power. Your mother's tiny kitchen may be fine for the family, but how will it handle ten people trying to prepare and serve massive quantities of food?

The Selection Process

No matter what type of caterer you decide on, you'll need to ask questions to make sure that they can provide the services you want. Don't play the part of the shy couple—your wedding (and your hard-earned money) lies in the balance. You don't want to kick yourself later for not asking a relatively obvious question when you had the chance.

The Cost

You'll want to know about the price of the food. Caterers can give you an estimate based on the number of guests you plan to have and your menu selections. You should also ask about price guarantees. You'll want to know if your overall estimate includes meals for your DJ (or an entire band), your photographer(s), your videographer(s), wedding planner(s), and anyone else you'll have on the clock that evening. Also ask whether the cost covers gratuities for the staff and the cost of the bartender, coatroom attendant, and anyone else who will be working at your reception.

ESSENTIAL

If you're looking for a caterer who can serve up killer hors d'oeuvres in plentiful amounts, get a price list. You'll also want to know the price difference between setting the appetizers out on a table (for the guests to help themselves) versus having the wait staff pass them around on trays.

Don't forget to ask about the refund policy. It's not a pleasant topic to broach, but what if, for example, a hurricane blew into town on the same weekend as your wedding? Or what if you and your fiancé decide next week that you're going to elope? What will happen to your down payment? Will you be held responsible for any additional payments?

The Food

Does the caterer offer plated meal options? A buffet? Stations? No matter how simple or fancy the service, you want to know whether this caterer can meet your needs. Ask if there are different options. Can your guests choose between fish or chicken? If you have vegetarian, diabetic, kosher guests, or guests with various allergies attending the reception, can special meals be prepared for them? What about the wedding cake? Can this caterer provide one, or will you need a baker on the side? What about the leftover food? Not too long ago, folks frowned upon their hosts taking that food home. Now it's more commonplace to see a caterer wrap up any extra meals—and considering what you're likely to pay for those meals, you shouldn't feel funny about asking about this option.

ESSENTIAL

Throw a little style into your menu by infusing a dash of color in your food selections. For example, use blueberries in your champagne flutes if your colors happen to include blue or add strawberries to your fresh summer salad to go with your gorgeous pink peony centerpieces!

The Contract

When you decide on a caterer who meets your budget needs and who has answered these questions to your satisfaction, *get every part of your agreement in writing*. Don't leave any stone unturned—you might get tripped up later. If you're not familiar with a caterer's work, or if it is a new business, ask for references. This is most important when you're planning almost a year ahead. You'll be asked to give a sizable deposit, and you want to make sure the caterer will still be in business when the date arrives!

FACT

You'll want to know what the ratio of staff to guests will be and what the staff will be wearing. You'll also want to ask about the linens, dinnerware, and related items. If they do not have the color of linens you desire or stemware that you love, you may have to rent some.

Different Service Styles

Once the menu is finalized, you will need to decide on the type of serving style you would like your caterer to use. Depending on the formality of your wedding (which can range from a backyard barbecue to a multiple course dinner), you will need to decide which style suits the occasion!

Plated

The most traditional style of wedding service is the plated meal. This is where servers come from the kitchen with meals already plated for a sit-down dinner. Depending on the type of menu, this can be a multiple course meal with multiple plates. The most common is a pre-set salad followed by the main course and finally dessert. Dessert can be the wedding cake or another dessert in addition to the wedding cake. Since not all couples choose to have wedding cake, desserts are almost always offered by caterers. You can also have a very complicated and amazing multiple course dinner paired with wines. The sky is the limit when it comes to plated meals. It is also easy to get creative with color and tabletop items.

French

French service is a very unique and formal dining experience. A waiter will bring out an entire tray for each table with all of the elements from your dinner menu. This requires a highly skilled server that can serve with one hand while holding the very large elaborate display of food with the other. Typically there is an additional server that will come behind the first to offer a variety of sauce selections. This service is typically more expensive due to the additional servers required for each table.

Russian Service

Similar to French service, a server will come around to each table with a tray. Only this time your guests serve themselves from the elaborate display of food. It is still quite formal and requires additional staffing as well.

Table d'Hôte or Family Style

Many cultures love this form of dining service for their wedding banquets. Typically the table does not have centerpieces—the food is the centerpiece! This type of mini-buffet, with plates full of your wedding menu for your guests to serve themselves, really encourages conversation. Family style can have a formal or informal feel to it depending on how you set the table.

ESSENTIAL

If you want a family-style meal that is formal with floral designs, the best option is to have long banquet-style tables. This way you can have tall centerpieces with room for food down the center of the table.

Tapas Style

Similar to the family-style service, a tapas-style dinner is more like mini-tastings for your guests at the table. Here, smaller plates and bowls of many different types of foods are passed around the table for your guests to nibble on, just like in a tapas restaurant.

Buffet and Stations

Buffets can either be done as round or long tables with various types of chafing dishes and platters on them, or you can go the route of various stations.

If you decide to go with a buffet, consider having at least two lines. Your guests will get to the food twice as fast, an especially nice touch if you're planning a rather large wedding. Though buffet service saves you the cost of wait staff, it does require more food than a sit-down meal, since portions are not controlled. You will want to have plenty of food visible so that no one will feel shy about taking enough to eat. The caterer should assign a few staff members to watch the table and replace any food that starts to run low. A big misconception is that you will save money by having a buffet.

Semi-buffet service is another option. With this service, the tables are already set with plates, flatware, and glasses. You can even have a pre-plated salad and have the guests go to the buffet for their dinner selections. The wait staff clear the tables and serve drinks.

Rather than presenting your guests with chafing dishes full of food that could start to look unappetizing once the bulk of the line has attacked, this option calls for several manned food stations to be set up around the reception venue. For example, you could have a pasta station, mashed potato bar, omelet station, carving station, salad station, veggie station . . . the list is truly endless depending on your style and theme.

ESSENTIAL

The beauty of the stations buffet arrangement is that guests get the hot, fresh food they want prepared by a professional. Make certain to arrange a serving timeframe with your caterer and agree that when that time is up, the food stations will be cleared.

The Bar

One of the hottest topics surrounding any wedding is whether to host a cash bar or an open bar. At the open bar, guests drink for free, courtesy of you or whoever is footing the bill. At a cash bar, they have to pony up for their own drinks.

Most people will suggest to you that it's rude to expect your guests to pay for their own drinks. After all, you wouldn't normally host a party at your home and expect your guests to pay for what you serve them.

On the other side of the debate is the sobering (as it were) fact that open bars can end up being extremely expensive. People are often wasteful with liquor that they haven't bought. Someone might order a drink, take a sip, and go off to the powder room. The drink is forgotten, or the guest assumes it's gotten warm and orders a fresh one. And why shouldn't this guest take full advantage of your generosity?

ALERT

Another thing to consider with an open bar is that you're more likely to have drunken guests wandering about. People who would never pay eight bucks for a glass of wine in a bar suddenly find that it tastes much better when it's on the house.

Other Options

If you really don't want to make your guests buy drinks, there are a few options that might work for you:

- Have an open bar for the first hour of the reception only. This will ease your guilt, help your guests pass the time pleasantly while you're off taking pictures, and minimize any problems with guests.
- Serve free champagne punch. This punch is fairly light in terms of alcohol content, and people aren't likely to pound down glass after glass.
- Serve beer and wine only (no hard liquor).

DIY Bar

If you're having a home or backyard reception you'll need to know what you need and how much of it to have on hand. Your caterer can send you a list of the quantities that you will need and will usually help you find a bar or a table to set up the bar with. Make sure that any table you use is sturdy and steady. Draping the table with nice linen that extends all the way to the ground not only dresses things up but also hides excess bottles and trash stored underneath. Now, what will you need?

The Soft Stuff

Always have nonalcoholic options on hand for guests who prefer to steer clear of the hard stuff. Every bar should be stocked with soft drinks and water. You can also include interesting nonalcoholic sparkling water concoctions mixed with various juices.

Champagne or *Non*?

Though people commonly refer to any sparkling white wine as champagne, only the wine made in the Champagne region of France carries this title. As you might expect, you'll pay more for champagne, but there are many varieties of sparkling wine that are reasonably priced. Unless you have a wine connoisseur (sommelier) on your guest list, nobody will know the difference. If you're like most couples, you'll only want enough sparkling wine to fill everyone's glass once for the first toast of the evening.

FACT

If your caterer is responsible for procuring the wine and other liquor, all you have to worry about is the bill. If you have to buy it yourself, assume that each bottle of champagne will yield six glasses.

The Setup

If you're setting up your own bar, you'll need more than liquor. You'll also need garnishes, like maraschino cherries, lemons, limes, celery, and olives. Add mixers, like juices, soft drinks, soda water, and tonic water to the list as well. And you'll also need ice, swizzle sticks, and cocktail napkins.

Now for the hard stuff: beer, wine, and liquor.

For anyone concerned about guests having a little too much to drink, here's a tip. Don't serve salty foods. They only make people thirstier. Do serve meats, fish, cheese, and other high-protein foods. They restore blood sugar, which is depleted when someone drinks alcohol, and they help sober up guests who have had too much. Coffee will only excite a drunk guest—it won't sober him or her. If you're trying to sober up some guests, have them drink water to flush out their systems. And don't forget the option of providing transportation with a shuttle for all of your guests and having taxis available.

ALERT

If you're serving alcohol at an at-home reception, it has to be an open bar. It's against the law to sell liquor without a liquor license.

Doing the Numbers

You may not care if you have a lot of liquor left over at the end of the reception. Somehow, some way, you'll probably find something interesting to do with it, no matter how hard it may be. (Actually, most liquor stores will let you return any unopened bottles of alcohol, but not loose cans or bottles of beer.) But how do you know how much to buy in the first place? There are some standard consumption guidelines.

On average, for a wedding reception of 100 guests for an evening reception, you will need the following:

- **Champagne**—18 bottles
- **Red wine**—10 bottles (just for the bar)
- **White wine**—18 bottles (just for the bar)
- **Wine with dinner**—4–5 cases (equivalent to roughly 2 glasses per person, since each case holds 50 bottles and each bottle yields 4–6 glasses). Depending on what you are serving for dinner, the wines you choose will vary. If you are serving surf and turf, you will most likely need half white and half red wines for dinner. If you are having chicken, fish, or seafood only, you may want to have more white wine on hand. Always ask your caterer for recommendations.
- **Beer**—4 cases
- **Whiskey**—1–2 liters

- **Bourbon**—1–2 liters
- **Gin**—2 liters
- **Scotch**—3 liters
- **Rum**—2 liters
- **Vodka**—6 liters
- **Tequila**—1 liter
- **Dry vermouth**—2 bottles
- **Sweet vermouth**—2 bottles
- **Tonic**—1 case
- **Club soda**—1 case
- **Cranberry juice**—2 gallons
- **Orange juice**—1 gallon
- **Grapefruit juice**—1 gallon

ESSENTIAL

Have you ever been to a wedding where the bride or groom was drunk? Not only is this embarrassing for guests to witness, but typically the drunken newlyweds regret the experience mightily. If you do drink, be sure to eat something and to drink nonalcoholic beverages, too. It's up to you to know when you're about to cross the line from happy newlywed to obnoxious Drunky Drunkerson.

In regard to equipment rental, you will need to know your crowd and again, figure 4–5 drinks per person. Some basic rental equipment you will need are highball and lowball glasses, wine glasses, champagne flutes, and cocktail napkins. You might also need martini glasses if you plan to serve martinis and cosmopolitans. You need a way to mix drinks and have containers or glasses for your bar condiments. In addition, you will need to have lots of ice (not only for the drinks, but to keep the beer, wine, and sodas cold). If you plan to serve margaritas and piña coladas, those require even more ice, frozen drink mixes or blends, salt, and blenders. Ask your caterer for some advice on quantities for all of these items. Remember, caterers do this every day and will be able to give you averages based on the number of guests.

Your Liability as Host

Rejoicing with the bride and groom does not have to mean drunken reveling. But it does sometimes happen that a few guests go beyond the limits of common sense and wind up incredibly drunk. In recent court decisions, this has become a serious problem for both hosts and caterers.

Be aware of your responsibilities. Liquor may not be served to anyone under the legal drinking age, even at a home party. Courts have ruled that hosts are financially liable when teenagers who are served liquor at parties in private homes become involved in auto accidents or criminal matters. Caterers and restaurants have been held to the same standard.

If any of your adult guests are too drunk to drive but do so anyway, and then have an accident after being served drinks at your party, the damage they cause could be your responsibility and liability. As a good friend, you should call a taxi or find someone else to drive the car in these cases. Caterers and bartenders could be held liable in these situations as well.

To avoid these situations, discuss with your caterer ways to limit alcohol consumption at your reception. Reliable caterers are happy to cooperate and to suggest options.

Caterer Worksheet

Name (if different from reception site): ....

Address: ....

Telephone: ....

Contact: .... Hours: ....

Appointments: ....

Date: .... Time: ....

Date: .... Time: ....

Date: .... Time: ....

Date of hired services: ....

Number of hours: .... Cocktail hour: ....

Overtime cost: .... Final head count due date: ....

Menu: ....
....

Sit down or buffet? ....

Includes the following services: ....
....

Includes the following equipment: ....
....

Cost: ....

Total amount due: .... Date: ....

Amount of deposit: .... Date: ....

Balance due: .... Date: ....

Gratuities included? ☐ Yes ☐ No   Sales tax included? ☐ Yes ☐ No

Terms of cancellation: ....

Notes: ....
....
....
....
....
....

Caterer Worksheet (continued)

Item	Description	Cost	Notes
Food			
Appetizers			
Entrees			
Dessert			
Other food			
Beverages			
Nonalcoholic			
Champagne			
Wine			
Liquor			
Equipment			
Tent			
Chairs			
Tables			
Linens			
Dinnerware			
Flatware			
Glassware			
Serving pieces			
Other			
Service			
Servers			
Bartenders			
Valet parking attendants			
Coat checkers			
Overtime cost			
Other			
Gratuities			
Sales tax			
Total of All Expenses:			

CHAPTER 14

Photography and Videography

A picture paints a thousand words. At no time in your life will this statement seem truer or more appropriate than on your wedding day. You'll be feeling things you can't even recognize, never mind describe—and thanks to the artistry of photography and videography, you won't have to. An investment in photography and videography may be a pricey one in the short term, but one that will last for generations and preserve the history of your family.

Finding the Right Photographer

Good photography is not about simply clicking on the autofocus feature and shooting away with the family camera. It's an *art*—it requires skill and planning. Needless to say, you don't want to put this huge responsibility in the hands of just anyone, so be very careful about whom you choose as your wedding photographer.

Beware of "professional" photographers who aren't experienced. Imagine how you'd feel after finding out the entire ceremony was photographed with the lens cap on. There are countless stories of couples that have received less-than-quality work for their money. Don't be the next!

ALERT

Don't take a risk on an unproven entity. Take the time to find a photographer who knows what they are doing. There is no substitute for the education and experience of a professional photographer. Go to wedding chat boards, local magazine reviews, local wedding planner blogs, and photographer websites such as *www.wpja.com* and *www.wppionline.com* to find more information.

Most photographers offer packages based on the number of hours you will need for the day of the wedding. In addition, most photographers offer *a la carte* services including things like engagement shoots and albums. Pick and choose a package that is right for you and your style of wedding. Go ahead and look for the best value, but remember: You will do yourself a big favor by opting to pay a little more for a quality job. The cost of having a bad photographer is considerably more.

In most cases good photographers will have an extensive website with galleries of the weddings and events that they have shot in addition to albums in their studios. Many experienced photographers are involved in various organizations like WPPI (Wedding & Portrait Photographers International) and WPJA (Wedding Photojournalist Association), which means they are actively involved in educating themselves. Since technology rapidly changes every day, so does photography. Again, an educated and experienced photographer is your best bet!

In the end, if you find several photographers that meet your specific criteria, it makes it easier. Why? Then it all just comes down to personality. Keep in mind your photographer is with you *all* day long on your wedding day. You want to make sure you like them and can be comfortable. Your photographer will be taking photos of you while you are getting dressed and while you kiss after saying "I do." Don't you want that person to feel like family that day?

FACT

Remember: A photographer's high price tag does not necessarily mean you'll be getting high quality. A low price tag, however, is a pretty reliable sign that you're likely to see low-quality results or that the photographer has less experience. This is one wedding expense that really is worth the money, time, and effort that it requires.

Second Shooters versus Assistants

A second shooter is not the same as an assistant. When you are in the midst of hiring a photographer, you will want to know if he or she is charging for a second shooter or an assistant.

A second shooter is exactly that: a second professional photographer at your wedding. A second shooter is typically needed for larger weddings and large wedding parties if you plan to have posed family portraits.

An assistant, on the other hand, does not typically look for other photos to take that day. Assistants help photographers get the lenses that they need, set up lighting, and carry their bags around all day. The assistant is not a vastly experienced photographer. Many assistants are interns and are learning the ropes.

Your photographer will likely charge you extra if a second shooter is needed, but not if an assistant is.

Questions for Your Photographer

Don't be afraid to ask your photographer questions (they are used to it). You're about to drop a huge chunk of change into their pocket if you decide to hire them. So find out *before* you sign a contract what you're getting into. Here are some questions you should ask:

- How long have you been in business?
- Do you specialize in weddings?
- Have you taken photos at my ceremony and reception sites?
- Are you a full-time photographer?
- What kinds of packages do you offer?
- What's included in each package?
- How many pictures do you typically take at a wedding of my size?
- What is your hourly fee if the wedding goes over time?
- Is there a fee for travel?
- Will I be able to purchase additional prints in the future?
- Can I see some of your recent work?

Things to Look For

There's more to this than asking the questions, of course, and since you may not have any experience in working with professional photographers, an explanation of some of the previous questions follows.

Steer clear of part-time photographers who only occasionally handle weddings. They're not likely to have the equipment and experience of an expert in the field, and their lack of commitment to this line of work will show in the final product. You want a full-time photographer, not someone who does this as a hobby, and not someone who's trying to line her pockets by doing this as a side job. If you're planning to work with a studio, choose one that specializes in weddings. Only experienced wedding photographers know all the nuances of photographing a wedding, like how to avoid problems, when to fade into the background, and the best way to compose a great shot when working with a crowd.

If you are on a tighter budget, less experienced photographers will typically be less expensive; just be sure to pick one with a good eye. One thing to look for in a less experienced photographer is if she has trained or interned with another more experienced photographer. Be sure to look thoroughly at less experienced photographers' portfolios and ask the same questions you would any other photographer. Be cautious and ask the photographer to go to your venue before the actual wedding day to find great spaces for photo locations.

ALERT

Avoid very large studios that appear to use the assembly-line approach. Often they employ anywhere from fifteen to 100 photographers and won't guarantee which one will show up on your wedding day, or how qualified she is to do the job.

If you find a studio you'd like to work with, always ask to see sample wedding images that were taken by the same photographer who will be working your wedding. If the studio can't or won't supply them, find another one to work with. A high-quality studio or photographer will take three times as many photos as you signed on for, to give you the best and broadest selection. Note that studios may charge for the photographer's travel time, or for overtime if the job runs longer than expected. Ask for prices up front. Be sure to find out what the prices are for additional prints you may want to order beyond your original album package (if you order one).

Photojournalistic versus Traditional

If you think that hiring a photographer is just asking the right questions and liking his personality, you have yet to come to the realization that there are two camps of wedding photography. While the majority of couples today are choosing photojournalist-style (or documentary-style) photography, there are still couples all over the world that prefer traditional wedding photography. What is the difference? Read on!

Photojournalistic Style

In a very simplistic statement, photojournalistic-style wedding photography is about taking photos as they happen at your wedding. The photographer's job is to simply tell the story of your wedding day without playing any role in it. The photographer is an observer who captures images. Photojournalistic wedding photography is all about being real and showing the facts of the day with no influence from the photographer (think newspaper-style). There are some distinct advantages and disadvantages to the true photojournalistic-style of wedding photography.

Advantages are:

- Your album will look like the story of your wedding day
- Photos tend to look natural and unposed
- Without posed photography, there tends to be less stress of herding wedding parties and families

Disadvantages are:

- There typically are no family portraits (for true documentary style)
- There is an incredible amount of unpredictability
- You may not always have the most flattering images of you and your family

Traditional Style

Traditional wedding photography is all about planned and posed photos with lots of control by the photographer. There is almost always a very definite timeline, schedule, and a detailed list of photographs that must be taken with lots of direction and possible lighting. If it requires a ton of setup and time, it typically means traditional photography. Like photojournalistic photography, traditional photography has its own advantages and disadvantages.

Advantages are:

- Your family will be elated to have all of the family posed portraits that they now don't have to pay for!
- With planning, there is a certain amount of control.

Disadvantages are:

- Posed images tend to be very time consuming and stressful for all of the people involved in the posing and the timeline of the day.

- Posing is not the first thing on everyone's list and it is not real. You don't pose in real life.

In reality, most weddings have a mix of photojournalistic style with a dash of traditional to keep all parties happy. Let the photographers you are interviewing know what style you want for your wedding day, whether it is one style or the other or a little bit of both. A good photographer should be flexible with you.

Photo List

Should you decide to go with at least a little traditional photography for your wedding day, you will need to sit down with your photographer and discuss your wants, needs, and expectations for your posed photos. However, there are always little things that you may have dreamed of photo-wise. Let your photographer know the special things that you want captured the day of your wedding. If it is just the posed family photos, then leave it at that. If it is the details of the reception, let her know. Give your photographer a list of all the special people you want included in the pictures, especially anyone who isn't in the wedding party. Your photographer may be exceptional, but she's not a mind reader. If your eighty-year-old aunt is famous for doing the twist at family functions, make sure to tell your photographer that you want that moment captured on film.

Formal Photos Before the Wedding

Although it's considered bad luck for the couple to see each other before the ceremony, many couples feel comfortable doing away with this superstition and taking the formal shots before the wedding. This makes life easier for a lot of people. The photographer doesn't have to rush to get all the shots on your list in between the ceremony and dinner and you get to enjoy more of the reception.

If seeing the groom before the ceremony is absolutely out of the question for you, try to take as many of the formal pictures as you can without your fiancé. For example: you alone, you and your parents, you and your attendants, and so on. At the reception, speed things up by making sure everyone who's going to be in a picture knows where he or she is supposed to be.

ALERT

If you don't want your photographer to bother with some of the standard poses (for example, you with your attendants or ushers), speak up. Why waste time on posing for pictures you don't want?

Special Locations

Some couples opt to take their formal wedding photos at a location other than the reception site. Sometimes the spot they select is of great sentimental value or a historical landmark or the scenery is gorgeous. If you do plan to take your photo shoot on the road, remember that your guests will have to wait even longer than usual to see you (and their dinner) at the reception. As a way to ease their impatience (and their stomachs), make sure that the reception site will be offering bar service and hors d'oeuvres during a cocktail hour while they wait for you to arrive.

Videography

Videography is equally as important as photography. Newlyweds, ironically, are the people who usually remember the least about their wedding. They're in a fog of emotion and excitement, in which hundreds of sensory impressions go by in a blur. Photographs will show them a story of still images of the day, but video will show how things *were*. When a couple finally gets the chance to watch their video, it will certainly bring back memories but it will also show them many things they hadn't seen before.

Don't leave the videotaping to a friend or a relative unless you've seen a sample of her work and were impressed by it. Your fiancé's sister may have the best intentions and even own a good video camera, but odds are she won't have the necessary sound and editing equipment to make a tape for posterity. She may miss some key moments while she is trying to enjoy the party herself!

ESSENTIAL

It may sound like no big deal to have your friend put a video up on a camcorder for you. However, this person will not get to enjoy the ceremony as much and you are really not guaranteed professional results. In an age where video streaming is king, it is also nice to have video to send to those who could not make it to your wedding.

When searching for a videographer, apply the same basic guidelines you would for a still photographer. The pictures may be moving this time, but the images should still be crisp and clear, and colors should be true-to-life. You want to be comfortable with your videography company, and confident that they won't be ordering your guests in and out of shots.

Confirm that your videographer has up-to-date, quality equipment, and not a thirty-year-old camcorder. Also ask about editing and dubbing capabilities, microphones (will one of you be wired for sound during the ceremony?), and lights. Find out how many cameras they have, and how many people will be assisting on the job and the costs associated with each individual.

Ask to view sample tapes. You're looking for smooth editing, clear sound, and an overall professional look and feel to the video. With all of the technology available today, you don't have to settle for anything short of broadcast-quality production values. When looking at videography, you can typically tell the difference between a novice and an experienced videographer by the quality of the audio and usage of excessive lighting in video samples.

Once you've found someone and verified references, get a written contract stipulating costs, services, personnel commitments, the date, the time, and the place.

The Videographer Interview

Again, it's in your best interest to ask as many questions as you feel are pertinent to the candidate at hand. Here are some questions to ask:

- How long have you been doing this professionally?
- Can I see some of your recent work?

- If the company is an agency-based, will I be able to meet the lead videographer before the wedding? If not, why?
- What kinds of packages do you offer? What are your rates?
- How long will it take to receive the final edit?
- Are there any other fees, such as travel, hourly, and so on?
- Are you shooting everything in high definition (HD)?
- Do you provide Blu-ray options in addition to DVDs? What is the price difference? How many copies will I receive?
- Do you use any special effects in the final product, such as titles, credits, graphics, music, and so on?
- May I have the names of some former clients so that I can talk to them about their experience with you?

QUESTION

Where should I start searching for a videographer?
If you're working with a studio for your wedding pictures, they should be able to recommend videographers. And don't forget your most precious resource in these situations: word of mouth.

When you're viewing samples of the videographer's work, consider whether the segments tell a story. In other words, does the video make sense to you? Is everything in chronological order? Are the big events like the ceremony, the cake cutting, etc., shown clearly? How's the sound? Is the editing smooth? Is the picture steady and focused?

ESSENTIAL

DVD technology can change at any time. If possible, try to hire a videographer that shoots in HD. Even if you do not own a Blu-ray disc player now—you can always upgrade a standard DVD to a Blu-ray disc later, but your original video must be shot in HD.

There are some very elaborate video formats out there, some featuring special lenses and special effects. You can get an Oscar-caliber video, but it won't come cheap. Before you get carried away with the idea of seeing your name in lights, remember that little technicality called a budget. Like the photo package, the typical wedding video package can really range in price depending on the quality of the equipment, the number of hours you've contracted the videographer for, the number of cameras, the amount of editing, and the amount of education and experience a videographer has. Remember to determine what's most important to you, figure out what you can afford, and go from there.

Videography Style

Like photography, there are traditional- and documentary-styles in regard to videography. A traditional style is one where cameras may be set up in a few locations and several of your guests may be interviewed about how the day was and how much they love you. Much like posed photography, traditional videography is about setting the scene.

A documentary format is the standard for wedding videos, and gives you a documentary-style account of your wedding day. It usually starts with you and your fiancé preparing for the ceremony, then proceeds to scenes of the wedding and the reception.

ESSENTIAL

If your videographer will be using a format that requires editing, ask if you can have the unedited footage as well. You may not watch this DVD as often, but you'll probably want access to the uncut version for those memorable moments that didn't make it onto the official DVD.

Remember to take your videographer to your ceremony and reception sites (if she has not been to them before) ahead of time to check out the lighting, possible angles, and so on.

You should also acquaint the videographer with the photographer, if they haven't crossed paths at a wedding before yours. This way each person can get an idea of how the other works and can establish an understanding of how to work together to get shots instead of stepping on each other's toes all evening.

Photographer Worksheet

Name of photographer/studio: .... Address: ....

Telephone: .... Contact: ....

Hours they can be reached: .... Directions: ....

Appointments:

Date: .... Time: ....

Date: .... Time: ....

Date: .... Time: ....

Date: .... Time: ....

Name of package (if applicable): ....

Date of hired services: .... Time: ....

Number of hours: .... Overtime cost: ....

Travel fee: .... Fee for custom pages: ....

Fee for black and white prints: .... Fee for sepia prints: ....

Fee for album inscription: .... Additional fees (if any): ....

Engagement session included? ☐ Yes ☐ No   Additional cost, if any: ....

Will attend rehearsal? ☐ Yes ☐ No   Additional cost, if any: ....

Cost of film, proofing, and processing included? ☐ Yes ☐ No   Additional cost, if any: ....

Type of wedding album included: .... Date proofs will be ready: ....

Date order will be ready: ....

Additional services included:

.... Cost: ....

.... Cost: ....

Total amount due: .... Date: ....

Amount of deposit: .... Date: ....

Balance due: .... Date: ....

Sales tax included? ☐ Yes ☐ No

Terms of cancellation: ....

Notes: ....

Photographer Worksheet (continued)

Included in Package:

Item	Number Included	Cost of Each Additional	Notes
8" x 10" engagement portraits			
5" x 7" engagement prints			
4" x 5" engagement prints			
Wallet-size engagement prints			
Wedding proofs			
Wallet-size prints			
3" x 5" prints			
4" x 5" prints			
5" x 7" prints			
8" x 10" prints			
11" x 14" portraits			
Other prints (list below)			
Preview album			
Wedding album			
Wedding album pages			
Parent albums			
Other (list below)			

Photographer Checklist

Give a copy of this completed form to your wedding photographer.

Name of bride and groom: ---------------- Address: ----------------

Telephone: ---------------- Wedding date: ----------------

Ceremony location: ---------------- Reception location: ----------------

Special instructions: ----------------

Portraits:

- [ ] You and the groom during the ceremony (if possible)
- [ ] An official wedding portrait of you and your groom
- [ ] The entire wedding party
- [ ] You, your groom, and family members
- [ ] You and your mother
- [ ] You and your father
- [ ] You with both parents
- [ ] You with your groom's parents (your new in-laws)
- [ ] The groom with his mother
- [ ] The groom with his father
- [ ] The groom with both parents
- [ ] The groom with your parents (his new in-laws)
- [ ] Combination photos of the attendants
- [ ] You and your groom with any special people in your lives, such as grandparents or godparents
- [ ] Other:

Photographer Checklist (continued)

Photos from the ceremony (if possible):

- [ ] Each member of the wedding party as he or she comes down the aisle
- [ ] The mother of the bride as she is ushered down the aisle
- [ ] The groom's parents
- [ ] You and your father coming down the aisle
- [ ] Your father leaving you at the altar
- [ ] The wedding party at the altar
- [ ] The ring exchange
- [ ] The vows
- [ ] The lighting of any candles or special ceremony features
- [ ] Any relatives or friends who participate in the ceremony by doing a reading or lighting a candle
- [ ] The kiss
- [ ] The walk from the altar
- [ ] Other:

Candids:

- [ ] Getting ready for the ceremony; putting on the veil, the garter
- [ ] The bridesmaids, and you with them before the wedding
- [ ] You and your father leaving
- [ ] You and your father arriving at the ceremony
- [ ] Getting out of the limousine/car
- [ ] You and your groom getting in the car
- [ ] Toasting one another in the car
- [ ] Reception arrival
- [ ] The first dance
- [ ] The cutting of the cake
- [ ] Tossing the bouquet
- [ ] Removing/tossing the garter
- [ ] Going-away dance
- [ ] Leaving for the honeymoon (possibly with a "just married" sign on the car)
- [ ] Other:

Videographer Worksheet

Name of videographer/studio: _____ Address: _____

Telephone: _____ Contact: _____

Hours they can be reached: _____ Directions: _____

Appointments:

Date: _____ Time: _____

Date: _____ Time: _____

Date: _____ Time: _____

Date: _____ Time: _____

Name of package (if applicable): _____

Date of hired services: _____ Time: _____

Number of hours: _____ Number of cameras: _____

Overtime cost: _____ Travel fee: _____

Additional fees (if any): _____

Will attend rehearsal? ☐ Yes ☐ No Additional cost, if any: _____

Length of video: _____

Date DVD(s) will be ready: _____

DVD(s) will include:

Pre-wedding preparations: ☐ Yes ☐ No Notes: _____

Individual interviews with bride and groom prior to ceremony: ☐ Yes ☐ No

Notes: _____

Ceremony: ☐ Yes ☐ No Notes: _____

Reception: ☐ Yes ☐ No Notes: _____

Photo montage: ☐ Yes ☐ No Notes: _____

Other: _____

Videographer Worksheet (continued)

Package includes:

Sound: ☐ Yes ☐ No   Notes:

Music: ☐ Yes ☐ No   Notes:

Unedited version of wedding events: ☐ Yes ☐ No   Notes:

Edited version of wedding events: ☐ Yes ☐ No   Notes:

Price of additional DVDs:

Other:

Additional services included:

Cost:

Cost:

Cost:

Cost:

Total amount due: Date:

Amount of deposit: Date:

Balance due: Date:

Sales tax included? ☐ Yes ☐ No

Terms of cancellation:

Notes:

CHAPTER 15

Flowers, Lighting, and Décor

After the venue has been chosen you can start dreaming of all the wonderful floral designs and décor that can make the space yours! Whether you are having a simple backyard wedding or the most formal *fête* your town has ever seen, flowers, lighting, and all sorts of décor will help you define your wedding style.

Ceremony Décor

Flowers and décor are an important part of the ceremony. Décor at the ceremony site creates atmosphere and a romantic mood. No matter what type of venue your ceremony will be in, you will need to incorporate some sort of décor that lets people know where the ceremony will actually take place. Here are a few ideas to indicate ceremony location:

- If you are getting married in a garden or a backyard, the garden might be all the décor that you need. You may want to add an arch or hanging flowers or lanterns from the trees that surround the area where you will exchange your vows. Another simple approach to a ceremony in a backyard or garden setting is creating a ring of petals where the two of your will stand for the ceremony.
- If you are getting married in a church, you can accent the altar with two floral designs or a candle display. Consider a pretty aisle runner and matching flowers, ribbons, or bows on the pews.
- If you are getting married in a synagogue or mosque, they might have their own *chuppahs*, *mandaps*, or other traditional decorations for you to use. If not, most event floral designers will be able to provide a *chuppah* or *mandap* for you.
- If you are getting married in a ballroom, restaurant, or other nontraditional venue, here are a few ideas to make your ceremony special:

  - **Backdrops and lighting**—You can rent fabric from a design and décor company for a little bit of drama or use lighting to either uplight the walls or project a pattern behind you.
  - **Candles**—Your floral designer might be able to rent beautiful candleholders or different-sized glass vases where you can have floating candles or large pillars or taper candles in sand inside the glass. Since many venues do not like open flames, glass-enclosed arrangements of candles or electric candles can replace traditional ones.
  - **Flowers**—Get creative with floral designs for your ceremony site. This can be as basic or as over the top as your budget and style allow. You can have anything from standard altar arrangements

on pedestals to something amazingly unique like an indoor garden scene complete with a trellis. If your venue has a way of hanging items, why not hang some lanterns or votive glasses filled with flowers for a pretty whimsical look?

Do a little research before you meet with a floral designer. If the whole idea of spending time with a florist seems a bit overwhelming and you're not sure where to start, there are many websites that have creative ideas and photos that you can pull from. Start with national websites like *www.theknot.com*, *www.brides.com*, and *www.marthastewartweddings.com*, or blogs like *www.stylemepretty.com*, *www.ruffledblog.com*, *www.oncewed.com*, or *www.eco-beautifulweddings.com*. Once you have had a chance to take a look at a few designs, you'll have a rough idea of what you're looking for prior to meeting a floral designer.

ALERT

When you visit a florist, make sure they specialize in weddings. A florist who is focused on doing daily deliveries for mass-produced bouquets is typically not the right fit for a wedding. Since weddings are highly time sensitive and color-centric, you will need a florist who understands the ins and outs of wedding deliveries in your area.

Be sure to check out a floral designer's website before you visit them. Most florists will show a sampling of their work on their website and might even have a blog that shows you what they are doing every week. Many experienced wedding floral designers will have connections with lighting crews and will know where to get certain rental items if they do not already provide them in-house.

ESSENTIAL

Be wary of the floral designer who makes you choose from an innocuous glossy stock photo catalogue. Your wedding should be unique and reflect you as a couple. Why would you want your wedding to look exactly like someone else's wedding?

If you need a complicated ceremony floral design scheme (like, for example, large floral displays or a *mandap*), be sure to ask your florist for possible photos of their own previous work that may be similar to what you want for your wedding day. Typically you can tell if a florist is capable if they have done similar items and are able to provide photos for you to peruse. The photos the florist provides may not be *exactly* what you are looking for, but if they are close, the florist can probably recreate your vision. If your florist can take your concepts and run with them (and has done similar design work in the past), start getting excited!

Personal Flowers

When planning your ceremony, you will need to consider floral designs for the two of you, your wedding party, and family. Depending on your culture and type of ceremony, the type of flowers you choose will vary.

If you are having a traditional Western ceremony you will need bouquets and lapel flowers for your wedding party along with immediate family. Depending on your family's heritage there are all sorts of other floral designs that may need to be incorporated (e.g., floral garlands for Indian ceremonies). Be sure to ask your family and officiant for ideas.

ESSENTIAL

If your bridesmaids are willing to part with their bouquets, you could use their flowers to decorate the wedding cake table or the head table. Discuss this possibility with your florist, to get recommendations on types of bouquets that would work best for this dual purpose.

Here are some unique ideas for creating bouquets that reflect you and your personality (and possibly your culture):

- **Family heirlooms**—If your grandmother cannot be with you on your wedding day, why not use one of her favorite brooches to stick either amongst the blooms or on the stems? How about tying his grandmother's pretty blue handkerchief around the stems for your something blue?

- **Personalized bouquets**—Tired of seeing all the bridesmaids with the same bouquet at every wedding? Incorporate each of your bridesmaid's favorite flowers into her bouquet. If you have any married bridesmaids, consider making smaller versions of their bridal bouquets (using your colors) for their bridesmaid bouquets.
- **History and culture**—Take a look at your mom's and your fiancé's mom's bouquets (and maybe even your grandmother's) and incorporate those flowers into your bouquet. Are you having an all-blue wedding but you are Chinese and red is a lucky color? Why not have an all-red bouquet for your bridal bouquet? Your bridal bouquet does not have to match the entire wedding, it can be a reflection of you and your heritage.
- **Eco-friendly options**—If you love flowers, but hate the waste, ask your florist for seasonal flowers that dry well. A few popular examples: roses, sunflowers, hydrangea, berries, echinacea, rosemary, lily grass, etc. Not a flower fan and you hate artificial flowers? Why not go for a bouquet made out of paper that you can keep in a scrapbook or in a cute vase in your home after the wedding? A lovely bouquet made of fabric that you can place on your mantel or on your dresser will last for generations. You can either make this yourself or if you'd prefer someone else's handiwork, check out *www.etsy.com*.

Keeping your personal flowers meaningful is not only appropriate but can be a lot of fun while doing the research. Remember, your bridal bouquet will be in all of your photos—make sure you spend the most time on that floral design!

Turn to the checklist page at the end of this chapter to help you think through all of the various personal flowers you'll need for your wedding day.

Reception Décor

The décor at the reception should have some sort of element that ties it to the ceremony. Even if you want to change the colors or the types of flowers from the ceremony to the reception, you want to make sure your guests know they are in the right place (especially if the ceremony is in a different location).

Depending on the type of reception you are having, you may need just a little décor for it or a whole production crew. Think about the flow of the reception and it will give you a greater sense of your floral design needs. Your floral designer and/or lighting crew may have already been to your reception site before and will be able to give you suggestions. If not, be sure to go to your reception site and take photos of it before you meet with your florist. If you can, send the photos to your florist via e-mail before you meet so they can start gathering ideas.

ALERT

If you don't like the color of the carpeting of your reception site, don't let this ruin your floral design dreams. Keep in mind by the time all of the tables, chairs, and guests are in there, the carpeting is the last thing people will notice.

The Guest Book

With advances in technology, gone are the days of the typical guest book. Many couples are choosing different guest book options such as:

- **Photo booths**—Have your guests take photos with a backdrop or an actual rented photo booth with scrapbooks for guests to write a note in to go with their photo
- **Wishing table**—Have your guests write out notes on colorful paper to place in pretty vases
- **Matted engagement photo**—Have your guests sign the matte around your photo to place on your wall at home after the wedding
- **Fingerprint tree**—Have someone draw a large tree (or buy one from an artist on *www.esty.com*) and then have inkpads for guests to use their thumbprints to add "leaves" to the tree. Include colorful pens for guests to sign their names next to the leaves.

Don't limit yourself to just a blank book with lines—get creative!

Cocktail Hour

When planning for your cocktail hour, use smaller floral designs or votive candles for cocktail tables. You may want to consider having flowers and a hospitality basket in the ladies room, as this will help guests freshen up after dinner. Other décor you may want to consider include: lighting, bar flowers, escort card table arrangement (if you are having assigned seating), gift table, table décor, and the guest book table.

Get creative when it comes to your cocktail hour and reception as well. Mingling is fine, but you might want to have activities for your guests to do while they wait for you to enter after taking photos. Some fun ideas include:

- A photo or video booth
- Games (both board and yard)
- Wine and cheese tastings

Centerpiece Options

When talking with your floral designer about centerpieces, make sure your centerpieces are either low enough or tall enough for your guests to be able to speak to one another from across the table. The last thing you want to see are your guests putting the centerpieces on the floor to be able to see one another!

A few guidelines when trying to choose which type of centerpiece to have:

- If your venue has low ceilings it is typically best to go with low centerpieces.
- If your venue has enormously high ceilings it is best to go with tall centerpieces.
- If you're on a semi-tight budget and you really want tall centerpieces, consider two to three different types of centerpieces. A couple of low centerpiece options and one type that is tall will keep costs down and create visual interest.

- Never choose highly-fragrant flowers (e.g., stargazer lilies) for center-pieces as you might have guests who are allergic to them or simply do not care for the smell disrupting their dinner.

If you don't want to have flowers as your centerpiece, there are various other options. Here are a few examples:

- **Candles**—For a tight budget, a bowl of water with floating candles and a few scattered petals is one of the least expensive options out there (be aware that your guests may know that as well). You can get a little more creative by getting different-sized vases to place in the center of the table with either taper candles or pillar candles inside the vases for a reflective glow. Stay clear of scented candles if you go for colored candles, as some guests may not like the scent you pick. You can also do floating candles with flowers submerged underneath the candles. Ask your florist for ideas and vases that you might be able to rent from them.
- **Food**—Again, if your budget is tight, food is an option for your centerpiece. Instead of putting edible favors at each place setting, you can stack them on a cake stand in the middle of the table. Instead of a three-tiered wedding cake, have different cakes as the centerpiece for each table with an explanation of what kind of cake each table has—you can even name your tables the flavors of the cakes. Your guests can mingle after dinner and sample all the different types of cakes you chose while getting to know each other. Some cultures have family-style celebratory feasts (meaning the actual dinner is placed on several plates in the middle of the table), where food is literally the centerpiece.
- **Photos and art**—If you are a crafty gal, you may want to be the DIY queen and make pretty arrangements with artwork or photos in the center of each table. Some great websites with beautiful DIY projects include:

  - *www.diybride.com*
  - *www.oncewed.com*
  - *www.weddingchicks.com*

- *www.ruffledblog.com*
- *www.100layercake.com/blog*
- *www.eco-beautifulweddings.com*
- *www.marthastewartweddings.com*

Does your home already have framed pictures of you and your fiancé scattered throughout? For a personal touch, bring these as the centerpieces, or ask your parents to bring framed pictures of the two of you as kids, placing one of each of you on every table.

QUESTION

How much should I allot for my floral designs and décor budget?
Typically in most metropolitan cities, décor will be between 9–12 percent of your overall budget. In other places, you should expect to pay between 7–10 percent. Remember, the flowers, lighting, and décor are the only things that will make the reception space reflect you as a couple (other than the food, which will quickly be consumed).

Tent Décor

If your reception is going to be in a tent, you will have a whole slew of other décor options to consider.

- **Lanterns**—Many couples love the look of hanging lanterns (either paper or glass). Just be sure they are securely fastened to the crossbeams of the tent unless you have a lighting crew that can bring in sturdy additional wiring.
- **Lighting**—Many tent rental companies will offer different packages in regard to lighting. Most tent companies provide perimeter lighting, while others can provide complete lighting packages.
- **Liners**—If you hate the look that the poles of the tent give off for your reception, many high-end tent rental companies provide tent liners to cover all of the poles.
- **Tent sides**—When choosing tent sides, keep in mind that many photos will be taken under the tent. Don't opt for cheap plastic sidewalls

as they will look like cheap plastic sidewalls in the photos! Most tent providers can offer white sidewalls or even decorative sidewalls like ones that have cathedral-style windows. All tent sides should be easy to open, rain proof, and closable in case of rain.

- **Foundation**—Depending on the ground where your tent is being erected, you may need to talk to your tent company about the area where the tent is going. If the tent does not have a solid, level foundation to go on, an experienced tent provider can work up a plan to level the ground.
- **Flooring**—Another issue to think about in addition to the ground not being level is if the tent is going to be on grass and dirt. You don't want your guests to trip or your tables to be lopsided and have your beautiful tall centerpieces tipping and glasses leaning. Another issue to consider is rain. You do not want your guests squishing across the floor or walking on muddy grass after a week of rainfall. Always invest in some sort of rental flooring if your tent will be over grass or dirt areas.

Talk to your tent representative to see whether or not you need to have someone available onsite for the duration of the reception. Should something go wrong with the tent, you do not want to leave your caterer, planner, and the guests trying to figure out how to fix the problem!

Linens and Other Décor

Many couples see linens as an afterthought. Depending on the number of guests you are inviting and the type of reception you plan on having, linens can really make an impact on the design of your reception space. If your budget allows, try to use specialty linens on your tables as opposed to just the standard white cotton linens that most venues provide. If you have multiple colors, consider changing up the colors of linens for your escort-card, cocktail, cake, and guest tables. With many venues, you might be able to use a colorful linen as well for your bar.

Some other popular décor items:

- **Pipe and draping**—Especially helpful for covering ugly walls and unnecessary doorways. Draping fabric between columns can create a romantic and whimsical look. For creating drama, hanging reams of fabric from different points in your reception space can really make a statement.

- **Ice sculptures**—These can be anything from monograms to martini luges. Some couples choose to provide ice sculptures for stationary hors d'oeuvres, cake, and buffet tables.
- **Cake, dessert, and favor bars**—See Chapter 17 for more details

There are other ways to decorate your reception site depending on what type of venue you have. Using hanging votives and paper lanterns works wonders for receptions under tents and nearby trees. If you can, look at pictures of previous weddings that have taken place at your venue for ideas.

Flowers and Seasonality

After you have figured out the style of your wedding and what sorts of floral designs you will need, you should sit down with a florist. Depending on the time of year, the types of flowers that will be available for your wedding will vary. The seasonality of your flowers will really affect the bottom line of your floral design contract as well. What does seasonality mean in the wedding industry? It means that certain flowers are only available at certain times of the year here in the United States. However, many popular floral designs today include flowers from all over the world—especially Canada, South America, Holland, and New Zealand.

Here is a simple guide to seasonality and colors available for each season and the most popular varieties of flowers. Always be sure to ask your local florist for other possibilities as this is by no means an exhaustive list with the thousands of varieties of flowers that are in the world!

Flower Name	Colors Available*	Months/Seasons Available
Peony	Pink, white, red, yellow, and peach	May and June (some varieties are available from Israel and Holland during winter months at a much higher price)
Rose	Every color except blue	Year round
Tulips	Every color except blue	Winter through spring
Anemones	White, red, pink, and purple	Spring and fall from various locations around the world

Calla Lilies	Every color—except blue—in the mini variety; white and green in the large variety	Spring through fall from various locations around the world
Gardenias	White and pink	Late spring through summer
Stephanotis	White	Year round
Hydrangea	White, pink, blue, green, antique mix of green/red, and purple/blue	Year round in various varieties and countries
Chrysanthemums	Every color except blue	Fall is when they are most abundant, but available year round in various varieties
Snapdragons	White, pink, orange, burgundy, and yellow	Year round from various countries
Delphinium	White, pink, blue (dark and light), purple, and lavender	Year round in various varieties and countries
Freesia	White, pink, red/orange, lavender, yellow, and cream	Year round in various varieties and countries
Hyacinth	White, pink, purple, yellow, orange, lavender, red, and orange; the Grape Hyacinth variety comes in white, blue, and green	Winter through spring
Sweet Pea	Purple, white, pink, red, peach, and yellow	Winter through spring
Lily of the Valley	White	Spring
Sunflowers	Yellow	Summer through fall
Orchids	Every color except blue	Year round
Dahlias	White, pink, red, orange, burgundy, and yellow	Summer through fall
Larkspur	White, blue, lavender, purple, and pink	Summer through fall
Carnations	Every color except blue	Year round
Daffodil	Yellow, white, and yellow/orange	Spring

*Many flowers can be dyed with special floral dyes. Only natural colors are listed in this table.

Perhaps you want to pick certain flowers for your wedding that convey a special meaning. Following is a list of some popular flowers and the symbolism they represent:

▼ **FLORAL MEANING**

Flower	Meaning
Chrysanthemum	Love
Daisy	Innocence
Forget-me-not	True love
Gardenia	Secret love
Iris	Affection
Ivy	Fidelity
Lily	Majesty
Lily-of-the-valley	Happiness
Rose (red)	Love
Rose (pink)	Perfect happiness; gratitude
Rose (yellow)	Friendship; joy
Rose (white)	Innocence; purity
Rose (peach)	Desire
Rosebuds	Beauty; youth
Rosemary	Fidelity
Violet	Modesty

Preserving Flowers

Many brides choose to preserve their bridal bouquet as a memento of the wedding. The odds are very strong that your bouquet will, after time, end up in storage (which often means someplace where you seldom look at it). Keep this in mind if you decide to take your bouquet to the florist for preservation. The process will probably cost you more than the bouquet itself. There are, however, cheaper and more practical ways for you to preserve your bouquet yourself.

Pressing Flowers

Pressing is the most popular method of bouquet preservation. The process of pressing your wedding flowers works best if you start it fairly soon after your wedding, *before* your flowers have had time to lose their fresh appearance. Take the bouquet apart and place the separate flowers in the pages of heavy books, between sheets of paper towels (if not cushioned by paper towels, ink from the book's pages will ruin the flowers and the book).

The flowers should be kept in the books for two to six weeks, depending on the size of the blossom. The bigger the flower, the more time (and the more books to stack on top) it needs. When the flowers look ready, glue them onto a mounting board in an arrangement that closely resembles the original bouquet. Place the board in a picture frame and hang it.

ESSENTIAL

If you are not a particularly crafty person, only use a few blooms to dry and then ask a professional framing company to take your dried flowers and frame them with your wedding invitation.

Hanging/Drying

First, take the bouquet apart. Next, hang the flowers upside down to dry to preserve shape and prevent drooping. Some color may be lost in the drying process—the loss is less if the flowers are hung in a dark room. Like pressing, the earlier you start the process, the more successful it's likely to be. Some flowers do not dry very well, so don't be surprised if you need to discard a few.

Wedding Favors

With the advent of the Internet came an explosion of wedding favor options. Some couples choose to make favors themselves, while the majority of couples opt for an easier route of having favors pre-packaged and ready to be placed at each place setting.

There is no specific etiquette that says that you must provide favors for your guests. However, there are certain cultural traditions and superstitions that dictate differently. The most common in several cultures is the use of Jordan almonds. This candy-coated almond is considered an important element of a wedding in many cultures. The most general meaning is the bittersweetness of marriage. It is especially traditional in Greek weddings, Italian weddings, French weddings, and Middle Eastern weddings.

Favors should really represent you and your fiancé. Most favors are typically placed at each place setting at the dining tables, handed out to guests during the reception, or placed near the door for guests to take on the way out. Here are some favor ideas:

- **Food**—The most popular wedding favor is one that can be eaten. Cookies, brownies, chocolates, hard candies—the list goes on and on. Try to find food that reflects your town. Do you live in the south? Why not give your guests a bottle of local barbecue sauce or hot sauce? Live in San Francisco? Ghirardelli chocolates should do the trick (especially if you have a lot of out-of-town guests).
- **Personalized**—Want your reception to really reflect you? Be sure to incorporate something about you for your favors. Are you a dentist? Why not give everyone a travel toothbrush? Love to travel? Give them luggage tags. School teacher? Give them personalized pencils and pens.
- **Eco-friendly options**—If you are not a fan of all the packaging and materialism of favors, there are eco-friendly options for favors. You can make a donation to your favorite charity and let your guests know about it at the escort card table. You can also provide seeds or actual potted herbs or tree saplings for your guests to plant in their own garden. Help your guests go green by giving them reusable grocery bags or reusable water bottles.

There are tons of websites dedicated to favors and websites that help couples make their own favors. The sky is the limit when it comes to favors, so be sure to set your budget ahead of time before you go shopping for them.

Lighting and Lanterns

If your reception is going to be at night, or in a room with no windows (or generally a rather dark location), consider adding lighting in order to create a warm and inviting atmosphere.

Lighting experts will be able to provide all sorts of options when it comes to illuminating your reception (and sometimes ceremony) spaces. You can choose from simple up-lights on the surrounding walls and/or columns of your reception space or consider pin-spotting each centerpiece with its own lighting fixture. With technology comes a whole range of lighting paraphernalia like custom gobos with monograms for your names on your dance floor and interesting patterns to splash across ceilings. Some advanced lighting companies can provide moving fixtures and, of course, provide help in installing lanterns. The amount of lighting you will need is really dictated by your budget and style.

You can purchase paper lanterns online at Asian-inspired websites such as *www.asianideas.com* and *www.paperlanternstore.com*.

If a lighting company is out of your budget range and paper lanterns won't work for your reception space, candles and twinkle lights are always economical options. Does your venue have a lot of outdoor steps? Consider luminaries and tiny votive lights to light the way at night. Luminaries and votives always work well for sidewalks and pathways. Just be sure to avoid any fire hazards. If there is a pool or a fountain, see if your venue will allow you to float candles in it. You can also rent large glass vases from your florist to place floating candles in and place them around outdoor spaces. You could also line your aisle with candles (if it's wide enough).

Ask your lighting expert and floral designer for interesting and creative ways to use lighting, lanterns, and candles for your venue.

Wedding Party Flowers Worksheet

Person/Item	Description	Quantity	Cost
Bride:			
Bouquet			
Flowers for Hair			
Toss Bouquet			
Garlands			
Maid/Matron of honor:			
Bouquet			
Flowers for Hair			
Bridesmaids:			
Bouquet			
Flowers for Hair			
Flower Girl(s):			
Flowers			
Basket			
Flowers for Hair			
Garland			
Pomander			
Mothers:			
Corsage			
Nosegay			
Grandmothers:			
Corsage			
Groom:			
Boutonnière			
Best man:			
Boutonnière			

Wedding Party Flowers Worksheet (continued)

Person/Item	Description	Quantity	Cost
Ushers:			
Boutonnière			
Ring bearer:			
Boutonnière			
Pillow			
Fathers:			
Boutonnière			
Grandfathers:			
Boutonnière			
Godfather(s):			
Boutonnière			
Godmother(s):			
Corsage			
Readers:			
Corsage			
Boutonnière			
Officiant:			
Boutonnière or Corsage			
Other (list below):			

Total of All Expenses:

Ceremony Flowers and Decorations Worksheet

Item	Description	Quantity	Cost
Aisle runner			
Altar flowers			
Garland			
Potted flowers			
Potted plants			
Pews/chair flowers			
Pews/chair bows			
Candelabra			
Candle holders			
Candles			
Unity candle			
Wedding arch			
Columns			
Trellis			
Wreaths for church doors			
Staircase			
Window Treatments			
Mantel Treatments			
Other (list below)			

Total:

Reception Flowers and Decorations Worksheet

Item	Description	Quantity	Cost

Guest tables:

Item	Description	Quantity	Cost
Centerpieces			
Garland			
Candles			

Head table:

Centerpieces			
Garland			
Candles			

Buffet table:

Flowers			
Garland			
Decorations			

Cake table:

Cake top			
Flowers			
Garland			
Decorations			

Guest book table:

Flowers			
Decorations			

Envelope table:

Flowers			
Decorations			
Candelabra			
Candle holders			
Candles			

Reception Flowers and Decorations Worksheet (continued)

Item	Description	Quantity	Cost
Archway:			
Columns			
Trellis			
Wreaths			
Garlands			
Potted flowers			
Potted plants			
Hanging plants			
Other:			
Other:			
Staircase			
Window Treatments			
Mantel Decorations			
Entryway			
Path Décor			
Bar Decorating			
Restroom Arrangements			
Wedding Cake Flowers			
Flowers for Special Guests			
Anniversary Dance Bouquet			
Flowers for Rehearsal Dinner			
Flowers for "Getaway Car"			
Thank-You Bouquets			
Other:			
Total:			

Lighting and Décor Checklist

Lighting for Ceremony:

Lighting for Reception:

Up-lighting:

Pinspots on:

☐ Centerpieces

☐ Head Table

☐ Cake

Gobo (logo) on Dance Floor:

Any other Décor Rentals:

Other Notes:

CHAPTER 16

Music and Entertainment

Have you ever been to a wedding where the music was so bad you wished there hadn't been any? You certainly don't want anyone to remember your wedding this way, so you will need to put some careful thought into this part of your big day. Remember that the right music adds emotion, drama, and fun to your wedding; the wrong music can completely destroy your reception and mood. Take your time in choosing not only the perfect music, but also the right musicians.

Ceremony Music

Carefully selected music can provide atmosphere and enhance the mood and meaning of your ceremony. You may already have a clear vision of the type of music you want for your ceremony. Depending on the type of ceremony you are having, you may need to have prelude music, processional music, music during the ceremony, and finally music as the wedding party recesses. Not all religious ceremonies allow music, so be sure to ask your officiant about the guidelines for yours.

If additional musicians, singers, and songs are an option you'd like to consider, consult with the officiant in charge of your ceremony. Some religions place restrictions on secular selections during the ceremony, but others may be very open. Ask about this well in advance before you start your search for ceremony musicians. Following are a few ideas for your ceremony.

Church Ceremonies

If you are having your ceremony in a church: Use what they have! An organist or a pianist can always do the trick. You can add some pomp and circumstance by including a trumpet for your entrance or a harp. Some couples may not like the idea of traditional church music. If you are in this category, ask your pastor or priest if you can bring in a string quartet, classical guitarist, or any number of other instruments and ensembles.

Jewish Ceremonies

Very traditional music for Jewish ceremonies includes a cantor to sing the *Sheva Brachot* also called the *birkot Nesuim* (traditional seven blessings) and other songs and chants. The recessional of most Jewish weddings includes a very festive ensemble of musical instruments including the clarinet, violin, guitars, and drums, though there could be an accordion and even a full orchestra. The sound of the music is typically folksy, stemming from European traditions, which encourages dancing and clapping by the wedding party and the guests.

Southeast Asian (Hindu/Indian) Ceremonies

The use of *Dhol* drummers for the *Baraat* is popular. Other instruments that can be found during the various stages of an Indian wedding (see Chapter 6) are: *sitar*, *tabla*, and *bansuri*. Many couples choose some of these same instruments for certain parts of their cocktail hour or reception.

Chinese Ceremonies

The use of stringed instruments such as the *Gu-qin* (which translates as "Ancient Musical Instrument" and is a seven-string, plucked instrument), *Er-hu* (also known as the Chinese violin with two strings and played with a bow), *Gu-zheng* (a fifteen to twenty-five stringed instrument that is plucked), and the *Pipa* (also known as the Chinese lute) are popular. Other traditional instruments include the *Dizi* and *Xiao*, which are both wind-blown instruments.

Japanese Ceremonies

The *Koto* and *Shamisen* are the two most popular Japanese musical instruments used for ceremonies. The *Koto* is a long zither with thirteen woven strings stretched over ivory bridges that are plucked and strummed, while the *Shamisen* is a skin-covered lute with three woven silk strings that are plucked with a *bachi* made of ivory.

Persian Ceremonies

A wide range of music can be played during your ceremony. Some more classical instruments for your ceremony include *Setar* (not to be confused with a *sitar*), which is a three-to-four–string plucked instrument that is part of the lute family; *Kamancha* (three silk stringed or four metal stringed bowed instrument); and *Santur* (a hammered dulcimer played with mallets).

Other Ceremony Music

If you are not religious and you really don't want to incorporate heritage in your ceremony—keep it simple. If you are having your ceremony in a garden or ballroom, consider one instrument or you can even have your DJ or band pipe in music from a speaker.

Also, don't worry if you think you don't know enough about classical music (should you choose to hire classical musicians for your ceremony). The musicians you eventually choose can offer suggestions based on guidelines you offer them. On the other hand, if you know exactly what you want and the musicians you want to hire don't have it in their repertoire, simply buy the music for them. Be sure to send the music to them way ahead of time so they can practice!

Bands versus Wedding DJs

When it comes to your wedding reception music, you really end up having one of two choices: go with a band or a DJ. The type of music that you choose really depends on the type of reception that you want to have. Whether you are going with a formal or informal wedding reception, the possibilities are endless when it comes to music selection.

Bands

Bands are often the first choice for most wedding receptions. Some couples love to show off their incredible swing dancing capabilities and could never dream of having anything other than a swing band orchestra complete with a horn section. Or there could be an amazing Frank Sinatra impersonator who will totally jazz-out your reception.

FACT

Some bands are called classical or jazz ensembles while others may simply be variety bands based on the type of musical era or genre you want to have played. You could choose, for example, an ensemble for your cocktail reception and eight-piece band for dinner and dancing.

Whichever type of band you choose, there are lots of logistics involved in having a band at your reception. First and foremost is space and power. Before you book a band, you need to make sure that your reception site has enough space for a band and sufficient power. The last thing you want is a large band and a tiny dance floor. The other incredibly important facet of having a band is making sure they are not going to blow an electrical fuse. Consult with your venue manager or your wedding planner to see how they have dealt with bands in the past to get the best advice.

If you have a particular song that you want to have played during the cocktail hour or for your first dance, you can almost always provide a disc or an MP3 for your band to plug into their sound equipment. While bands are not DJs, they are aware that they may not be able to play every song you want at your wedding. If you have multicultural music that you would like to have played over dinner and then switch to the band after dinner, let that be known before you sign up with a band.

Whatever type of band you choose for your reception, you should always keep in mind that they will typically cost more than a DJ.

ALERT

A large band that is charging less than a DJ is typically a band that rarely does weddings (or has never done one). Why is this important? Although they may be cheaper, they may not be sensitive to the time constraints of a wedding and the flow of most receptions. Be sure you are ready to take on this risk!

There are a few other logistical things to keep in mind when you hire a band. Most bands require at least one break and must be fed. Be sure to plan out your timeline with the best possible breaking point for them to eat. Typically a good time is while you are eating and they can have band members switch playing while others eat. Another great time is when you are cutting the cake or doing toasts (if they are not during the dinner portion of the evening). However, you need to make sure that there is never a long break without music while no one is talking. A lack of music is a huge signal that something is wrong or it is the end of the reception.

When hiring your band of choice, be sure to ask them the following questions:

- What sort of power needs do you have? (This becomes especially important if you are having a band play in your backyard or at a venue that does not typically host weddings, or even a historical site that might have old circuits.)

- How many breaks will you take? (You will want to make sure that at least one of the breaks that they take is during a time that you can have recorded music playing—such as during dinner or during the cake cutting and toasts.)
- Do you need a stage? Will you provide one? (If they do not provide one, this may be something they stipulate in their contract. Be sure to ask this question as you may faced with footing the bill for a stage after the fact. Some bands require a stage and will make specifications for it up front.)
- Will you stay late if the party should extend? What is the fee for that?

After asking all the questions, ask if you can see them play live either at a club or a party/wedding. Most bands will be hesitant to have you come to another wedding, as they are only trying to safeguard the privacy of their clients. You wouldn't want a bunch of random engaged couples at your wedding, would you? If you can't see the band live, ask if they have any of their work recorded so you can see them on DVD.

ALERT

If you are considering using an MP3 player or another type of personal music device in lieu of a band or DJ, try to talk yourself out of it. MP3s, no matter how advanced, need to have someone to stop and start them. Computers and MP3s always have a magical tendency to freeze up when you need them the most! Don't leave your wedding music to fate.

DJs

For many couples, a DJ is an easier and less expensive option compared to a band. Most reputable and experienced wedding DJs are able to provide a wide range of music. A DJ is all about having a mix of music, which typically will be able to please everyone in your crowd.

A DJ can also make a change in the style of music you want as the night goes on. This is especially important as the dancing portion of the evening starts to ramp up. If you are mixing two cultures, you may want to have a DJ that can play music from both throughout the night. Only a DJ will be able to infuse radio mixes, some of the oldies but goodies your parents adore, and an amazing hymn from your homeland, all in one night!

ESSENTIAL

There is a distinct difference between a wedding DJ and most other club and party DJs. A wedding DJ understands that you want them just to play music and not try to create a club-like atmosphere. Unless you want a club-like atmosphere, in which case, you should hire a club-style DJ. Otherwise, a wedding DJ will just make announcements as needed.

Although a DJ is not like a band in his needs for electrical power—you may end up needing additional equipment. Some typical extra needs are multiple speakers, wireless microphones, and a separate set of sound equipment for your ceremony and cocktail hour.

Since your DJ will possibly be your only form of entertainment at the reception, be sure to ask the right questions before signing a contract. Here is the best list to start off with:

- Ask your DJ about pricing on any extras before you sign a contract. If you need extra speakers, microphones etc., know what the costs are up front.
- How much time do you need for setup?
- How many hours will you play?
- What is the fee for staying late if additional time is needed?
- Do you have a list of references?
- Will you protect your song list? (Meaning, if you have a list of songs that you do not want played, will he be sure not to play any of those songs even if your long-lost uncle begs for one?)
- What kind of backup system do you have?

Dancing

Some couples may opt for a reception with no dancing, while the majority of couples can't wait until the dancing begins. Depending on your culture and the timing of your event, there are all sorts of special dances you may want to incorporate at your reception.

First Dance

You might already have a song that's special to the two of you that you'll want to use for your moment in the spotlight on the dance floor. Obviously, the possibilities are endless, not only because there are millions of songs to choose from (Old? New? Fast? Slow? Blues? Country? Any and all of these are fair game), but because your personalities *should* come into play in choosing the right one for you. If you're a silly, playful couple, you might want to choose something that's a little more lighthearted than you would if the two of you were very serious-minded people. The important thing is to choose a song that you both love. Don't worry about whether anyone else will feel it's an inappropriate or odd choice. This song is all about the two of you!

Father-Daughter/Mother-Son Dances

Here's where you might want to get a little more traditional—unless you and your parents have a special song already. Base this choice on your relationship with your parents individually, and not on what anyone else would like to hear during this dance.

Many couples choose to have one song for the father/daughter and mother/son dance. You can either dance at the same time or have your fiancé join in with his mother halfway through the dance.

Classic father/daughter dance songs:
- "Brown Eyed Girl" by Van Morrison
- "Butterfly Kisses" by Bob Carlisle
- "I've Got the World on a String" by Frank Sinatra
- "I Loved Her First" by Heartland
- "My Father's Eyes" by Eric Clapton
- "The Way You Look Tonight" by Frank Sinatra or Tony Bennett
- "You Are the Sunshine of My Life" by Stevie Wonder

Classic mother/son dance songs:
- "What a Wonderful World" by Louis Armstrong

- "Forever Young" by Rod Stewart
- "Georgia on My Mind" by Ray Charles
- "I Wish You Love" by Natalie Cole
- "I'll Be There" by Jackson 5

ALERT

A word to the wise: If you can find out where the speakers are located in the reception room, try to seat your older guests away from them and away from the area where the musicians will be playing. This should help prevent your elderly relatives from being made uncomfortable by the volume of the music.

Other Dances

If you're getting the whole wedding party out onto the dance floor, you might want to choose music that lets them cut loose a little and get the party rolling. Again, the choices are really endless. If you do choose to go with a peppy song here, make sure it's one that your wedding party can actually dance to (instead of trying unsuccessfully to catch a beat for several minutes). Oldies such as "The Twist" by Chubby Checker or "ABC" by the Jackson 5 are great dancing songs, or go with music that's currently popular at clubs.

Always take suggestions from your DJ as to what is current and will get guests on the dance floor. If you know of a particular song that will really do the trick, just let your DJ know. The more information he has about the style of music you and your guests like, the better your party will be.

In many cultures there are special dances. Find out from your officiant and your families about which one is appropriate for you and your wedding. A few examples include:

- The Hora (Jewish Culture)
- Lion Dancers (Chinese Culture)
- Belly Dancing (Middle Eastern Cultures)

Ceremony Music Worksheet

Organist's name:

Address:

Telephone: Fee:

Soloist's name:

Address:

Telephone: Fee:

Name of other musician, if applicable:

Address:

Telephone: Fee:

Part of Ceremony	Musical Selection	Performed By
Prelude		
Processional		
During the ceremony (list specific part below)		
Recessional		
Other		

Reception Music Worksheet

Name of band/DJ:

Address:

Telephone:

Manager/contact:

Hours he or she can be reached:

Number of performers:

Description of act:

Demo tape available? ☐ Yes ☐ No

Notes:

View live performance? ☐ Yes ☐ No

Date: Time: Location:

Appointments:

Date: Time:

Date: Time:

Date: Time:

Date of hired services: Time:

Number of hours: Cocktail hour:

Overtime cost:

Includes the following services:

Equipment provided: Equipment rented:

Rental costs:

Total amount due: Date:

Amount of deposit: Date:

Balance due: Date:

Sales tax included? ☐ Yes ☐ No

Terms of cancellation:

Notes:

CHAPTER 17

Cake and Desserts

Gone are the days when you could only have cake as dessert for your wedding day. In fact, in many cultures no cake is ever served. When looking for a way to satiate the sweet-toothed guests at your wedding, your options are limitless now. Cake, cupcakes, dessert bars, and a whole slew of other options are waiting for you!

History of Wedding Cakes

Wedding cakes have been around since ancient times. In Rome, a loaf of wheat bread (*farreus panis*) was broken over the bride's head to symbolize hope for a fertile and fulfilling life. The guests ate the crumbs, which were believed to be good luck. Later, a variation of the custom found its way to England, where guests brought small cakes to the ceremony. The cakes were put into a pile, and the bride and groom stood over the pile and kissed. Eventually, someone came up with the idea of stacking the cakes neatly and frosting them together—an early version of today's multitiered wedding cakes. Since then, the cake has lost most of its significance as a fertility symbol and is seen primarily as a decoration and the main dessert for many weddings.

Finding the Right Baker

Depending on where you live, the availability of bakers there, and which season you're planning your wedding for, you may want to contact your baker up to a year in advance, or at least a few months before the big day. Bigger, full-service bakeries simply have more resources available and will be better staffed and equipped to handle a wedding on short notice.

If you want that cute little bakery around the corner to make your wedding cake, get on the phone as soon as possible, and be prepared to fork over a big deposit for them to save the date for you. And though this phrase is getting very familiar at this point in your wedding planning, the best way to find a baker is through *word of mouth*. There's simply no better way of knowing whether a baker can make a delicious and beautiful cake than to talk to someone who has bought one.

If you're at a complete loss as to what style of cake you want, your baker will have photos available to help you pick out your cake design. Once you've found one you like, you can move on to questions of size and price.

The Interview

To get a baker's undivided attention (something you really want and need in order to discuss plans for your wedding cake), call the shop to make an appointment. You can't pop in during their busiest time and expect that someone will just drop everything to conduct an elaborate style consultation.

Also, by calling ahead, you're giving the bakery time to prepare batters and icings for you to try and approve (or disapprove). If you want your cake to include your wedding colors, bring a swatch of fabric with you. If there's a definite style of cake that you're after, bring a picture or sketch. You'll also need to bring along the names and numbers of your florist and photographer, as well as all the relevant information regarding your reception site (location, contact name and number, and directions).

ALERT

Your cake could be lovely to look at, but that won't count for much if 200 people can't quite manage to swallow it. And this brings you to one of the most fun parts of wedding planning: cake tastings! Be sure to taste a sample of any cake *before* you order it.

Here are some issues to address with the baker:

- **Size**—You'll have to know approximately how many guests you're expecting to attend to nail down what size cake you'll need.
- **Flavor, filling, and icing**—You'll be given a list to choose from. If you want different flavors on different tiers, ask your baker if they can do this for you.
- **Specialty**—Does this baker have one? Can you taste it?
- **Backup plans**—If your cake should suffer an unforeseen tragedy on the morning of your wedding (a delivery van accident that totals your confection, for example), will this bakery have another cake or dessert ready to go?

Of course, the other big issue you'll want to discuss is price. Most bakeries will base their prices on a plain cake with buttercream frosting—*each slice* will cost you X number of dollars. (If you're having 200 guests and the cake is $4 dollars a slice, you're looking at an $800 cake.) From there, you'll add to the price of each slice with each upgrade.

Fillings will cost you so much per slice, while rolled fondant frosting will cost you so much *more* per slice. And if you want any fancy design work on your cake, you're looking at paying even *more*. (Have you always wondered how the cost of wedding cakes can spiral completely out of control?) If you decide to incorporate pillars, a stand, and other added décor for your cake, you will probably be charged a rental fee for these items.

ESSENTIAL

How much cake will you need? Your baker is your best resource here. You don't want to have too little cake, after all. Your cake can be cut into three-inch or four-inch slices, with a corresponding change in yield. A sheet cake will yield about forty servings.

Delivery is typically added as well. Each bakery has its own specific delivery area (a radius of fifty miles from the bakery, for example). If your reception falls outside that area, an extra charge may be added. Also, some bakeries have minimum order amounts. If you fall short of that amount on your order, the bakery will make its money by charging a minimum fee or additional delivery fees.

You Take the Cake!

Make sure the baker arrives at the reception in time to set up the cake before the guests arrive. Multitiered cakes usually need to be transported in sections and assembled at the reception site. Unless you want this phenomenon to be part of the reception entertainment, make arrangements with the site coordinator to allow the baker plenty of time to get in early and do their work. And remember to touch base with the coordinator about where the cake will be placed. Though traffic patterns and simple space restrictions may dictate where the cake goes.

Saving Cake

You may want to preserve the top layer of your cake for tradition's sake. There is a tradition of freezing the top layer of your wedding cake so that you and your fiancé can thaw it out and enjoy it on your first anniversary. Your baker will probably address this issue with you. If she doesn't, and you're interested in saving the cake, make sure you bring it up. Some bakers will even offer to make you another small top tier on your anniversary instead (typically a better tasting option)!

Cut It Down

Rest assured, there *are* ways to cut costs. Your decorated cake does not have to serve all the guests. Save money by ordering a smaller decorated cake, along with a supplemental sheet cake (which is kept in the kitchen and not on display) to feed your guests. On the other hand, if dessert is already included on your wedding menu, there's really no need for a wedding cake except for the traditional cake-cutting ceremony. If that's the case, you can cut costs by making it as small and simple as possible.

Cake Design, Flavors, and Fillings

Once upon a time, a wedding cake was white inside and out, but today there are countless options for decoration and consumption. The cake can be garnished with fresh flowers, fruits, or greenery, and the icing or trimming can be made to match the wedding colors you've selected. The choices for cake flavors, frostings, decorations, and garnishes are plentiful—and tempting.

Don't forget that your cake is edible; it's perfectly appropriate to serve it as dessert. Why spend tons of money and weeks of a baker's time to create the Mona Lisa of wedding cakes, only to have it sit uneaten in a corner of the room?

Cake Design

You truly have limitless options when it comes to the actual design of your cake. While the traditional wedding cake is round and three-tiered, many couples opt for square cakes or a combo of both. You are also not obligated to have a traditional wedding cake at all. Several cultures use pastries as part of their cake design and you may want to have a cheesecake. Whatever the shape of the cake you go with, the design on your cake can be as simple as smooth icing with clusters of flowers or as intricate as replicating the lace that is covering your gown. Choose your cake designer based on the design you are looking for in addition to the taste of it.

Flavors

Bakers have come a long way over time. Although many couples choose to have the traditional white or yellow cake, chances are you'll be presented with a long list of choices: chocolate, chocolate hazelnut, double fudge, Italian rum, French vanilla, lemon, orange, spice, carrot cake, cheesecake, red velvet, raspberry swirl, and the list goes on.

Your baker may also have her own specialty that's out of this world. In addition, you can choose to have a different flavor for each tier of your cake, just to accommodate the different tastes and needs of your guests. You may have some guests whose stomachs just can't handle a heavy rum cake, for example, or who are allergic to carrot cake.

QUESTION

What about the frosting?
The standard icing for most wedding cakes is butter cream. You can also get rolled fondant or a combination of butter cream with fondant artwork and sugarpaste, but these are more expensive options.

Fillings

Some people love cake with a little something extra. Your baker will probably be able to offer you a wide variety of wedding cake fillings, which may include lemon, custard, raspberry, strawberry, almond crème, chocolate fudge, chocolate mocha, chocolate mousse, pineapple, etc.

And then, you may have *another* opportunity to add a little extra oomph to the cake, with sauces or toppings such as ice cream/sorbet, fresh fruit or fruit sauce, or chocolate.

Cake Toppers

Back in the day, every wedding cake had a miniature newlywed couple on top of it. It didn't even matter if the couple on top of the cake bore the slightest resemblance to the real-life couple they were representing. They were there to stay.

Now you have an amazing array of other options. You can still go with the bride and groom perched upon the top layer of your wedding cake, but they don't have to be a perky plastic couple. You can buy a keepsake china or porcelain cake-topper, monograms, or fresh or sugar-paste flowers to top your cake with. If you want to have a fun and less traditional cake topper, you can use cartoon characters! Whatever you put on top of your cake should only be limited to who you are as individuals.

Allergies and Alternatives

Many people have allergies to milk, eggs, gluten, and all sorts of various ingredients that can go into a cake. Don't let that stop you from having a cake at your wedding. Some cake designers are able to create cakes that are vegan, lactose-free, gluten-free, flourless, and eggless. You will be amazed at what is available. It takes some ingenuity and patience to find the right baker who knows how to make a gluten-free cake that tastes delicious. Check around on the Internet for cake designers who specialize in just cakes in your area. Ask questions and see what kind of alternatives they have available. If you can't find the right baker to make the gluten-free wedding cake you have been searching for, ask your mom or a friend to possibly make a small cake or cupcakes just for you or your guest to eat that day, so you can have your cake and eat it too!

You may also have guests who are diabetic. For guests that need a low-sugar option, you may want to consider having a delicious fruit display available.

Cake as Décor

With so many options and choices for your cake, it can truly become a piece of art. Placing your cake in an area where it will be seen and possibly lit up with lighting will truly help to embrace your cake as being part of the décor for your wedding. Since wedding cakes can be anything from simple three-tiers with flowers to colossal towers of confection, make sure your cake reflects your style and that your venue has the space to place the cake. In addition, going for a groom's cake (see next section) can also really be part of the décor as well, and can add a conversation piece to the reception.

Be aware that if you place your cake next to a window on a sunny summer day, you run the risk of it melting and becoming damaged. Take note when you create the layout for your reception.

ALERT

Your cake will be the center of attention when you cut it. Be sure the cake is situated in a place that has a simple background so the two of you (with your cake) will stand out—not the background.

Groom's Cake

The groom's cake gives you another opportunity to work more décor into your wedding day. Long ago, the groom's cake was referred to as the wedding cake, and what we now call the wedding cake was known as the bride's cake. The groom's cake was traditionally a dark fruitcake—a symbol of the sweet life that lay ahead for the newlyweds—and the slices were packaged in monogrammed boxes as a wedding favor for each guest. According to superstition, if a single woman sleeps with the cake box under her pillow that night, she'll dream of the man she is to marry.

Of course, as with all wedding traditions, this one has evolved with time. Since very few people actually like fruitcake, you should choose a flavor that will please the masses.

The groom's cake is supposed to give the groom *his* moment in the spotlight, so it should reflect his interests. Get creative here. If he's a hockey player, order a cake in the shape of a hockey stick or a puck; if he loves to make things, maybe a pile of wood with hammer and nails. The groom's cake is supposed to be more fun than the wedding cake, so nothing is off limits.

The groom's cake can be served at the reception, but you may want to serve it at the rehearsal. This way, he really gets his time to shine, and your wedding guests won't be bombarded with cake, cake, and more cake.

You can order a groom's cake from the same baker who is doing your wedding cake—and if you want to keep it a secret from the groom, that's all right, too.

Although groom's cakes are more common in the southern regions of the United States, this does not preclude you from offering one at your wedding if you don't live in the south. Just be prepared to explain the purpose of the cake to your guests who have never heard of this tradition.

Dessert and Favor Bars

Some people are just plain tired of the traditional wedding cake for dessert. Not everyone eats cake and not every wedding cake actually tastes good! To make matters worse, some wedding cakes can be so expensive simply because the word *wedding* is tacked on to the front of the word cake. There are a slew of different options other than wedding cake for your sweet tooth. Many couples are opting for an actual dessert or favor bar. This is where you can have a combination of various dessert options mixed with cake (e.g., fruit tarts, cookies, brownies, mini cheesecakes, mini wedding cakes, chocolate mousse, petit fours, etc.).

Another wildly popular option is to have a favor or candy bar. These bars give your non-cake eating friends a place to placate their sweet tooth. The bar is a display of various sized and shaped candy jars (or vintage glass jars) filled with assorted candies. Provide your guests with scoops and little bags and stickers or twist ties and your favor bar is complete. You can also mix in nonedible favors so your diabetic friends have some options. Of course you could always label a few jars with sugarless candy. The idea behind a favor bar is simply to give your guests some options and also to add a bit of whimsy to your day!

Cupcakes

A fun option is to do away with the wedding cake all together and provide a mix of cupcakes for your guests. To keep in tune with the style of your wedding, make sure the frostings match the colors of your reception. Mix up the flavors so all your guests can choose their favorite kind. Some cupcake designers will be able to provide you with a cupcake tower so your cupcakes can be arranged like a wedding cake. If you do not want your cupcakes to look like a wedding cake, consider using fun and vintage wire cupcake stands or small pedestal cake stands to artfully display your cupcakes. In addition to your cupcake frosting colors, you can also insert fun décor items like paper circles with the design from your invitations on them or silly cartoon characters that you and your fiancé adore. Keeping your cupcakes playful and colorful can also add to the décor of your wedding reception.

Late-Night Snacks

If your guests have not had enough to eat since the onslaught of food from the cocktail hour to the wedding cake—you can still bring more food out. Some couples believe it is the best thing in the world to bring out another late-night pass of goodies just before the party ends. Here are a few delicious examples:

- **Milk and cookies**—A nightcap shot glass of milk and chocolate chip cookies could do the trick. See if your caterer can use your mom's chocolate chip cookie recipe and surprise your mom at the reception.
- **Brownies on a stick**—Mini brownies on a stick can come in a variety of colors if you use icing and sprinkles.
- **Popcorn and candy**—If both of you love the movies, why not pass around gourmet popcorn in cute personalized bags and movie size candy boxes for your guests to snack on in their hotel rooms (instead of the $10 bag of pretzels their mini bar offers)?
- **Cotton candy**—It takes a seasoned caterer, but a late-night pass of colorful cotton candy in paper cones will impress your guests and bring a sense of nostalgia to the end of your night.

Whatever the extra sweets that come out later in the evening, make them fun and be sure they reflect your style as a couple.

The Cake Checklist

Item	Description	Cost
Wedding cake:		
Size		
Shape		
Number of tiers		
Number cake will serve		
Flavor of cake		
Flavor of filling		
Flavor of icing		
Icing decorations		
Cake top		
Cake decorations		
Other		
Groom's cake:		
Size		
Shape		
Number cake will serve		
Flavor		
Icing		
Cake top		
Cake decorations		
Other		
Cake serving set		
Cake boxes		
Delivery charge		
Other		

Total:

CHAPTER 18

Green Your Wedding

Weddings can produce an enormous amount of waste. If you are not careful, your wedding runs the risk of being a local eco-disaster. Asking questions and finding ways to have an eco-friendly wedding is easier than you think. Whatever style wedding you are planning, making at least one green choice can make all the difference. Once you make one decision, the likelihood is you will want to make more eco-friendly choices. Starting small is how every bride and every groom can make a difference.

Reduce, Reuse, and Recycle

The triple-R motto of eco-friendly living and working is: reduce, reuse, and recycle. There are simple ways to apply these three green words to your wedding.

Reduce

Since the advent of modern society there have been modest and opulent weddings. No matter the size, style, and design of your wedding, you can make an eco-minded decision to reduce the impact your wedding has on the environment.

Here is a general list of ways to reduce the waste your wedding can create. The idea of this list is to jumpstart your mind to think differently about the wedding-planning process; it is by no means a definitive list. Just choosing one item from the following ideas is a big step toward making your wedding eco-friendly.

Reduce the Number of Guests Coming to Your Wedding

Reducing the amount of people you invite means fewer people will have to travel to your wedding. Transportation is typically one of the largest wedding-related issues that affect the environment. The fewer people you invite, the fewer people who will have to take a plane, train, or automobile to your wedding. For you, this could mean looking at your list and simply cutting out the people that live out of the country. It could also give you the greatest excuse to not invite every single person who invited you to his or her wedding (even though you had not spoken for over six months). Whichever way you look at it, take a hard look at your list and see if you can reduce it.

ESSENTIAL

A good way to rule out guests from your list (if they are not family) is to look at whether you have communicated with those prospective guests in the last six to twelve months and whether they will be in your lives the year following your wedding. Why invite someone if they really are not part of your life?

Reduce the Number of Locations

If you are able to have your ceremony and reception all in one location, it can truly make a difference. If you are unable to have your ceremony at your reception site, try to choose a reception location that is as close as possible to your ceremony location.

Reduce the Amount of Trash That Can Be Created

This particular way of reducing the impact of your wedding will take a little more effort on your part. It will also require in-depth conversations with your caterer and florist.

Your caterer is typically the one who creates the most amount of trash. Ask if they can use recycling and composting bins. Ask where the majority of their food is coming from. Ask if they can buy locally as opposed to ordering from a large food distributor.

ALERT

Just simply asking your caterer questions about their environmental impact will either get them starting to think about reducing waste or will give you a sense as to whether the company is even aware (or cares) about the waste they create. You could actually be an agent of change for their operation!

When it comes to your florist, the same idea holds true: Ask questions! Ask them where they source their flowers from and if they plan to use floral foam in your arrangements (which can have a significant environmental impact). Are they composting and recycling as well?

At the very least, if you are planning on doing wedding favors, try buying them locally and with as little packaging as possible. If you are buying something online, you not only have the packaging waste for sending the items to you, but your items could have been made in a foreign country and shipped all the way to the website's headquarters and then shipped all the way to you.

Reduce the Number of Wedding Party Attendants

This can either be a really easy decision or a very difficult one. In most cases, if you are having a lot of people in your wedding party, it means that you have a lot of friends and family. However, if you can, make it simple and just have one attendant on each side. This reduces the amount of limos/forms of transportation you will need to contract; gifts you need to buy (and cart around); tuxes that need to be rented; and a whole slew of other things that go along with a wedding party.

Reduce the Amount of Paper to Be Used

It is simple, the environment needs trees to help offset carbon dioxide and paper products require trees. If you are able, send an online invitation to those who are Internet savvy and then purchase paper invitations for those who are not. Don't print menus and consider forgoing the ceremony program. Another easy way to reduce paper waste at a wedding is to use linen cocktail napkins at your bar instead of paper napkins.

FACT

There are some tree-free papers, post-consumer waste (PCW), and Forest Stewardship Council (FSC) certified papers on the market to help reduce the impact paper can have on your wedding. New technologies emerge every day. The key is to ask questions about the paper you are buying.

Reduce the Amount of Red Meat to Be Served

If you are a meat lover, this may be one you just can't swallow. However, if you can forgo red meat and replace it with chicken/fowl or fish, you can greatly reduce the environmental impact of your wedding. Red meat, simply put, requires an enormous amount of energy to produce, prepare, and digest.

Reuse

The second green "R" is reuse. There are so many great ways to reuse items from your wedding or even reuse items you (or someone else) already own and incorporate them into your wedding. Here are a few ideas to help you get excited about reusing.

FACT

Cows are currently the largest producers of methane gas in the United States. Methane gas contributes to global climate change. If every wedding in the United States switched to chicken or fish instead of beef, imagine the incredible difference it would make!

Rent or Share Items before Buying Them

No matter how unique your wedding is, there will be elements of your wedding that you can rent in addition to the tables, chairs, linens, and tabletop items. You can rent items like glassware for your centerpieces and lanterns for lighting and décor. You can even rent wedding dresses and jewelry. There are great places on the Internet that can help you find ways to share items as well (e.g., your local newspaper, and wedding chat boards, blogs, and websites).

Buy Used Items

Someone bought a $10,000 couture wedding gown and now wants to sell it for $1,000. Yes, this can happen! People are sometimes in a hurry to get the clutter that a wedding creates out of their life once the wedding is over. There are wonderful places online and possibly in your own town where you can buy a used wedding gown. You can go online to places like *www.tradesy.com* and *www.oncewed.com* as well as wedding chat boards and blogs. Go to that local consignment or thrift shop and you might actually find the tie you have been looking for or some beautiful vintage ribbons for your bouquets. You might even end up finding something to design your whole wedding around.

Reuse the Flowers and Décor

If you plan on having a brunch the day after your wedding, take some of the centerpieces from the wedding day to reuse. Then after the brunch take the flowers to a local hospital or a nursing home. Or make sure your florist gets his vases and other décor back. After all, what will you *really* do with seventeen identical vases?

Borrow Items from Friends and Family

Does your aunt have a pair of earrings to die for? What about your mom's pearl necklace? Did your best friend just get married? What could you borrow from her wedding day? Sometimes borrowing can mean small things like jewelry, or it could mean something as large as borrowing china from all of your relatives to give your buffet that sweet vintage style. Borrowing can really make your wedding unique and incredibly sentimental—and at the same time—green!

ESSENTIAL

Make sure you have assigned someone for your wedding day to have a list of items that can be reused and that should be taken. If you don't, these items might end up in the trash.

Look Inside Your Own Home

Typically your home reflects your style and most weddings reflect each couple's personal style. Why not take something that you already own in your home and use it at the wedding? Have a pretty set of silver from your grandmother? Why not use it for the coffee station? There are probably all sorts of décor items in your home that can be used on your wedding day. Then after the wedding (every time you see them) they will remind you of your wedding day!

Recycle

Everyone knows about recycling, but many people forget about this "R" when it comes to their weddings. Recycling at your wedding can make an incredible impact on the environment. Here are a few ways to help recycling work at your wedding.

Ask Your Caterer to Recycle and Compost

Ask if they will have recycling bins at the bar(s) and in the back with the kitchen staff. If they can compost (not all know how to do this), even better.

ALERT

If you can, ask your caterer to not use bottled water at the bars. In most places water from the tap is drinkable. If the water is not safe for regular consumption, consider buying three or four water filter pitchers for the caterers to use. This could save hundreds of bottles from having to be recycled and you can reuse the pitchers after the wedding.

Enlist the Help of Friends and Family

If your caterer looks at you sideways about the whole recycling thing, consider taking care of the recycling yourself. Have a friend who is committed to the environment? Ask her if she will take all the recyclables with her at the end of the night. Yes, it is not the most glamorous thing to ask someone to do, but in the end you will see the amazing amount of trash you saved! Don't forget about all the paper products like programs and menus too.

Buy Recyclable Products

This may sound like a no-brainer, but take a look at the things you are buying and ask yourself "Are they even recyclable?" If your caterer or baker (or you) are providing to-go packaging, make sure it is recyclable. Is the packaging your favors come in recyclable? How about the packing materials the items you order online come shipped in?

Recycling is a relatively easy thing to do for your wedding, you just have to be mindful that not all facilities are recycle-friendly (including your hotels, ceremony site, and reception site).

Simple Ways to Go Green

There is simply not enough room in this chapter to go into depth about all of the many ways you can green your wedding. In addition to all of the items previously mentioned, here are few concrete ideas on how to go green for your wedding day.

Buy Locally

Another misconception about going green is that it will be expensive, especially when it comes to food. A lot of the catering expense is from the use of organic items that are not produced locally or within a reasonable distance of where your wedding will take place. For example, an organic Japanese plum flown in from Japan is certainly going to be more expensive and create more waste (shipping-wise) than trying to buy plums from a local farmer (unless of course you live in Japan). Another example is to hire a local seamstress or gown designer to make your wedding gown or headpiece. Not everything that is beautiful and couture has to be flown in from other countries! Buying locally is a huge component in going green for your wedding.

Social Justice

The idea of giving back to the local and global community is sometimes missed by brides and grooms when it comes to their weddings. Just like buying locally, giving back locally or globally can really take your wedding to a whole darker shade of green. Why not give a donation to one of your favorite nonprofits (whether local or global) instead of giving away favors?

You could also make sure your caterer wraps up all the leftover food from your wedding for a local shelter. In most cases a caterer might not be able to do this due to liability reasons. However, if the caterer gives the food to you to give to the shelter, most shelters will gladly take what you have and will be able to manage the food in such a way that it will not be harmful to those who come and eat it. The biggest catch to this is that you have to have someone assigned to this project once your wedding is over. He will have to leave immediately afterward to take the food to the shelter. Find someone who is committed to doing this and you will know that very little was wasted on your wedding day.

Carbon Offsetting

An easy way to ease the tension of greening your wedding is carbon offsetting. While there is a little bit of controversy over this topic, it is still worth exploring. There are a few reputable carbon offsetting firms (like

Carbonfund.org Foundation and TerraPass) that have great wedding calculators. The calculators help you see how many metric tons of carbon dioxide your wedding will create. The idea is to help you to think about the amount of waste that you can reduce on your own and simply offset the rest by donating to help further reforestation efforts and alternative energies.

Research

There is simply nothing more valuable than just doing some plain old research and asking questions. If you are reading this chapter, you obviously care about the environment. So use the Internet to do a little research and ask your vendors about what they are doing to be proactive in the green department.

How to Find Green Vendors and Products for Your Wedding

The topic of going green for all aspects of living and working is gaining interest every day. Going green is no longer thought of as a trend, but more of a necessity as we continue to see how the waste that is being created by humans is affecting the earth. There are several organizations that are leading the way to help educate about how to go green. Here are few sources that can help you go green for your wedding day:

- **Eco-Beautiful Weddings (*www.eco-beautifulweddings.com*)**—the first magazine dedicated to eco-friendly weddings. A magazine along with a daily blog giving nothing but eco-friendly wedding ideas for weddings all over the world.
- **Elegance & Simplicity, Inc. (*www.eleganceandsimplicity.com*)**—a wedding planning firm based in Washington, D.C., that focuses on eco-friendly weddings around the world and also owns and operates Eco-Beautiful Weddings. The staff educates wedding professionals around the world on how to be eco-friendly wedding professionals.
- **Eco-Chic Weddings (*www.ecochicweddings.com*)**—a website (written and maintained by eco-author Emily Anderson) dedicated to eco-friendly weddings, registries, and living.

- **Tradesy (*www.tradesy.com*)**—a website dedicated to helping brides sell their used wedding gowns and educating couples about how to go green on their wedding day and after.
- **The Broke-Ass Bride (*www.thebrokeassbride.com*)**—funny and witty website all about creating eco-friendly weddings inexpensively (with lots of giveaways).
- **Green Bride Guide (*www.greenbrideguide.com*)**—another great vendor resource guide for budget-conscious green brides and grooms getting married in the United States. Created by eco-author Kate Harrison.
- *The Everything® Green Wedding Book* **by Wenona Napolitano**—a comprehensive and approachable source to lowering your wedding's carbon footprint.

The Green Checklist

Vendor/Item	Questions to Ask	Notes
Wedding Planner	Can they focus on helping you find green vendors in your area? Do they have experience planning eco-friendly weddings?	
Pre-Wedding Parties	Vendors involved in reducing waste, items to be reused and recycled? Will recycling and composting bins be available?	
Ceremony Location	Is it close to the reception site? Can the flowers be reused at the reception site?	
Wedding Jewelry	Can they be borrowed or rented? Are the materials used eco-friendly?	
Formalwear	Can you buy a used gown? Is there a consignment shop nearby? Where are the dresses or suits made? Does the tux rental location use PERC-Free cleaning agents?	
Accessories	Can you buy locally? Are the materials made from all natural fabrics or vintage/recycled materials?	
Gifts for Attendants	Are you buying them something that they will actually use after your wedding? Can you purchase something locally?	
Reception Site	Do they provide recycling bins? Do they compost? Can you have your ceremony there as well? Does the facility give back to the community through educational programs? Is the building historic? Is the building LEED certified?	
Paper Products	Can you go without programs and menus? Are tree-free, PCW, or FSC invitations available?	
Catering	Will they recycle? Do they compost? Where do all of their food items come from? Do they buy from local and sustainable producers/farmers?	

Vendor/Item	Questions to Ask	Notes
Photography	Is your photographer local? What kind of albums do they provide that are eco-friendly?	
Videography	What kind of packaging does the final product come in? Can copies be held online?	
Transportation	Pedicabs available? Buses equipped with propane gas tanks? Possibility of renting a hybrid or biodiesel powered vehicle?	
Cake	Can local and fresh ingredients be used? (Be sure to not add any food coloring or fondant.)	
Hotels	Are guest accommodations close to both the ceremony and reception sites? Does the hotel provide recycling bins in each room? Does the hotel have a green mission statement?	
Honeymoon	Any great eco-tourism packages available?	
Carbon Offsetting	Where is your donation being invested?	

PART III

Beyond the Wedding Day

CHAPTER 19

Post-Wedding To-Do List

So the wedding is over and all of the guests have gotten on the last shuttle back to the hotel. All you have to do now is hop on a plane to your honeymoon, right? Wrong! You really need to think and plan to make sure you are prepared for all the little things that will need to be taken care of once the wedding is over.

Thank-You Notes

As soon as the news of your engagement goes live to the world, you will need to run to the store and get some thank-you notes. You may have never been fond of the written word, but you will need to get used to it now. In some cases, an e-mail might work, but in most cases a handwritten note is appropriate and greatly appreciated. Not all thank-you notes need to be written on letterpress custom thank-you cards. You can always just have a few different types of thank-you notes handy and when it comes time to order your stationery for your wedding, throw in some thank-you notes as you are going to need them!

Thank-you notes should be sent right after you receive the gift. Whether you are getting gifts for a bridal shower or for the actual wedding, remember to sign with your maiden name before the wedding takes place. Always be sure to mention the gift and how you plan to use it in the thank-you note.

Dear Ann and Billy,

Thank you so much for the beautiful painting. We plan to hang it over the living-room fireplace for everyone to see. The colors really brighten up the room.

Fondly,
Ann Cooper

Dear Aunt Mary:

Thank you for the lovely wine glasses; they really round out our bar set. Jim and I are looking forward to your next visit, when you can have a drink with us.

Warmest regards,
Ann Cooper

Remember the gifts may start arriving as soon as you announce your engagement and may continue in a steady stream until one year after the wedding. The gift organizer in the back of this chapter helps you to keep a record of what you receive, from whom, and when. Organizing things this way will be a great help when you sit down to write those thank-you notes.

Rental Returns

Once you have planned every single detail of your wedding, you need to go back and comb through all of the contracts and see where and when rentals need to be returned. Following are a few of the most common items that will need to be returned.

- **Tuxes**—Typically tuxes will need to be returned by the first business day following your wedding day. Check your contract. If you have out-of-town attendants who are unable to return the tuxes, you will need to assign someone from your wedding party or family to be sure they are returned in a timely matter.
- **Linens**—Depending on how your reception site or caterer works, they should be taking care of the linen rental returns for you. However, if you have rented linens on your own, make sure you have assigned someone to pull all linens at the end of the night and give them clear directions on how to return the linens in a timely manner.
- **Décor**—As with all other rental items, check your floral design, cake, lighting, and décor contracts to see what you need to return. In most cases, they will come back and retrieve their rented items. If you are responsible for returning cake stands or vases, be sure you have assigned someone to gather and return them, as those items are easily misplaced and you will be responsible for the replacement cost.
- **Equipment**—As with other rentals, depending on the type of equipment you are renting, most equipment rental companies will come to retrieve their items. However, if you want to save money on delivery costs by picking up the chairs yourself, someone will need to return them afterward.

ALERT

Take note that many rental companies, no matter what you are renting, will charge more money if you return the items past their due dates. See the rental worksheet in the back of this chapter and give it to the person in charge at the end of the wedding.

Announcements

If you and your fiancé are like most couples, you will not be able to invite everyone on your original guest list. Business associates, friends and family living far away, and others may have been squeezed off the list due to budget or space constraints. Wedding announcements are a convenient way to let people know of your recent nuptials. They are not sent to anyone who received an invitation. (Note that people receiving announcements are under no obligation to buy you a gift.) Announcements should be mailed immediately after your wedding.

You and your fiancé should have them ready before you leave for your honeymoon, and your maid of honor or best man can mail them while you are gone.

Whoever was named on your invitation as the wedding's host should also be the person or persons announcing the marriage.

The traditional wording of announcements

> *Mr. and Mrs. Joseph Moran*
> *proudly announce*
> *the marriage of their daughter*
> *Margaret Ann*
> *and*
> *Mr. Justin James McCann*
> *on Saturday, the twelfth of July*
> *Two thousand and fourteen*
> *Holy Trinity Lutheran Church*
> *Chicago, Illinois*

The Dress: Preserve It, Donate It, or Sell It

When it comes to your dress, you typically have three options as to what to do with it after the wedding. If you plan to keep it for a future daughter, you will need to take it to a dress preservation specialist. Since it will need to be stored for years to come, you can't just go get it dry cleaned and keep it in a plastic bag. A dress preservation specialist will use acid-free tissue and boxes and fold the dress in such a manner that it will unfold easily out of the box. Find the best gown preservation specialist near you on the Association of Wedding Gown Specialists' website (*www.weddinggownspecialists.com*).

However, since a very small percentage of brides actually wear their mothers' gowns, you may want to consider donating your dress. Donating your dress is becoming easier and easier with several nonprofits popping up all over the place. The most popular is Brides Against Breast Cancer (*www.bridesagainstbreastcancer.org*), which is an organization that provides opportunities for metastatic breast cancer patients' dreams or wish fulfillment. You can also donate your dress to the Salvation Army, which can resell your dress to raise funds for its broad mission.

If you are strapped for cash and simply want to make more room in your closet, there are many ways to sell your dress. See if your area has a local bridal consignments shop. If not, there are several reputable online websites that will help you sell your gown (e.g., *www.tradesy.com* and *www.oncewed.com* or even eBay or craigslist). Just keep in mind that you will need to clean your dress or make any minor repairs to it in order for it to be wearable by another bride.

Keepsakes and Mementos

Once you come back from your honeymoon, you will be anxious to look at the video and the photography. However, there are lots of things that will be left over from the wedding that you might want to make sure you have samples of. Try to see if your parents or your attendants can remember to safeguard your guest book, a favor, programs, menus, your place cards and escort cards, invitation, Save the Date, announcement, and anything else that might help bring back memories from your day. Store them in an airtight box or find a way to scrapbook the items. You are creating history for your family and future generations. The photos and video are important to be able to visually maintain the memories of your day. These few precious extras are typically things people inadvertently throw away, but they cannot be replaced!

Gift Organizer

Name	Description of Gift	Thank-you note sent?
		☐
		☐
		☐
		☐
		☐
		☐
		☐
		☐
		☐
		☐
		☐
		☐
		☐
		☐
		☐
		☐
		☐
		☐
		☐
		☐
		☐
		☐
		☐
		☐
		☐

Rental Worksheet

Name of rental company: .... Address: ....

Telephone: .... Contact: ....

Hours: .... Order date: ....

Date: .... Time: .... ☐ Delivery? ☐ Pick up?

Special instructions: ....

Total amount due: .... Date: ....

Amount of deposit: .... Date: ....

Balance due: .... Date: ....

Cancellation policy: ....

Damaged goods policy: ....

Notes: ....

....

Item	Description	Quantity	Cost	Total Cost (Quantity x Cost)
Formalwear & Accessories:				
Bridal Gown Rental				
Tuxedos				
Jewelry Rentals				
Shoe Rentals				
Ceremony Equipment:				
Aisle runner				
Candelabra				
Canopy/Chuppah				
Lattice arch				
Microphone				
Other				

Rental Worksheet (continued)

Item	Description	Quantity	Cost	Total Cost (Quantity x Cost)
Tents:				
Size				
Size				
Flooring/Carpeting				
Lighting				
Decoration				
Other				
Chairs:				
Style				
Style				
Style				
Other				
Tables:				
Size				
Size				
Size				
Other				
Linens:				
Table				
Chair covers				
Napkins				
Other				

Rental Worksheet (continued)

Item	Description	Quantity	Cost	Total Cost (Quantity x Cost)
Dinnerware:				
Dinner plates				
Salad plates				
Bread plates				
Dessert plates				
Cake plates				
Soup bowls				
Fruit bowls				
Cups and saucers				
Other				
Flatware:				
Dinner forks				
Salad forks				
Dinner knives				
Steak knives				
Butter knives				
Spoons				
Soup spoons				
Serving spoons				
Meat forks				
Carving knives				
Cake serving set				
Other				
Glassware:				
Wine glasses				
Champagne glasses				
Water goblets				

Rental Worksheet (continued)

Item	Description	Quantity	Cost	Total Cost (Quantity x Cost)
Glassware (cont):				
Highball glasses				
Double rocks glasses				
Snifters				
16 oz. glasses				
8 oz. glasses				
Punch cups				
Other				
Bar Equipment:				
Ice buckets				
Ice tubs				
Bottle/can openers				
Corkscrews				
Cocktail shakers				
Stirring sticks				
Electric blenders				
Strainers				
Cocktail napkins				
Other				
Serving pieces:				
Serving trays				
Platters				
Serving bowls				
Punch bowls				
Water pitchers				
Salt and pepper sets				

Rental Worksheet (continued)

Item	Description	Quantity	Cost	Total Cost (Quantity x Cost)
Serving pieces:				
Butter dishes				
Creamer/sugar sets				
Bread baskets				
Condiment trays				
Other				
Miscellaneous:				
Coffeemaker				
Insulated coffee pitchers				
Hot plates				
Microwaves				
Grill				
Coolers				
Coat racks				
Hangers				
Ashtrays				
Trash cans				
Other				

Total of All Expenses:

CHAPTER 20

Your Honeymoon

After all of the planning, coordinating, organizing, worry, and stress that is involved in getting married, you will be more than ready to just take a break from it all! When it's all over with, you'll need more than just an ordinary vacation to recuperate. Your honeymoon is the perfect occasion to plan the vacation of your dreams.

History of the Honeymoon

The term *honeymoon* comes from ancient times. Teutonic couples would marry beneath a full moon, and then drink honey wine for thirty days after; hence the name. Too bad today's honeymoons rarely last for thirty days!

Now many see the honeymoon beginning when the bride is carried over the threshold. This wedding custom originated in Italy. The bride had to be carried across the threshold because she was (or pretended to be) reluctant to enter the bridal chamber.

Anyway you see it, once you are married, you are considered newly-weds for a year and you should consider planning some time to get away!

Planning the Getaway

On the surface, a honeymoon is no different from any other vacation. You pack your bags, make your reservations, and leave home for fun in the sun, snow, or wherever. But to a pair of newlyweds, a honeymoon is much more than that—it's the first getaway together as a married couple and the ultimate romantic experience. Whether it ends up being the best vacation or not, your honeymoon will most likely have more staying power in your memory than any other vacation you end up having. While you can't get a guarantee on perfection, you can eliminate a lot of potential problems by planning carefully—and early.

Where Are You Going?

You might have your honeymoon all planned out in your head right now. However, your fiancé might have vastly different ideas. First, you'll need to pinpoint what you both expect from this trip. Make a pact that you can each insist on the inclusion of *one* activity (other than snuggling up to each other, that is).

And if this doesn't help, you'll either have to plan a two-part honeymoon (where you'll spend the first part of the week on the beach and the second part of it in Nepal), or, more realistically, you'll have to find a happy compromise. Maybe you could forgo Everest in favor of hiking up a mountain in Hawaii.

ALERT

> Honeymoon or not, everyone has their limits. You don't want your honeymoon to be marred by an argument over who's calling all the shots. Make sure whatever you're planning is going to keep *both* of you entertained for the entire vacation.

Fair and Square

Keep in mind that the activities you're planning should be enjoyable to both of you. Many couples plan their honeymoons by saying, "Whatever you want is fine with me," until one partner takes that ball and runs with it. The ensuing honeymoon turns out to be filled with activities that the planner finds interesting. And even though he may have genuinely thought that his spouse would enjoy the various outings, the nonplanner ends up bored or annoyed instead.

It's fair to expect a certain amount of compromise on your honeymoon. For example, you might want to introduce your wife to waterskiing, a sport you mastered long ago. But you can't expect your spouse to spend the entire week giving in to your every demand. Likewise, if you really despise museums and your new husband loves to spend the day looking at abstract art, you might agree to accompany him for a day or two, but after that, chances are you'd be bored and a little miffed.

Money Talks

Ultimately, of course, your budget will have a big influence on your choice of destination. Consult a travel agent or the Internet to find low-priced airfares, reduced-rate package deals, and other ways to save money. You may be pleasantly surprised. Check out the following websites for tips and advice on planning your honeymoon:

- *www.honeymoons.com*
- *www.unforgettablehoneymoons.com*

Perhaps you can afford a trip to Hawaii by staying at a less-than-four-star hotel, or travel Europe via hostels and bed and breakfasts. Remember, however, to confirm that *inexpensive* lodging does not mean: without running water, dilapidated, or situated in the red-light district (though all of these situations, in their own way, may add some excitement to your trip). A few websites that give great advice from other fellow travelers, experts, and honeymooners are:

- *www.tripadvisor.com*
- *www.frommers.com*
- *www.smartertravel.com*

Some couples choose to postpone the trip for several months, either for financial reasons or because one partner just can't get the vacation time from work right after the wedding. If you're still in the early stages of planning your wedding and you just know that you won't be able to afford any sort of honeymoon, your travel agent might be able to help you by setting up a honeymoon registry.

ESSENTIAL

A honeymoon registry is similar to a gift registry, but instead of buying you pots and pans, your friends and family make monetary contributions to your vacation fund. Some agents can even set up a website for your registry, which makes things infinitely easier on everyone concerned.

A few ways to save money and still have a honeymoon are the following:

- **Staycations**—If you don't have a dime to your name after the wedding, you can always stay at home and have a staycation. Yes, that means staying at home and going to the local places that you always wanted to check out, but never have. For example, if you live in New York but have never been to the Empire State Building or the Statue of Liberty, make a plan to do so during your staycation. There are all sorts of things you can do on your staycation. Start new traditions of cooking together or maybe a new hobby together. Go hiking on your local trail, or simply rent all of your favorite movies and eat ice cream in bed together!

- **Off-season**—Traveling during the off-season is the best time to save money. If you are getting married during high-peak season, there is nothing wrong with postponing your honeymoon for a few months to save money.
- **Weekend getaways**—Don't get trapped into thinking that your honeymoon has to be two weeks in order for it to be your honeymoon. Just being together and away from the masses for a few days is enough to be called your honeymoon. One day, when you are rolling in the dough, you can get away for two weeks for your dream vacation. Your honeymoon can be a bed and breakfast weekend getaway or a fun weekend at a quiet mountain cabin. Just the two of you and a bottle of champagne is all you need!

Honeymoon Hot Spots

Are you at a complete loss as far as picking a destination is concerned? Here are some of the most popular spots for newlyweds:

- **The Caribbean**—Punta Cana or Playa Dorada, Dominican Republic; Palm Beach, Aruba; Grand Cayman, Cayman Islands; Grace Bay Beach, Turks and Caicos; Shoal Bay, Anguilla; Gold Coast, Barbados; Negril, Jamaica; St. Croix; Nassau, Bahamas; Diamond Beach, Martinique; Luquillo Beach, Puerto Rico; Tortola, British Virgin Islands; Grand Anse Beach, Grenada; St. Jean Beach, St. Barthelemy; St. Maarten/St. Martin; Canouan, The Grenadines; Pigeon Point, Tobago; and Trunk Bay, St. John.
- **Mexico**—Los Cabos, Baja California, Isla de Cozumel, Cancun, Puerto Vallarta, Ixtapa Guadalajara, and Tulum, Maya Riviera.
- **South Pacific**—The Marquesas and Tahiti.
- **Europe**—Greece, Spain, Ireland, Switzerland, England, France, Italy, Monaco, and Germany.
- **United States**—Alaska, Hawaii, Grand Canyon National Park, Disneyland or Walt Disney World, Cape Cod, Martha's Vineyard, and Nantucket.

Of course, this list only scratches the surface. You have the entire globe to choose from, every state, every country, every region—and, by definition, anywhere newlyweds choose to vacation is a honeymoon spot. The main thing is to find a place that you both love, as it will be in your memories for the rest of your lives!

FACT

You shouldn't feel pressured into choosing a spot because everyone else goes there, nor should you shy away from a place because you don't want to follow the crowd. You want to go to St. Louis and see the Gateway Arch on your honeymoon? Go for it.

Once you and your fiancé agree on where you'd like to spend your honeymoon, you should start making your reservations, either through your travel agent or by scouting out the Internet travel sites. Some of the resorts in the more popular tourist and honeymoon spots can be booked solid up to a year in advance, so start as early as you can—especially if you've got your heart set on a particular location.

Book It!

Perhaps you're used to handling your vacation arrangements by yourself, without anyone's help. Or maybe you have a great travel agent and you'd never make a move without him or her. No matter which method you prefer, make sure you start early enough so that you can book the hotels, activities, and flights that you want.

Making Your Own Arrangements

If you're making your own travel arrangements and you're taking off soon after your wedding, don't forget that your plane tickets should be booked in your maiden name. You'll need a valid photo ID to board your flight, and the name on the ID must match the name on your ticket.

Also, if you're taking off immediately following the reception (or the morning after), try to arrange for smooth travel connections. As you're looking at tickets online, an eight-hour layover may seem like a bit of a hassle, but you may think you're willing to accept it for the sake of saving a few hundred bucks. But keep in mind that you're likely to be exhausted and anxious to get on with the honeymoon—and a long layover (or a series of them) on the day after your wedding might get your trip off on the wrong foot. Fatigue can breed irritability and forgetfulness. Add the stress of travel to that, and you have the recipe for potential disaster.

ALERT

If either of you is generally not a good traveler, you might want to keep things as close to home as possible. You could find a nice resort that's within driving distance, for example, instead of hopping flight after flight (which will only add to any travel-related misery).

Even if you get to your destination without mishap, you certainly don't want to risk bickering with your spouse your first full day as a married couple. Moods could swing, tears may be shed, and you'll lose almost an entire day to travel in the process.

If possible, try to get at least six hours of sleep the night before you take off. You may not wake up totally refreshed (given that weddings have a way of making you feel like you've run a marathon), but you'll be better off than if you only slept for two hours. Make some time for a long hot shower and a hearty breakfast, and you should have a good start to the first day of your honeymoon.

Using Travel Agents

Maybe you scoff at the very idea of travel agents, reasoning that you can do all of this yourself. If you're going out of the country, however, you might benefit from working with an agent who can enlighten you as to the finer points of international travel. Because foreign vacations can get very complicated—with connecting flights that have to meet boats that have to meet trains—putting all the responsibility into the lap of a trained professional might be a good idea. After all, you've already got enough to think about with planning the wedding.

Your agent will be able to tell you which paperwork, identification, and other necessities you will need in order to travel abroad. With the exception of visits to some parts of the Caribbean (from the United States), you'll need a passport, which takes at least six weeks (and sometimes longer) to obtain. (More on passports in the next section of this chapter.)

Documents you will need to track down if you're planning on leaving the country include:

- Birth certificate
- Driver's license (or other picture ID)
- Proof of marriage
- Proof of citizenship

Travel agents are also on the ball as far as alerting you to potential troubles. You might not want to risk traveling to a spot during its rainy season. Or you might find out from your agent, who's in the know, that your four-star resort is planning on adding another entire wing during your stay, which will add up to lots of round-the-clock noise. This would be enough to make you want to stay across town. Nowadays, some foreign countries post travel alerts for U.S. citizens, which you'll obviously want to know about before you attempt to board a plane to a restricted or dangerous area.

Of course, you can find this information on your own, but it will take a considerable amount of time to research the things that your travel agent already knows. Just consider whether the time it will take is worth it, or if it could be better spent focusing on the wedding itself.

If there was ever a time to consult a travel agent—this is it! Most travel agencies are not as expensive as you think and it is usually best to try to find a travel agency that specializes in honeymoons. Remember, in the end, when you pay a professional to take care of a major investment item (your honeymoon), you usually end up saving money. Travel agencies know the ins and outs of travel and will be alerted to deals. In fact, some resorts only release deals to certain travel agencies. Have an open mind and you might discover more things you can do on your honeymoon with a travel agency.

Passports

Passports are relatively easy to obtain. You'll need to give yourself a minimum of six weeks, but you should really start the process as soon as you can to avoid any last-minute problems. It is possible to pay extra for expedited service, which generally takes about two weeks.

Your first step is to fill out an application, which can be found online at *www.state.gov/travel*. If you're applying for the first time, you'll have to take the application to a passport agency or a passport acceptance facility. This isn't as hard as it sounds—many of these facilities are located inside larger post offices, some libraries, and county offices. You'll bring proof of U.S. citizenship (your birth certificate or naturalization certificate will do); a photo ID (such as a valid driver's license or government ID); two passport photos (unless the post office where you are going does that for you); your Social Security number; and money (check the website for current fees).

Travel Tips

If you're leaving town, as most honeymooners do, you may be entering foreign territory—literally or not. Even if you're not leaving the country, if you're visiting a place you've never been to, it might feel as though you've been transported to another planet. Here is some advice on how to take care of yourselves in strange surroundings.

Do Your Homework

Before you take off on any vacation, you should acquaint yourself with the area you're traveling to. If you're going to Chicago, for example, you might not need to rent a car, because public transportation is around every corner, and you'll never find a parking spot, anyway. If you're headed to New York City, you'd better start studying the subway system, unless you want to drop a fortune in cab fare. If you're going to land in a foreign airport, get yourself a map of its layout so that you'll know where to find the baggage claim and where you'll have to go to grab a taxi.

Do your research before you leave for your vacation. You can always buy maps in any city you visit, but if you *look* like a lost tourist—and you will if you're walking and reading that map—you're an easy mark for a pickpocket or a less-than-honest merchant. Avoid the additional stress, and review the maps before you go.

Know what kind of weather to expect. You're headed to the Caribbean, and you think that all you're going to need is a bikini and some sunscreen, right? But if you're vacationing during hurricane season, you might want to bring a raincoat . . . *and* inquire as to your resort's money-back guarantee. Beware that if you are on the ocean, it might get chilly some nights as well.

If you're headed to an all-inclusive resort, find out what that means, *exactly*. Have you paid for your lodging and food only? Are water sports and entertainment included? What about gratuities? Alcohol? Do you have to shell out for transportation to and from the airport?

You'll also want to research whether you'll need any vaccinations before traveling abroad, and you should try to work in a physical and dental checkup before you take off. Get yourself a good travel guide for any region you'll be traveling through. These books are updated constantly and offer some of the best, most realistic information on foreign travel.

Better Safe Than Sorry

There will be no lecture on the use of credit cards during the course of your honeymoon. It's actually safer to use your credit cards (or traveler's checks) than to carry around huge wads of cash. The regular stipulations apply. Don't go wild charging everything just because you're on vacation, and keep track of how much you're spending. Be aware that you will need some cash, however, if you're planning on hitting the smaller inns and restaurants in foreign countries, many of which operate on a cash-only basis. Wear a money belt for the safekeeping of your money.

Confirm your hotel reservations the week before you leave. There's nothing quite like dragging all your heavy luggage into a hotel lobby in some exotic locale, dreaming of a nice, long nap—only to find that you don't have a room (and there's not a vacant room on the island). If the room you thought you booked isn't the room you're being given, speak up. Ask for the manager on duty, and don't take "no" for an answer. Once you arrive at your hotel, don't be afraid to tell the management if the service or accommodations are not to your satisfaction. And *don't* wait until you're leaving. Most reputable hotels will go out of their way to rectify any problems as soon as possible, whether that means having your room cleaned again (the right way), or moving you to another room if possible, one that's not right next to the vending machines.

FACT

Packing for your honeymoon will likely overlap with last-minute wedding stuff. Even if you're not the type of girl who packs a week before a trip, make an exception this time. That might mean buying things like brand-new toiletries specifically for the trip, instead of packing things you already have and will need during the week before your wedding—like lotion and shampoo.

Gratuities

It's raining tips! Or so you would think, especially if you've ever sat in the lobby of a grand hotel, watching the bellboy and the doorman collect their rewards; or gone to a fancy restaurant, where seemingly every employee has his or her hand out. Who gets tipped, why, and how much? In some situations you can ask your companions at the dining table in a hotel or on shipboard, or the management. However, it's *always* best to be armed with the knowledge before you're faced with a sticky situation and want to avoid any awkwardness.

On Cruises

Your cruise line will probably provide you with tipping guidelines, but you should know what you're in for. The room steward cleans your cabin, makes the bed, supplies towels, soap, ice, and room service. Some people like to tip on the first day, "**t**o **e**nsure **p**erfect **s**ervice"—a slogan said to be the origin of the word *tips*.

Dining room waiters are generally tipped. The maître d' is the head-waiter in charge of the dining room. No tip is necessary unless he has handled special requests for you. As for bartenders, wine stewards, pool and deck attendants, and so on, check the bar bill. On almost all ships, a service charge is automatically added, making a tip unnecessary. Other service personnel should be tipped when the service is given, at the same rate as for service ashore, usually 15 percent.

ESSENTIAL

At the airport, tip the porter when you check in at the curb or have bags taken to check-in for you. If he goes way out of his way for you—like if you're cutting things close and he points out to you that you don't have to wait in that long line at the ticket counter, which you had every intention of doing—give him a little extra.

Some cruise lines advertise a no-tip policy. People still tip for special service on such ships, but it is not necessary if you do not ask for anything above and beyond. Doing a little research online before you leave is always a must to see what the going rate is for tipping on cruises.

At Hotels

Bellboys get tipped per bag and for hospitable gestures (turning on lights, opening windows). If you send the bellboy on an errand, tip him extra. In most major cities, the doorman gets tipped for hailing a cab, and for helping you out with your incredibly heavy suitcases or shopping bags.

Chambermaids are tipped for each service, and you should try to leave the tip every day. You may not have the same maid for the entire week. Room service is pricey: you'll tip 15 to 20 percent of the bill in addition to a room service charge. But *check the bill* to make sure that the gratuity hasn't already been added in.

Valets get tipped for retrieving your vehicle. The concierge is tipped if he provides you with special service (for instance, books tickets for a show or makes dinner reservations).

In Restaurants

The headwaiter (or maître d') is a tricky little character. While he basically plays the role of host, he's in full control of the dining room. How much you tip him depends on how badly you want to eat in this particular restaurant, where you want to sit, and how long you want to wait. It's not unusual for headwaiters to receive $50–$100 tips at the best restaurants in the biggest cities. For guidance on the norms in the particular area you're staying in, ask your hotel concierge.

Wine stewards are tipped 15 to 20 percent of the wine bill. Your server is tipped 15 to 20 percent of the food bill (as long as the gratuity hasn't already been included). Buffet servers are tipped as long as the service (clean plates, drinks, etc.) was decent.

ALERT

Remember, these are only guidelines for good service. Keep in mind that people in the service industry are sometimes paid less than minimum wage and depend on tips. However, if you get lousy service *anywhere*, you're not obligated to reward the person who provided it.

Note that in a foreign country, the amount of the tip should be calculated in the local currency. It may be less or more than you would tip in dollars, depending on the exchange rate. And in many foreign countries, the gratuity is added into the bill.

The more you plan out your honeymoon in advance, the more relaxing it will be. Book a travel agent or do the research ahead of time and avoid stress while honeymooning!

The Honeymoon Checklist

Item	Description	Projected Cost	Actual Cost	Balance Due
Transportation:				
Airfare				
Car rental				
Moped rental				
Bike rental				
Train pass				
Taxi				
Parking fees				
Other				
Accommodations:				
Wedding night				
Honeymoon destination				
Other				
Food				
Meal plan				
Meals				
Drinks				
Entertainment:				
Souvenirs				
Spending money				
Tips				
Other				

Total:

Travel Services Worksheet

Travel Agency:

Address: _____ Telephone: _____

Fax number: _____ Contact: _____

Hours: _____ Directions: _____

Notes: _____

_____

_____

Car Rental Agency:

Address: _____ Telephone: _____

Fax number: _____ Contact: _____

Hours: _____

Description of reserved vehicle (make/model): _____

Terms: _____

Notes: _____

_____

Transportation:

Destination:	Destination:
Carrier:	Carrier:
Flight/Route:	Flight/Route:
Departure date:	Departure date:
Time:	Time:
Arrival date:	Arrival date:
Time:	Time:
Confirmation number:	Confirmation number:
Date:	Date:
Notes:	Notes:

Travel Services Worksheet (continued)

Accommodations:

Hotel: _____ Address: _____

Telephone: _____ Fax number: _____

Check-in date: _____ Time: _____

Check-out date: _____ Time: _____

Type of room: _____ Daily rate: _____

Total cost: _____ Confirmation number: _____

Date: _____

Notes: _____

Hotel: _____ Address: _____

Telephone: _____ Fax number: _____

Check-in date: _____ Time: _____

Check-out date: _____ Time: _____

Type of room: _____ Daily rate: _____

Total cost: _____ Confirmation number: _____

Date: _____

Notes: _____

Hotel: _____ Address: _____

Telephone: _____ Fax number: _____

Check-in date: _____ Time: _____

Check-out date: _____ Time: _____

Type of room: _____ Daily rate: _____

Total cost: _____ Confirmation number: _____

Date: _____

Notes: _____

CHAPTER 21

The Married Life

The idea of moving in together sounds so wonderful, and you probably can't wait. But there are a lot of things to take into consideration when you start planning this part of your future. You'll need to have a sound financial plan (and a knack for compromise) in order to make a smooth transition. Then there are the pesky legalities of regular life that need attention and should not be ignored.

Changing Your Name

Now that you are back from your honeymoon, the time has come to take care of that little legality of changing your name. But you might not want to change your name. If you do decide to change your name, be sure to check out Chapter 5 to learn all the ins and outs of changing your last name.

ESSENTIAL

If you are having trouble getting your name changed or you simply do not have the time, there are a few services that can get the job done for you. One of the easiest ways is through Name Change Express (*www .namechangeexpress.com*). Last case scenario: get help from your lawyer.

Wait until you've received a copy of your marriage license before you attempt to change your name on any accounts or documents. In many instances (when changing your name on bank accounts, for example), you'll need proof that you are who you say you are, and your marriage license is confirmation of your new title.

Post Office and Paperwork

If one of you ends up moving to the other's home after you are married, you will have to deal with changing your address at the post office immediately. You might even want to consider doing this before the wedding. This way you can live your life as normally as possible after the honeymoon without worrying if all your bills (and wedding gifts) are coming to your new home on time.

The best place to start is the U.S. Postal Service's website (*https:// moversguide.usps.com*). All of the information you need to change your address should be found there. You should allow the post office at least two weeks for the address change to take effect. Make sure you check out the worksheet at the end of the chapter for more details.

As in all life changes, you will need to inform your employers, insurance agents, and other relevant agencies about your marriage. It could actually save you money. Depending on the type of health insurance you have, combining the policies will most likely save you money—especially if you had an individual policy prior to getting married and his or your company provides it for a minimal monthly fee. Same thing goes for car insurance—combining your car insurance policies will most likely at least save you time and leave things less complicated (who wants two car insurance bills?). You will not only be sharing the same bed now, you will also be sharing the same living space and bills. Make sure you are on the same page and start planning and preparing yourself for all the paperwork you will need to fill out.

Children and Family Concerns

Some women who keep their maiden names will still choose to use their husband's surname for their children. If you're losing sleep worrying that your child will be ostracized in elementary school because of *your* decision to keep your maiden name, find something else to stress over. It's not an uncommon occurrence these days for kids to have different surnames from their parents, for a variety of reasons. Chances are whatever decision you make about your surname and your kids' surnames won't seem all that unusual when they enter school.

If you already have children from a previous marriage, the hope is that you have discussed your impending marriage with your child and possible ex-spouse and extended family. If you haven't, you really should. Some couples find it necessary to plan for family counseling as their family is now a combination of two families coming together. Although this may sound and feel wonderful to you, some children feel scared and are not capable of fully understanding what is about to happen. Be prepared for this and take a proactive stance for your child before problems begin after your marriage.

Family blending can either be extremely stressful or just a simple adjustment depending on the families that are blending and the circumstances. A few websites and books with incredible insight are:

- Blended-Families (*www.blended-families.com*) is a great resource that comes from Emily Bouchard's three books
- *Happily Remarried: Making Decisions Together Blending Families Successfully* by David Frisbie and Lisa Frisbie
- *The Smart Step-Family: Seven Steps to a Healthy Family* by Ron L. Deal

After you have found ways to work on blending your family, the next clear issue you will come up against is how to handle family members who constantly give you unwanted advice or interfere with the decisions or plans that you and your new spouse make. First and foremost, you and your new spouse will have to present a united front on how you want to tackle this issue. You will need to pick your battles, and the ones you choose to fight will have to be handled tactfully and simply. The simplest way to nip unwanted advice in the bud is to say: "I really appreciate the advice you are giving, but my husband and I are working through this issue and we will find the best way for us to resolve it on our own. Once we have reached a decision, we will be sure to let you know. Thanks for the help though!" There are all sorts of ways to tactfully tell someone you are not looking for their advice—some of it will work, some of it won't. The most important thing is to stick to your guns and know that you and your spouse are on the same page. If the two of you are not on the same page, it is a recipe for disaster. Communication (as in all things) is key!

Your New Home and Budget

Moving into a new home is a huge expense, whether you're renting or buying. Buying is usually technically a bigger expense, but if you're having trouble coming up with the rent for a dirt-cheap apartment, it feels the same either way. To make things easier on yourselves in the long run, make sure you know what you can afford. Lay out your budget *before* you go house hunting, and don't expect to find the perfect place on your first day. Finding the right place can be an emotionally draining and time consuming process.

Setting Up Your Budget

You'll be combining your income with someone else's in a joint budget, which may be the first time you've ever shared your income and spending. What this means, in plain English, is that you need to know how much money your fiancé is earning. Maybe the subject has never come up. Or maybe you've been afraid to ask—whatever the reason, if you don't have a clear idea of what this person's net pay is at the end of each week, now's the time to find out.

If you're like most people, though, you probably already have a good idea of how much your fiancé brings home each paycheck. But do you know how he *budgets* his money? That may be the trickier part of the picture. And on the flip side, have you relayed how you spend your earnings each month? Make a date to sit down with your fiancé and talk frankly about how you might go about setting up a budget you both can live with.

ESSENTIAL

You'll also want to discuss the use of credit cards. There's nothing scarier than assuming you're in the black, only to see a lot of numbers (and a few commas) in the "balance due" box on your credit card statement.

When setting up the budget, you'll add your paychecks together, plus any other regular source of income, and then subtract the following expenses:

- Rent/mortgage
- Utilities (electric, heat, phone, cable, water, and so on)
- Food
- Debts (student loans, car payments, credit cards, and so on)
- Insurance (car and/or homeowners')
- Other expenses (child support, commuting expenses, home business expenses, and so on)

The balance you end up with should not have a minus sign in front of it. If it does, you're paying out too much, and you need to find someplace to cut back. What this means for you in terms of housing is that you should not take on a bigger rent or mortgage payment—or one that will increase the cost of your living expenses—if you can't pay the bills you have now.

Dealing with the Budget

If you're moving into a new place, you'll want to ask if any utilities are included in the rent, and take it from there. If you're moving into an apartment in an old house, you might want to ask the other tenants what they typically pay for heat (the insulation might not be up to par) and air conditioning. You'll be able to get some idea of what a new apartment is really going to cost you in the end. To be on the safe side, consider padding the amounts when estimating your budgetary needs.

QUESTION

How much should you be spending on the rent or on a mortgage?
As a rule of thumb, the amount you spend monthly for rent or a mortgage should not exceed 33 percent of your total income (totaling both paychecks). Some estimates go as high as 36 percent—any more than that is too much.

Spending more than one-third of your income on housing is risky. Sure, you'll have a beautiful home, but if you can't afford to furnish it (or eat, for that matter), it will lose its luster in your eyes very quickly. The danger of buying more house than you can reasonably afford intensifies if one partner loses his or her job. This is exactly the way in which many people find themselves dealing with foreclosures and stressing their marriages at the same time.

Living Together

If you're lucky, you or your fiancé already lives in a place that's large enough for two and that both of you love. That certainly makes your life a lot easier, at least until the two of you decide that you need more room, or that you'd like to be in a different neighborhood, or until some other reason for moving creeps into the picture. But if you're like many couples, you'll want to (or have to) start fresh. One of the first decisions facing you will be where you want to live.

Your vision of married bliss may be a cozy little house in the country, hours from the bustling city. But what if your job means commuting back into the bustle five days a week? Chances are, you'd rather spend time with your new spouse than on the road between your office and your home. Likewise, if it's your spouse who's doing the commuting, you don't want to be stuck at home drumming your fingers on the table as you wait for him to finally walk through the door. Unless you simply can't live without that country house, you'll be better off searching for a place that's more convenient to both your workplaces—and saving that dream home for a time in your life when commuting isn't as big an issue (or when kids suddenly *are*).

Research the Area

When choosing a place to live, you'll want to be sure it has at least some of the amenities that are important to your and your partner's daily life. If you like a good game of tennis on the weekends, make sure there are public tennis courts available. Maybe you're a gourmet cook who needs ingredients found only in specialty markets. If so, then the typical supermarket chain probably won't suit you. Do you need a place where you can easily launch your boat? Make sure there's water nearby.

Once you've decided what your town or neighborhood must have, drive through a few possibilities to check them out more thoroughly. Park the car in the downtown area and take a stroll to get a feel for the place. Strike up a conversation with the person who serves your coffee. Pick up a copy of the local paper. Time the commute from the town center to your office.

ESSENTIAL

If you know someone who lives in a town you're considering, pump him or her for information. Do they like what the town has to offer? What are the pluses and minuses? How long have they lived there? Does the community have several housing options to choose from?

Your Home!

Determining the type of housing you should be looking at usually comes down to two factors: money and time. Generally speaking, apartments are the least expensive option and the easiest to find. Go through the apartment listings in the paper and make some calls to set up appointments to check them out. First and last month's rent plus a security deposit are the standard upfront financial requirements. You hand over a check, sign some papers, and move in. Unless you choose the most luxurious apartment in the ritziest part of town, chances are your monthly rental costs will be less than any mortgage you would pay for a house or condo.

Condominiums and houses are more expensive for several reasons. First, in order to purchase one you might need to come up with a down payment (usually 20 percent of the total cost). On top of that, there are other fees to pay when the final paperwork is processed, at the closing—fees that will likely run into the thousands of dollars. (You will need to hire a real estate agent or lawyer, for one thing, who will pretty much sit back during the closing and tell you to write all sorts of checks to people and agencies you've never heard of, and will never hear *from*, and then you'll write *her* a check to top it all off.) Finally, monthly mortgage payments are generally higher than rent. For newlyweds, these costs can be prohibitive, often making a nice apartment more attractive than a house or a condo in the early years of marriage.

FACT

Since condos and houses are more permanent residences than apartments, you'll want to spend time finding the perfect place. That can take as little as a week (if you're extremely lucky) or as long as a year, depending on what's available on the market and on your personal preferences.

Prioritize

Once you've decided what fits your budget, you'll have a narrowed down list of possible homes to choose from. You'll be faced with some decisions, which may mean that you'll have to make some big concessions.

How many rooms do you need? Must you have cathedral ceilings? Do you or your husband need an at-home office? What about a gourmet kitchen? A first-floor laundry room?

If you're on a tight budget, you may ultimately have to decide on the *one* most important feature of prospective homes, whether it's space, style, or convenience. It's best to have relatively meager expectations of your first home or apartment when you're pinching pennies.

If you have a slightly larger budget to work with, your house needs will be determined more by your lifestyles and personalities. If you like to entertain, for example, you'll be on the lookout for a home with a spacious kitchen and dining room. You might opt for a place with a spare bedroom if you hope to have frequent overnight guests or need a separate office space. And everyone has heard stories of how fights for closet and bathroom-counter space have ruined relationships. If you're concerned you and your spouse will fall into this category, go for the place with the walk-in closets and the bath and a half.

In the end, you might have to give up a few wish-list items in order to find a good place to start your future together. But if you're armed with a solid idea of what both of you really must have, you can save yourself time and aggravation as you search.

ESSENTIAL

Don't forget to include your outdoor expectations in the list. If you love to barbecue, you'll want to be sure you have a place to do it. Two cars might not need a garage, but they will need parking. And if you love gardening, you probably won't be satisfied with just a window box or two.

The Timing

If parental reaction isn't an issue for you, the time that the two of you choose to move in together depends on what's most practical. The most logical time to move is when your current living arrangements need to change.

For instance, if your lease is up, and it makes more sense to move than to renew it; your roommate is leaving, and you don't want to look for a new one; or you just have to move out of your parents' house now because they're driving you crazy.

Unless you and your fiancé are both faced with these decisions at the same time, you'll need to coordinate your move carefully. It would be expensive and wasteful to be paying for your new apartment together if you still have to pay rent on an old place where you couldn't get out of the lease. If that's what you're faced with, ask your current rental agent if he or she would consider letting you sublet your apartment. It will be up to you to find a suitable tenant, and any problems that tenant causes become *your* problems.

Or, if your lease is up, see if you can remain in your apartment on a month-to-month basis until you're ready to move.

You Already Live Together

It may be that you and your fiancé have been living together, or will be living together for some time before the wedding. This can make certain aspects of the wedding planning a lot less complicated.

If you're coordinating the bulk of the wedding yourself, you can have RSVPs mailed to you instead of your parents. Your gifts will be transported from your shower(s) directly into your home, and you won't have to worry about having to pack and move right after the honeymoon.

Living at the same address for a period of time before the wedding means you and your partner have a better understanding of each other's finances. You won't have to set up billing procedures for your utilities or cable or figure out a system for paying those bills. With the potential tension surrounding the planning of a wedding, not having to deal with the mundane tasks of everyday life can be really nice.

Distance Makes the Heart Grow Fonder

While living together before the wedding does have its practical side, many couples prefer to stick with tradition. They don't want to experience what it's like to be married before they've taken their vows. For these couples, the excitement and romance of the first night in their new home (and starting the budgeting and buying furniture) is a continuation of the excitement and romance of the pre-wedding season.

FACT

Give yourself plenty of time to prepare for the big move. You don't want to end up leaving your apartment in a huge rush because you waited until after the wedding to start packing. You'll never find anything in those boxes if they aren't labeled accurately and packed carefully.

Waiting until you are officially husband and wife can be a wonderfully romantic way to go. If this is your decision, you'll just be on a time-delay behind the couples that have chosen to set up house before the wedding. Getting yourselves organized is key here. You'll be moving (presumably) right after the honeymoon, which means that you'll likely be packing as you're preparing for your wedding day and your vacation.

Home Sweet Home

Whether you're moving in together before the wedding or waiting until the ink is dry on the marriage license, learning to live with someone else can be a rocky transition. If you're finding, suddenly, that your fiancé (or new spouse) has some questionable hygiene rituals or that he is obsessive-compulsive about where the condiments can be placed in the refrigerator ("they go on the door, not on the big shelves!"), you might be wondering what the heck you've gotten yourself into. How could you have agreed to spend all of eternity with this person?

This is one thing that many newlyweds (or new roommates) don't talk about. To admit that the bloom is off the rose, so to speak, would be lessening your relationship in the eyes of others. You definitely don't want anyone to think that what you and your guy have is anything less than perfect, right?

You'd probably be surprised at how many of your friends feel the same way. One day, someone will admit to a little something (that her husband hogs the entire bed every night, for example, and that she doesn't find it the least bit endearing), and the floodgates will be opened.

Be Honest with Each Other

The worst thing you can do, if your partner has a habit that really, truly irritates you, is to pretend that you love it. Chances are a hundred to one that by suppressing your true feelings, you're setting yourself up for a big blowout one day down the road. If you want him to pick up his own socks and put them into the laundry basket, ask him to do it. If you don't want her long hair in the bathroom sink, tell her. If your spouse is unaware that it bothers you, how will they have a chance to honor you and change it?

Division of Domestic Duties

Once you move in together you will need to take the time to figure out maintenance and chore duties.

Things you'll be faced with include the following:

- Maintenance (anything from clogged sinks to painting to cleaning the gutters)
- Everyday cleaning
- Laundry
- Cooking
- Grocery shopping
- Childcare

Ask anyone who runs a household on their own if it's possible for one person to successfully tackle all of these items without help. It isn't.

Nor should one spouse be expected to make the attempt to do everything on his or her own. You're *partners* now, for better or for worse, for home repairs or for grocery shopping.

How can you find a middle ground and ask for the things you want without somehow crossing the line into nagging territory? Just remember this: There's a right way to ask for something and a wrong way. You don't need to address your mate as though she is a six-year-old (even if she's acting like one). Treat her with the same respect you'd expect.

There's no right way to divide chores. Play to each other's strengths. Whatever works in your house is the right way to do it. You can also make tradeoffs on the really undesirable chores. Above all, realize that this is an ever-evolving process. You'll be working on these issues for a long, long time. Don't expect the perfect solutions to pop up the day after you've moved in together.

Moving Forward

Once you have your financial outlook and you are in your new home together as a married couple, the rest is up to you and your relationship. Always keep in mind that your wedding day is only the beginning of the rest of your lives together. All of the planning for this one day of your life is really just setting the tone for the rest of your marriage. Were you able to compromise and make decisions based on what the two of you wanted for your wedding day? Then you are ready to enter marriage. Try to always remember what brought the two of you together in the first place. And if you forget, ask for help!

Bride's Name and Address Change Worksheet

	Name of Institution	Notified of		
		Name Change?	Address?	Marital Status?
401k accounts				
Automotive insurance				
Bank accounts				
Billing accounts				
Car registration				
Club memberships				
Credit cards				
Dentist				
Doctors				
Driver's license				
Employment records				
Homeowner's/Renter's insurance				
IRA accounts				
Leases				
Life insurance				
Loans				
Medical insurance				
Other insurance accounts				
Passport				
Pension plan records				
Post office				
Property titles				
Safety deposit box				
School records				
Social Security				
Stocks and bonds				
Subscriptions				
Telephone listing				
Voter registration records				
Wills/Trusts				
Other (list below)				

Groom's Name and Address Change Worksheet

Name of Institution	Notified of		
	Name Change?	Address?	Marital Status?
401k accounts			
Automotive insurance			
Bank accounts			
Billing accounts			
Car registration			
Club memberships			
Credit cards			
Dentist			
Doctors			
Driver's license			
Employment records			
Homeowner's/Renter's insurance			
IRA accounts			
Leases			
Life insurance			
Loans			
Medical insurance			
Other insurance accounts			
Passport			
Pension plan records			
Post office			
Property titles			
Safety deposit box			
School records			
Social Security			
Stocks and bonds			
Subscriptions			
Telephone listing			
Voter registration records			
Wills/Trusts			
Other (list below)			

Index

We Have
EVERYTHING
on Anything!

With more than 19 million copies sold, the Everything® series has become one of America's favorite resources for solving problems, learning new skills, and organizing lives. Our brand is not only recognizable—it's also welcomed.

The series is a hand-in-hand partner for people who are ready to tackle new subjects—like you!

For more information on the Everything® series, please visit *www.adamsmedia.com*

The Everything® list spans a wide range of subjects, with more than 500 titles covering 25 different categories:

Business	History	Reference
Careers	Home Improvement	Religion
Children's Storybooks	Everything Kids	Self-Help
Computers	Languages	Sports & Fitness
Cooking	Music	Travel
Crafts and Hobbies	New Age	Wedding
Education/Schools	Parenting	Writing
Games and Puzzles	Personal Finance	
Health	Pets	